Tennessee
1850 Agricultural Census

Volume 2

Linda L. Green

WILLOW BEND BOOKS
2007

WILLOW BEND BOOKS
AN IMPRINT OF HERITAGE BOOKS, INC.

Books, CDs, and more—Worldwide

For our listing of thousands of titles see our website
at
www.HeritageBooks.com

Published 2007 by
HERITAGE BOOKS, INC.
Publishing Division
65 East Main Street
Westminster, Maryland 21157-5026

International Standard Book Number: 978-0-7884-3822-0

INTRODUCTION

The year 1850 brought a new kind of census. Not only was it the first US Census to name all people in a household on the regular US Census, but this was the first time the Agricultural and Manufacturing Census was taken on a widespread basis. Although this second census names only head of household, often times when an individual was missed on the regular census, they would appear on either of these two census reports. Unfortunately, many of these Agricultural and Manufacturing Census records have not survived. But, those that did survive yield unique information about how people lived. There are 46 columns of information. I chose to transcribe only six of the columns. The six are: Name of Owner, Improved Acreage, Unimproved Acreage, Cash Value of the Farm, Value of Farm Implements and Machinery, and Value of Livestock. Below is a list of all other types of information available on this census.

OTHER DATA COLUMNS
(not transcribed)

Column/Title

6.	Horses
7.	Asses and Mules
8.	Milch Cows
9.	Working Oxen
10.	Other Cattle
11.	Sheep
12.	Swine
14.	Wheat, bushels of
15.	Rye, bushels of
16.	Indian Corn, bushels of
17.	Oats, bushels of
18.	Rice, lbs of
19.	Tobacco, lbs of
20.	Ginned Cotton, bales of 400 lbs each
21.	Wood, lbs of
22.	Peas and Beans, bushels of
23.	Irish Potatoes, bushels of
24.	Sweet Potatoes, bushels of
25.	Barley, bushels of
26.	Buchwheat, bushels of
27.	Value of Orchard Products in dollars
28.	Wine, gallons of
29.	Value of Produce of Market Gardens
30.	Butter, lbs of
31.	Cheese, lbs of
32.	Hay, tons of
33.	Clover Seed, bushels of
34.	Other Grass Seeds, bushels of
35.	Hops, lbs of
36.	Dew Rotted Hemp, tons of
37.	Water Rotted Hemp, tons of
38.	Flax, lbs of
39.	Flaxseed, bushels of
40.	Silk Cocoons, lbs of
41.	Maple Sugar, lbs of
42.	Cane Sugar, hnds of 1,000 lbs
43.	Molasses, gallons of
44.	Beeswax and Honey, lbs of
45.	Value of Home Made Manufacturers
46.	Value of Animals Slaughtered

TABLE OF CONTENTS

Robertson County TN
1850 Agricultural Census

The Agricultural Census for 1850 was filmed for the University of North Carolina from original records in the Tennessee State Library and Archives.

The following are the items represented and separated by a comma: for example, John Doe, 25, 25, 10, 5, 100. This represents:

Column 1 Owner
Column 2 Acres of Improved Land
Column 3 Acres of Unimproved Land
Column 4 Cash Value of Farm
Column 5 Value of Farm Implements and Machinery
Column 13 Value of Livestock

The following symbol is used to maintain spacing where there are no numbers: (-) In addition, the left margin has been bound too close to the edge causing some first names or initials to not be completely visible.

Robert Draughon, 150, 195, 1710, 150, 200
George Cohea, 125, 80, 1200, 100, 300
John S. Hutcheson, 50, 80, 1000, 30, 200
Jacob H. Hoffman, 12, 38, 250, 12, 50
Larkin Crutcher, 35, 70, 330, 25, 100
Geo. W. Morris, 150, 350, 1800, 200, 600
William Pepper Sr., 50, 60, 800, 15, 150
William Woodard Jr., 38, 69, 800, 5, 135
David Herring, 70, 132, 1000, 20, 325
Gravit Edwards, 80, 70, 600, 50, 200
P. B. Watson, 60, 46, 425, 5, 400
Thomas Krisle, 100, 200, 2500, 50, 300
Benj. P. Porter Sr., 200, 154, 3000, 500, 700
Henry Porter, 200, 100, 1300, 25, 500
David Porter, 150, 120, 1600, 100, 250
Sarah Duncan, 45, 120, 1600, 100, 250
Baxter Powel, 60, 250, 642, 500, 150
Stephen Pepper, 50, 65, 600, 20, 200
William Bridgess, 100, 230, 2000, 100, 500
Wm. L. Bell, 100, 240, 1200, 40, 200
Alfred Pike, 40, 116, 600, 25, 200
Robert Mantlo, 60, 200, 900, 75, 200
A. J. Morris, 14, 46, 50, 2, 40
Jas. H. Holland, 35, 64, 800, 75, 300
Jesse Davis, 60, 310, 800, 75, 650
Lynch Mantlo, 10, 149, 164, 10, 100
Asa Harper, 44, 386, 400, 10, 300
Jacob Cibb, 60, 166, 500, 20, 200
William Huddleston, 27, 303, 630, 7, 150
Thomas Kiger, 35, 50, 246, 7, 100

D. D. Holman, 200, 50, 2000, 150, 600
Thomas Cibb, 80, 129, 1500, 100, 500
William Crockett, 75, 125, 1200, 50, 400
W. D. Crunk, 50, 50, 400, 25, 190
Soloman Fiser, 75, 255, 3000, 100, 290
Volantine Fry, 42, 40, 3000, 10, 400
H. D. Ruffin, 75, 25, 800, 100, 600
W. W. Pepper, 100, 75, 3000, 100, 300
Eldad Porter, 150, 150, 1500, 75, 250
John Draughon, 150, 369, 2000, 150, 500
John Flood, 40, 60, 500, 10, 75
Richard Boren, 4, 25, 100, 6, 50
Robert Green, 300, 230, 4000, 100, 1000
Thomas Frey, 40, 55, 200, 50, 100
Richard Farthing, 50, 33, 300, 15, 125
Josiah Taylor, 40, 30, 240, 15, 150
Henry Highsmith, 20, 122, 500, 15, 150
Edward C. Garrett, 100, 80, 837, 40, 250
Isaac Farmer, 75, 65, 1000, 40, 250
William Edding, 30, 31, 305, 20, 150
Joseph Edding, 50, 93, 600, 18, 150
James Highsmith, 30, 29, 250, 10, 150
Elijah Highsmith, 40, 64, 312, 40, 140
Thomas Woodard, 200, 466, 2400, 50, 1000
Meredith Woodard, -, -, -, 15, 300
Joseph Inscore, 40, 60, 400, 20, 150
William Huddleston, 40, 60, 450, 10, 80
Alfred Jones, 90, 25, 400, 10, 292
Jeemiah Fyke, 30, 20, 300, 150, 252
Nancy Fyke, 60, 40, 500, 50, 150
John Jones, 50, 70, 700, 75, 300
John Y. Perry, 175, 285, 1700, 150, 600

Azariah Dunn, 75, -, 1200, 90, 100
Cordy Mason, 45, 30, 400, 60, 225
Daniel Holland, 130, 130, 400, 100, 200
Thos. J. Willis, 3, 97, 850, 10, 200
Pleasant Holland, 3, 189, 850, 5, -
D. W. Taylor, 250, 300, 3300, 200, 1000
Elizabeth Madon, -, -, -, 5, 100
G. B. Mason, 60, 40, 1000, 50, 332
_. G. C. Mason, 100, 70, 1020, 60, 463
Robert Thompson, 100, 130, 900, 150, 280
Henry H. Turner, 70, 60, 400, 75, 250
Thomas Stark, 60, 60, 700, 100, 400
S. M. Johnson, 150, 100, 1240, 200, 1000
Jeremiah Stark, 60, 90, 1000, 400, 500
Wm. H. Jones, 35, 25, 300, 40, 150
Thomas Dean, 60, 45, 500, 20, 300
P. C. Holland, 75, 25, 350, 85, 300
Wm. A. Holman, 70, 70, 1400, 80, 500
Armstead Akin, 40, 17, 200, 150, 400
Willie Holland, 200, 225, 3500, 250, 500
James Lipscomb, 40, 100, 700, 10, 200
Elbert Williams, 60, 30, 360, 60, 200
James Benson, 100, 143, 900, 75, 500
Riley Dean, 15, 10, 125, 10, 100
Nicholas Thompson, 60, 40, 400, 10, 150
Calvin Holman, 100, 125, 1630, 200, 695
Ephraim Roberts, 140, 75, 1600, 100, 400
Mills Taylor, 75, 75, 700, 30, 400
William Roberts, 100, 133, 1000, 100, 300
Meredith Long, 95, 111, 1648, 30, 500
Dicy Holman, 35, 5, 320, 25, 150
John Jackson Jr., -, -, -, 100, 350
P. B. Roberts, 100, 180, 1600, 150, 500
A. McIntosh, 100, 310, 1600, 150, 800
Elizabeth Johnson, 170, 165, 2000, 25, 200
Richard A. Benson, 75, 65, 1000, 150, 400
Richard Holland, 115, 103, 800, 30, 540
J. B. Taylor, 100, 50, 1000, 50, 700
David Brakefield, 120, 255, 648, 50, 400
Nathan Russel, 140, 125, 2000, 150, 500
Jacob Smith, 700, 1600, 7225, 500, 1907
Henry Wells, 60, 24, 600, 40, 400
Robert Rrose, 100, 100, 1200, 150, 500
Presly Stark, 36, 48, 500, 65, 150
Jarratt Ivy, 120, 480, 2300, 150, 500
R. A. Ivy, 80, 50, 600, 5, 250
Jas. J. Reynolds, -, -, -, 10, 100
R. B. Rose, 70, 80, 1500, 175, 500
Wm. H. Mason, 40, 44, 400, 15, 300
John R. Pitt, 60, 45, 400, 25, 350
Daniel Chapman, 100, 143, 1600, 25, 400
John Chapman Jr., 35, 30, 300, 25, 400

Bennet Rose, 100, 50, 750, 30, 150
G. P. Bagwell, 35, 25, 325, 5, 60
Noah Woodard, 50, 40, 1000, 75, 300
David Taylor, 70, 120, 1000, 25, 300
Vincent Williams, 300, 400, 3500, 100, 500
James Woodard, 350, 350, 7050, 400, 2000
John J. Pope, 200, 230, 8000, 400, 1265
Joseph Holman, 50, 150, 1200, 150, 700
Joseph Shelton, 70, 80, 850, 15, 400
Mary Neal, 90, 96, 1000, 10, 200
William Harris, 80, 80, 700, 75, 300
Willie Roberts, 100, 90, 840, 185, 500
Jas. B. Smelser, 40, 30, 500, 150, 500
John Dean, 55, 100, 650, 150, 500
Giles Chapman, 40, 105, 900, 50, 150
Jas. O. K. Willis, 70, 30, 345, 100, 150
John Timberlin, 60, 25, 500, 15, 100
John Smelser, 80, 100, 1200, 75, 250
John Benson, 35, 90, 400, 12, 150
George Bargee, 60, 53, 400, 20, 200
Elizabeth Barbee, 80, 40, 500, 100, 300
John Holland, 100, 140, 1400, 150, 300
Samuel Fuqua, 80, 100, 1200, 200, 500
Elizabeth Keller, 80, 70, 800, 10, 200
William Traughber, 80, 170, 1000, 100, 250
Jas. B. Barber, 110, 179, 2500, 200, 1000
W. S. Baldry, 150, 200, 2500, 150, 1000
Julia Adams, 20, 30, 250, 10, 100
Jane Pitts, 70, 160, 800, 5, 400
John Ashbranna, 35, 65, 400, 60, 150
Thomas Traughber, 20, -, 100, 5, 100
William Fuqua, 50, 65, 1000, 200, 200
Henderson Beasly, 50, 65, 800, 10, 150
F. J. Beasley, 40, 30, 400, 80, 200
Elijah Willis, 100, 100, 500, 75, 300
Simpson Dorris, 125, 60, 1000, 150, 500
J. J. Dorris, -, -, -, 20, 100
John Ashbranna, 75, 40, 700, 20, 400
John Hampton, 45, 115, 60, 100, 250
Franklin Moore, 200, 214, 3300, 50, 700
John Chapman, -, -, -, 15, 100
Harvey Chapman, 32, -, 300, 10, 150
Alfred Moore, 276, 121, 3970, 200, 1000
Washington Ryburn, 150, 50, 1000, 100, 400
Wm. D. Scoggin, 150, 100, 2500, 100, 420
W. V. Lewis, 15, 120, 300, 15, 215
W. B. Dorris, 80, 70, 1500, 75, 340
George Babb, -, -, -, 75, 104
Harrison Akin, 50, 41, 600, 25, 200
Joseph Webb, 30, 20, 400, 25, 300
Sarah Moore, 150, 500, 4000, 150, 1000

W. R. Drake, -, -, -, 75, 150
B. B. Stark, 75, 83, 600, 40, 50
James Robertson, 120, 260, 1552, 150, 200
K. H. Jones, 65, 77, 700, 100, 150
Reuben Jones, 60, 65, 700, 75, 250
John Holman, 70, 90, 500, 40, 300
Pendleton Holman, 70, 66, 600, 60, 300
Henry Hart Sr., 500, 500, 15000, 250, 2335
Alfred Chapman, 50, 63, 500, 15, 150
D. G. Baird, 550, 850, 11500, 400, 2015
R. J. Williams, 125, 125, 1000, 50, 200
Elizabeth Walton, 125, 275, 2000, 50, 300
E. M. Dean, 65, 55, 500, 100, 252
Carrol Huey, 150, 208, 2000, 150, 400
John M. Pope, 50, 50, 600, 20, 350
Jas. W. Powel, 70, 40, 600, 30, 200
W. A. Willis, 55, 85, 850, 75, 400
Elisha Willis, 110, 90, 764, 100, 400
Curdy Holland, 190, 206, 1775, 200, 600
A. H. Dorris, 40, 60, 400, 15, 165
Jackson Jordan, 55, 80, 600, 40, 75
A. G. W. Gordon, 100, 100, 1000, 40, 450
Richard Clayton, 140, 140, 1500, 75, 400
Daniel Clayton, 40, 70, 600, 60, 130
Thornton Clayton, 50, 80, 1000, 100, 300
Tyler Edward, 100, 121, 1000, 125, 650
J. O. Samuel, 70, 30, 350, 100, 400
Thomas Jones, 35, 40, 140, 5, 100
William Sayle, 100, 94, 735, 75, 200
L. W. Willis, 115, 140, 2500, 200, 600
Josephus Armstrong, 75, 125, 825, 150, 500
Leonard Dozier, 200, 250, 2000, 100, 800
Margaret Flood, 75, 77, 300, 15, 100
Ephraim Farthing, 45, 25, 280, 10, 250
Mathew Freeman, 40, 85, 375, 15, 150
Jno. N. Brewer, 30, 27, 400, 90, 500
Jones Brewer, 175, 100, 1000, 150, 1000
Ira Fulton, 70, 40, 600, 150, 300
Jno. W. Pearson, 50, 50, 400, 15, 250
Milly Biggs, 60, 122, 800, 15, 200
Willie Biggs, 80, 100, 1800, 20, 350
Dawson Bell, 75, 75, 800, 30, 200
William Clayton, 40, 40, 300, 15, 100
William Pearson, 40, 45, 400, 15, 75
Alsy Babb, 70, 130, 900, 100, 500
Isaac Steel, 90, 50, 1000, 100, 400
A. Barker, 60, 64, 400, 60, 150
G. B. Babb, 35, 55, 500, 50, 300
Wm. K. Stone, 40, 95, 800, 12, 300
John Mcdonald, 50, 85, 400, 50, 400
Samuel A. Doss, 100, 112, 1400, 25, 400

William Turner, 35, 73, 650, 70, 250
Richard M. Rose, 90, 90, 900, 75, 250
Reese Johnson, 100, 196, 1400, 150, 500
Dempsy House, 25, 50, 350, 5, 150
Jacob House, 100, 200, 1200, 100, 600
Edmund Brewer, 170, 500, 2680, 300, 500
Michael Rose, 50, 50, 500, 10, 100
Harman Kelly, 25, 15, 400, 50, 200
Mary Simmons, 70, 235, 1500, 75, 500
Daniel Johns, 40, 40, 600, 75, 300
James Babb, 75, 135, 2000, 25, 400
Elizabeth Babb, 300, 600, 5000, 150, 400
Benj. Kelly, 15, 35, 500, 60, 120
Elvert C. Williams, 100, 600, 4000, 150, 400
Aaron Elison, 45, 112, 900, 100, 250
Thomas Williams, 50, 60, 700, 100, 300
R. D. Richmond, 100, 120, 1100, 150, 650
Larkin C. Griffin, 50, 30, 500, 60, 250
J. L. Yates, 80, 85, 1000, 50, 600
David Binkley, 65, 236, 900, 75, 400
Asa Benly, 100, 300, 4000, 150, 600
Charles Howard, 100, 100, 2000, 60, 500
Willie Howard, 25, 10, 250, 20, 150
Jas. C. Griffin, 117, 183, 1530, 75, 200
David Clark, 80, 93, 810, 100, 400
Elizabeth Jones, 60, 40, 400, 50, 300
Wm. F. Randolph, 80, 150, 800, 150, 600
Robert Randolph, 80, 40, 800, 150, 500
William Randolph, 100, 200, 2000, 150, 1000
Thomas Randolph, 25, -, 200, 10, 200
Bayless Randolph, 60, 110, 850, 60, 400
Tabitha Foot, 24, 24, 240, 20, 100
Elizabeth West, 60, 100, 800, 50, 200
Jones Proctor, 10, 54, 320, 20, 125
Alex C. Cook, 25, 171, 1000, 10, 150
Catharine Cook, 75, 225, 1500, 100, 400
Abel U. Babb, 15, -, 120, 15, 150
Jeremiah Cook, 20, 30, 500, 15, 400
John Samuel, 150, 70, 3000, 200, 600
Benj. Gambill, 100, 900, 6000, 200, 1000
Young Babb, 50, 54, 500, 20, 200
Reddick Rose, 25, 54, 500, 20, 200
Temperance Griffin, 40, 78, 600, 50, 200
George Randolph, 400, 400, 4000, 500, 1000
Lucinda Krisle, 100, 383, 2000, 75, 150
Thomas Yates, 110, 50, 1400, 50, 400
Kissiah Henly, 70, 90, 700, 20, 300
Samuel J. Henry, 250, 250, 2500, 200, 1500
Thomas Baird, 400, 400, 3200, 150, 750
Levi Zeck, 60, 40, 500, 60, 150

Jacob Zeck, 50, 50, 500, 15, 150
John Sevan, 80, 139, 900, 75, 700
W. B. Gorham, 100, 161, 2100, 100, 380
Anthony Fisher, 150, 350, 2500, 130, 500
Elenor Doss, 100, 120, 800, 50, 1000
G. B. Kelley, 40, 68, 400, 30, 300
Wm. J. McKisic, 150, 350, 1500, 200, 1200
Azariah Doss, 125, 80, 2000, 150, 1000
W. C. Richmond, 100, 100, 1600, 100, 1000
Peter Farthing, 40, 45, 550, 40, 250
Jno. C. Richards, 60, 40, 500, 60, 200
Jno. A. McMillan, 80, 96, 1600, 200, 150
William McMillan, 50, 55, 725, 40, 150
William Yates, 100, 100, 1000, 150, 400
Robt. W. Carr, 70, 79, 580, 15, 50
Geo. K. Link, 70, 30, 700, 15, 500
James Yates, 35, 15, 500, 15, 150
Charles Yates, 150, 300, 4500, 300, 1500
Richard Randolph, 70, 160, 600, 150, 620
William Jones, 40, 45, 600, 10, 90
Jas. M. Somverville, 30, 50, 400, 40, 300
Jno. C. Patterson, 120, 382, 5200, 150, 900
Rhody Redfeam, 70, 120, 660, 40, 150
Richard Readfeam, 50, 25, 400, 55, 120
James Hamilton, 25, 75, 550, 36, 360
George Featherstern, -, 70, 280, 12, 220
W. B. Kelly, 28, 122, 112, 25, 180
Henry Brewer, 70, 165, 1140, 50, 400
Caroline Wilson, 70, 108, 1225, 100, 500
John Brewer, 35, 65, 350, 10, 200
Kindred Wilson, 50, 100, 1500, 40, 500
James Wilson, 180, 390, 350, 50, 250
Toliver Hewlet, 100, 400, 2400, 150, 400
John Williams, 150, 150, 1500, 100, 500
John H. Price, 55, 45, 800, 10, 300
Warren Price, 60, 30, 700, 40, 600
Mathew _. Williams, 130, 220, 1800, 60, 700
Joshua Clark, 70, 135, 2000, 150, 700
Berry Wilson, 55, 95, 1000, 150, 700
Richard B. Smith, 35, 37, 400, 90, 500
James Hewlet, 35, 31, 448, 10, 200
Elisha Redfeam, 80, 60, 700, 80, 40
Thomas G. Baird, 80, 50, 1200, 40, 300
Thomas Stringer, 75, 45, 700, 125, 400
Jno. W. Woodard, 30, 60, 700, 50, 400
Allen Groves, 45, 45, 800, 150, 400
C. N. Woodall, 25, 25, 150, 25, 200
Henry Davis, 70, 40, 1100, 75, 200
Reuben Wright, 60, 103, 1000, 30, 150
Francis Wright, 70, 60, 500, 40, 200
F. Wright, 30, 30, 500, 20, 300
Pinkney Berry, 50, 79, 800, 100, 150

Thomas Groves, 85, 65, 1000, 100, 400
W. C. Bigbee, 45, 75, 800, 120, 250
Pleasant Berry, 80, 80, 800, 60, 150
William Weir, 120, 280, 3200, 75, 500
Thos. W. Payne, 100, 130, 5000, 150, 400
W. M. Jarnagan, 80, 95, 1500, 100, 350
Christopher Woodall, 140, 50, 2000, 270, 680
Bolivar Payne, 30, 120, 1000, 20, 200
John Stringer, 77, 100, 1239, 100, 100
Thomas Swan, 40, 55, 1000, 30, 300
Wm. W. McMunn (McMann), 100, 200, 1500, 125, 1200
William Mcguier, 40, 40, 400, 100, 400
John Maguier, 115, 85, 1600, 125, 1000
Isaac N. Wright, 50, 50, 700, 60, 200
Rachael Candle(Caudle), 40, 71, 700, 15, 150
Moses Caudle (Candle), 115, 135, 2000, 150, 1810
Milly Ponds, 20, 20, 300, 20,3 00
Obediah Chisum, 80, 80, 800, 150, 350
Nancy Somers, 100, 700, 1000, 125, 300
Thomas White, 200, 300, 4000, 200, 1000
Elijah Eubank, 75, 117, 2000, 250, 600
Leroy Gosset, 50, 130, 860, 10, 150
M. L. Huffman, 300, 300, 4500, 200, 3000
Robert Stovall, 30, 70, 700, 25, 200
W. M. C. Barr, 100, 200, 500, 75, 250
James Groves, 100, 70, 1000, 150, 500
Marcus Stovall, 30, 170, 2000, 100, 400
Nancy Clark, 60, 58, 600, 25, 100
Moses Byram, 350, 700, 4000, 250, 3550
James Duvall, 200, 140, 2500, 150, 400
Wm. C. Wright, 15, 73, 500, 100, 150
John Bunton, 1000, 3000, 13000, 500, 6000
William Cook, 80, 70, 600, 75, 300
John Horton, 45, 55, 300, 15, 200
Isaac Groves, 80, 60, 700, 130, 400
Albert C. Byram, 60, 58, 590, 25, 225
Willis Wilkins, 100, 97, 700, 50, 800
Lavina Cummings, 100, 150, 1600, 30, 300
Wilkerson Cummings, 25, -, 125, 15, 200
Mary A. Duvall, 400, 500, 9000, 500, 1000
Susannah Groves, 40, 57, 500, 90, 375
Alfred Groves, 100, 100, 800, 500, 400
James L. Williams, 40, 68, 500, 8, 100
Jas. B. Wright, 50, 65, 350, 15, 100
Jas. H. Riddle, 30, 30, 240, 8, 100
Arthur Williams, 55, 52, 1000, 5, 100
James W. Swan, 40, 40, 500, 10, 200
Jas. M. Roney, 60, 90, 1000, 125, 250

W. D. Payne, 50, 83, 1000, 50, 200
Wm. B. Burch, 30, 63, 335, 25, 300
Samuel Gilbert, 140, 120, 2000, 150, 1420
A. B. Young, 90, 50, 1000, 50, 710
Dudley E. Brook, 150, 216, 1400, 200, 1000
James Glidewell, 60, 60, 725, 30, 150
B. F. Young, 300, 200, 1700, 250, 1420
Wilson Hutcheson, 90, 110, 1400, 250, 1420
Elizabeth Stewart, 70, 60, 800, 75, 300
Jacob F. Young, 200, 150, 3000, 200, 1200
James Ponds, 100, 99, 1000, 75, 300
Sarena Nimmo, 70, 160, 1500, 50, 300
Jno. W. Gowen, 50, 68, 400, 15, 150
Daniel Malloy, 65, 100, 1000, 150, 200
Robt. H. Harrison, 35, 45, 700, 75, 300
Joel Hudson, 50, 60, 700, 30, 115
Alex. Johns, 75, 145, 2000, 50, 100
Andrew Johnson, 40, 70, 1000, 60, 300
Sarah C. Pack, 60, 50, 1000, 75, 500
James Eubank, 200, 300, 2000, 200, 825
Willie Groves, 30, 45, 450, 40, 300
Jno. J. Wright, 75, 97, 1000, 150, 500
Thomas West, 50, 100, 1000, 150, 500
David West, 40, 60, 400, 30, 250
Benj. Gossett, 30, 60, 450, 10, 250
Mildred Payne, 100, 206, 1500, 150, 600
Jane Wright, 350, 171, 600, 75, 150
A. F. Berry, 80, 73, 800, 100, 300
W. L. Payne, 150, 150, 3000, 200, 1500
Albert West, 40, 40, 500, 150, 500
Andrew Est, 100, 200, 850, 100, 400
John Hutcheson, 150, 200, 1500, 150, 500
F. L. Young, 150, 204, 1200, 100, 680
Joseph Swan, 100, 90, 1200, 150, 600
Benj. Patterson, 80, 250, 3300, 175, 600
Robert C. Patterson, 130, 320, 3000, 225, 1500
Soloman Payne, 200, 600, 3000, 150, 1200
Thomas J. Payne, 36, 140, 700, 100, 200
Pleasant Wright, 170, 150, 2000, 52, 600
Leroy Covington, 100, 130, 1500, 150, 600
Gideon Payne, 100, 400, 6000, 200, 1500
John Cook, 150, 200, 1810, 100, 600
Jas. L. Jones, 250, 126, 3000, 150, 1300
William Jarnagan, 100, 70, 1200, 150, 500
William Armstrong, 50, 70, 600, 25, 250
William L. Armstrong, 100, 200, 1000, 75, 400
William George, 60, 90, 600, 100, 200

William Johnson, 110, 130, 800, 150, 300
David Jones, 200, 100, 1500, 200, 1400
Jas. M. Pinson, 80, 10, 400, 100, 200
Thos. F. Cothern, 60, 30, 300, 30, 200
C. L. Birney, 60, 40, 500, 75, 500
William Williams, 40, 35, 400, 10, 100
A. J. Shannon, 5, 25, 100, 10, 50
William Tate, 100, 130, 1050, 75, 250
Jas. H. Birney, 90, 50, 900, 100, 500
Jno. G. Armstrong, 25, 105, 400, 25, 200
Kelly Shannon, 80, 75, 800, 60, 200
Stephen Jones, 100, 50, 400, 25, 200
R. C. Turner, 75, 55, 375, 75, 300
Wm. W. Moss, 120, 120, 1000, 150, 400
Campbell Jones, 140, 110, 800, 100, 300
Richmond Cole, 100, 120, 1000, 100, 300
O. (Q.), B. Stone, 70, 140, 1150, 30, 400
William Birney, 200, 100, 1500, 200, 700
Noah Byram, 40, 60, 300, 60, 100
John Durret, 50, 50, 300, 75, 200
William Long, 70, 240, 1500, 150, 400
Geo. W. Stone, 60, 70, 400, 25, 200
Edward Stone, 30, 60, 200, 30, 300
Frederic Luten, 75, 75, 800, 30, 200
Jesse Strickland, 70, 200, 200, 50, 500
Alex Lucas, 45, 45, 400, 100, 200
Stephen Cole, 75, 125, 1000, 150, 600
William Roberts, 140, 60, 2000, 300, 800
Isaah Warren, 50, 254, 1000, 100, 350
John H. Cole, 100, 366, 1000, 80, 400
John Gilbert, 70, 187, 780, 100, 400
William Empson, 30, 40, 500, 25, 200
Richard Jones, 100, 400, 2 000, 100, 500
James Jones, 140, 115, 2000, 15, 200
Reuben White, 35, 120, 500, 15, 150
Champ T. Cole, 50, 150, 400, 100, 150
William Jones, 100, 124, 448, 50, 250
Sandy Jones, 35, 108, 615, 20, 175
Thomas H. Williams, 110, 170, 1000, 75, 400
Anderson Jones, 70, 100, 316, 50, 250
John Jarnagan, 125, 125, 1500, 100, 350
Braden Jarnagan, 200, 110, 1800, 100, 300
William Elks, 40, 18, 250, 15, 150
R. H. S. Tate, 150, 250, 2000, 150, 800
Lewis Merrit, 60, 40, 500, 30, 200
Isaac Freeling, 75, 100, 500, 75, 400
William Roney, 25, 50, 300, 15, 100
Nicholas Covington, 70, 105, 700, 125, 400
Henry Covington, 20, 30, 250, 15, 200
Winneford Covington, 80, 50, 700, 30, 250
Francis Durret, 50, 41, 275, 15, 150
Wm. P. Jarnagam, 50, 25, 315, 100, 150

John Ellison, 80, 50, 600, 20, 300
Wm. R. Seal, 55, 140, 1475, 10, 250
Adam H. Frey, 45, 70, 550, 50, 250
Mary Shannon, 100, 100, 1000, 150, 300
Elisha Jarnagan, 80, 110, 600, 75, 300
Jacob White, 50, 25, 500, 15, 100
Jesse Shannon, 90, 90, 1000, 50, 300
James Boyles, 80, 50, 800, 50, 400
John Strain, 50, 75, 700, 75, 500
James Shannon, 120, 340, 2200, 150, 500
Thomas Randolph, 60, 110, 700, 50, 250
Geo. W. Cook, 50, 54, 600, 25, 100
Thomas Jones, 30, 40, 250, 40, 250
Velantine Simmons, 100, 325, 2000, 75, 500
Ann Chowning, 75, 125, 2000, 75, 200
Robert Chowning, 75, 125, 1500, 150, 600
John Tucker, 90, 90, 500, 75, 300
Simpson Warren, 25, 5, 100, 10, 75
James Moss, 25, 25, 100, 20, 150
Elijah Warren, 35, 95, 500, 15, 125
Stepto Chiat, 50, 75, 500, 25, 300
William McCarley, 50, 30, 500, 15, 200
Thomas Cheatham, 320, 360, 8000, 150, 500
James Sawyers, 150, 170, 1200, 100, 400
James Wallis, 250, 420, 1500, 200, 600
John Elmore, 300, 70, 500, 75, 150
Thomas Savage, 350, 45, 600, 150, 300
Jno. F. England , 130, 250, 1500, 15, 50
William Adams, 30, 122, 300, 75, 150
William Balden, 38, -, 200, 50, 60
Robert McMurry, 125, 275, 1500, 75, 300
Eli Baggett, 150, 163, 2000, 150, 500
John Halcomb, 150, 307, 3200, 100, 600
Allen Jones, 40, 75, 800, 75, 300
J. B. Bagget, 150, 55, 525, 25, 125
Anson Frey, 30, 100, 1000, 50, 320
Thos. C. Payne, 95, 100, 1000, 30, 400
Robert Savage, 90, 75, 1000, 75, 200
Elizabeth, Colgin, 100, 266, 1400, 75, 200
A. A. Swift, 20, 45, 200, 75, 150
Wm. P. Dorris, 30, 220, 850, 100, 300
Wm. D. Baulden, 60, 45, 300, 75, 300
John Baulden, 50, 100, 1000, 75, 300
Abraham Baulden, 40, 90, 600, 40, 300
James Jones, 150, 150, 1500, 200, 500
Thomas Sawyers, 50, 124, 1000, 15, 200
James Sprouse, 100, 200, 3000, 150, 800
Joseph Dorris, 50, 55, 2300, 125, 400
R. J. _. Dorris, 125, 100, 3000, 260, 650
Titus England, 45, 100, 750, 15, 150
W. O. Carter, 40, 70, 700, 80, 400
Elisha Wilson, 140, 230, 2150, 75, 340

William Bagget, 88, 100, 900, 50, 400
Elizabeth McMurry, 130, 10, 200, 20, 200
Reuben Elmore, 30, 53, 400, 100, 200
Joseph Crawford, 30, 120, 700, 30, 210
William Couts, 137, 67, 1800, 35, 500
Lewis Wells, 130, 160, `000, 40, 500
Jasper Clark, 50, 70, 700, 100, 400
Lewis Nuckolls, 340, 600, 5000, 150, 800
A. B. Couts, 400, 400, 8000, 100, 550
Mary McMurry, 75, 75, 600, 50, 200
Jno. P. Simmons, 150, 230, 1200, 200, 500
Grafton Winfield, 40, 30, 221, 20, 400
Thomas Cook, 110, 110, 700, 75, 500
John Cook, 50, 150, 1100, 25, 150
Joseph Winfield, 100, 250, 320, 35, 300
William Shaw, 100, 111, 300, 100, 200
William Chandler, 60, 205, 300, 25, 150
Miles Baird, 65, 54, 450, 75, 300
Meredith Walton, 150, 430, 2000, 250, 600
F. R. Durrett, 60, 100, 500, 25, 250
Taylor Cone, 100, 100, 250, 80, 150
James Owen, 60, 352, 1000, 150, 500
John W. Warren, 60, 60, 1000, 75, 200
R. S. Welch, 25, 275, 1500, 40, 200
Samuel McMurry, 25, 12, 275, 75, 200
Abraham Broderick, 40, 66, 600, 25, 200
Jesse True, 90, 47, 1500, 100, 700
Thomas Henry, 50, 80, 700, 50, 400
B. B. Porter, 115, 107, 1500, 100, 500
Elizabeth Pitt, 50, 70, 1000, 30, 300
David Chapman, 50, 120, 850, 75, 600
John Couts, 250, 145, 1500, 200, 1500
Malachi Krisle, 130, 108, 1150, 150, 1000
Nancy Couts, 400, 272, 3500, 200, 1000
Willie Woodard, 150, 250, 3000, 250, 1000
James Woodard Jr., 75, 65, 600, 100, 500
Wilson Pitt, 180, 170, 2500, 140, 1000
Amos L. Moore, 90, 123, 2000, 100, 600
William Pitt, 150, 240, 3000, 150, 500
John Long, 90, 245, 3000, 200, 600
John Byrns, 120, 240, 1500, 200, 630
Joshua Gardner, 80, 80, 600, 75, 200
Henry Bartlett, 60, 60, 500, 75, 400
James Long, 150, 375, 2000, 125, 600
Francis Pride, 100, 150, 1200, 100, 500
Samuel Braswell, 70, 60, 600, 100, 400
Jas. M. Gunn, 120, 100, 600, 100, 500
Wm. J. Winn, 100, 75, 600, 75, 500
Barbry Gunn, 120, 80, 1500, 200, 500
Joseph Gunn, 100, 100, 600, 100, 300
Thomas Gunn, 300, 340, 2600, 200, 1000
Alexander Gunn, 200,300, 3000, 100, 700

Henry H. Sugg, 500, 400, 9000, 300, 3000

Catharine Grymes, 60, 40, 1000, 75, 300

Richard Williams, 80, 220, 4000, 40, 500

John Lipscomb, 40, 64, 450, 20, 200

A. J. Bell, 55, 89, 1000, 50, 250

Edward Porter, 70, 250, 1200, 50, 300

B. S. Holland, 22, 24, 150, 15, 150

William Mason, 75, 75, 800, 50, 200

E. W. Hughs, 100, 116, 800, 75, 300

John McHenry, 87, 100, 800, 50, 500

Milton Wells, 25, 30, 500, 75, 150

D. M. Wells, 250, 390, 3000, 100, 1500

Phenby Pope, 100, 360, 4000, 200, 600

James Farthing, 10, 20, 150, 30, 100

Coleman Farthing, 50, 90, 1000, 75, 600

J. H. Gullet (Gallet), 25, 25, 500, 100, 250

Amanda Watts, 40, -, 360, 100, 200

M. M. Wall, 150, 194, 3300, 125, 1400

Uriah Young, 250, 245, 3000, 175, 700

Geo. E. Standback, 60, 40, 800, 50, 400

Moses Barham, 35, 20, 440, 20, 300

Daniel Ireland, 50, 70, 500, 25, 200

Silas Thomas 200, 194, 3940, 25, 200

Francis Dillard, 40, 20, 350, 25, 350

Thos. W. Ruffin, 50, 118, 1500, 50, 300

Joseph Small, 110, 215, 2500, 200, 700

Drewry Bell, 100, 124, 2000, 200, 1500

Wm. B. Porter, 150, 236, 1500, 150, 800

Crawford Hughs, 35, 15, 200, 20, 300

Jas. T. Rose, 22, 8, 125, 20, 100

Samuel Sneed, 40, 43, 300, 25, 200

F. L. Warren, 70 30, 300, 50, 500

Lemuel Ayres, 150, 150, 1500, 150, 700

Peter Fiser, 110, 190, 1100, 125, 500

Thos. B. Mathews, 160, 190, 2000, 150, 1000

Peter Frey, 65, 40, 550, 20, 100

Jas. Draughon, 80, 80, 800, 20, 400

Henry Stoltz, 50, 112, 500, 15, 200

L. B. Wright, 80, 172, 1250, 80, 400

Martha Bartlett, 50, 50, 300, 25, 150

Christopher Manlove, 222, 380, 5000, 200, 2150

Thomas Stoltz, 35, 89, 600, 125, 300

Samue Long, 80, 100, 600, 75, 500

Michael Fiser, 75, 150, 1300, 50, 300

Richard O. Mantlo, 50, 150, 600, 75, 200

Joseph H. Fiser, 60, 200, 2400, 75, 200

Christina Stoltz, 70, 100, 800, 100, 300

George Black, 80, 120, 1000, 75, 400

Willie Harris, 75, 25, 375, 40, 150

Henry Redmond (Richmond), 20, 80, 350, 25, 100

Francis Armstrong, 14, -, 100, 5, 100

Aaron Maner, 140, 200, 2000, 150, 500

Isham Black, 60, 90, 750, 40, 200

S. Q. Trotter, 150, 100, 1050, 100, 500

B. F. Chance, 35, 85, 700, 20, 100

Jas. E. Ruffin, 150, 200, 1000, 150, 400

Jas. Holman, 75, 125, 1000, 150, 600

Mathew Fyke, 60, 40, 400, 150, 500

J. J. Barnes, 60, 50, 800, 50, 400

L. S. Barns, 40, 30, 400, 50, 300

Jesse Glissen, 75, 50, 650, 50, 200

William Nipper, 50, 30, 350, 75, 200

Mary Morris, 60, 50, 400, 75, 300

Larkin Cellers, 100, 66, 500, 75, 300

Richard Jones, 50, 50, 500, 75, 300

John Newton, 75, 122, 800, 50, 200

Miles Draughon, 45, 45, 500, 30, 200

Temphey (Temsty) Dunn, 50, 75, 500, 30, 200

Josiah Farmer Sr., 150, 180, 1500, 50, 500

John C. Menees, 70, 175, 1100, 60, 400

Joshua Fyke, 3, 40, 160, 30, 175

Josiah Darden, 100, 56, 468, 50, 250

Moses Woodall, 35, 45, 400, 100, 200

Wm. F. Roland, 60, 30, 200, 10, 100

Robert Bartlett, 125, 45, 540, 250, 800

Jno. T. Batts, 115, 105, 1200, 20, 300

Jonathan Famer, 60, 43, 400, 40, 200

William Hollaway, 4, 90, 150, 15, 200

Patience Barns, 15, 120, 1000, 30, 300

William Jones, 75, 48, 360, 100, 500

Jno. W. Newton, 35, 48, 300, 20, 135

Reuben Ward, 60, 26, 200, 20, 150

Jeremiah Batts, 90, 160, 2000, 50, 400

Alexander Robertson, 40, 60, 500, 15, 175

Robert Mays, 60, 43, 400, 20, 100

Wm. W. Batts, 163, 100, 1200, 150, 300

Jeremiah Batts Sr., 60, 90, 600, 80, 200

Archer Winn, 50, 109, 700, 50, 300

John Riad, 20, 100, 2000, 150, 600

Jesse S. Ellis, 150, 150, 1500, 150, 800

B. M. Ellis, 200, 89, 700, 50, 400

Soloman Cobb, 70, 145, 1500, 50, 500

Thos. J. Menees, 40, 80, 600, 40, 300

Jas. Murphey, 125, 272, 1500, 200, 800

G. A. Washington, 2000, 2700, 20000, 1000, 5000

Henry Wells, 35, 40, 500, 10, 200

Alcy Sorey (Soxey), 40, 15, 200, 20, 150

Elbert Woodard, 80, 100, 1225, 40, 450

Wm. S. Adams, 100, 100, 1000, 50, 400

B. B. Batts, 140, 130, 2000, 150, 800

Abner Dunn, 80, 70, 800, 100, 300

Wm. B. Calhoun, 14, 110, 450, 15, 300

Micajah Agg (Ogg), 40, 55, 300, 45, 350

Edward Newton, 75, 167, 700, 13, 200
John Johnson, 250, 300, 3500, 250, 1000
Wm. W. Laprade, 100, 200, 2500, 200,
600
Samuel Parker, 60, 100, 1000, 75, 300
Elisha Cannon, 100, 212, 2000, 200, 500
James T. Gunn, 250, 380, 4300, 200,
1000
Wm. M. Bell, 200, 250, 2500, 200, 700
A. H. Gooch, 200, 150, 4200, 350, 1200
Thomas Williamson, 300, 150, 10000,
300, 1200
Ann Reasons, 30, 55, 400, 75, 200
Robert Shanklande, 80, 234, 5000, 50,
300
Richard Laprade, 420, 15, 3300, 200, 500
Joel B. Fort, 400, 460, 8000, 400, 3000
Elias Fort, 300, 200, 4000, 400, 1000
Joseph Wimberly, 230, 180, 5000, 200,
1200
Alexander Broom (Bourn), 100, 155,
1500, 150, 600
W. H. Adams, 50, 160, 500, 40, 223
Miles Jackson, 80, 280, 1500, 50, 700
Jas. G. Byrns, 150, 190, 2500, 50, 300
Willie Heflin, 80, 90, 1000, 50, 300
Andrewson Newton, 30, 10, 200, 15, 150
Paschal Knight, 40, 30, 300, 20, 200
Josiah Lawrence, 50, 150, 2000, 50, 300
Clement Chambers, 100, 90, 1750, 10,
300
Wills Draughon, 80, 50, 1050, 10, 350
Jas. I. Polk, 200, 440, 6000, 200, 2500
W. L. Norfleet, 2000, 325, 5000, 300,
1800
G. H. Whited, 50, 60, 1100, 60, 500
Thos. H. Gardner, 250, 180, 4600, 100,
1000
Jno. L. Whited, 35, 61, 800, 40, 250
W. H. Sherrod, 80, 80, 1000, 50, 400
A. L. Miles, 100, 200, 1500, 50, 500
Levi Pitt, 200, 242, 1300, 30, 800
W. D. Alford, 65, 65, 800, 20, 200
Anna Byrns, 80, 35, 1000, 25, 300
William Sherrod, 70, 126, 1000, 35, 400
Robert Sherrod, -, -, -, -, 300
Benj.(Berry), Darden, 100, 200, 1500,
100, 700
L. M. Jackson, 75, 85, 500, 100, 350
G. D. Dunn, 40, 44, 500, 25, 300
Samuel Dunn, 150, 100, 1200, 200, 1500
N. J. Dunn, 75, 45, 500, 50, 400
George Adams, 150, 100, 2000, 75, 800
Norfleet Dirch, 150, 175, 2000, 25, -
William Watson, 100, 60, 800, 50, 500
D. B. Allen, 100, 67, 800, 100, 500

Samuel Northington, 500, 400, 8000, 300,
2100
Wm. C. Gossett, 80, 37, 900, 100, 400
Andrew Atkins, 50, 65 1100, 25, 400
R. R. Gill, 60, 70, 1000, 50, 200
Benj. Mallory, 200, 200, 2500, 50, 1500
A. L. Vanhook, 60, 98, 800, 50, 400
H. A. Conly, 50, 25, 600, 10, 150
William Stroud, 70, 139, 1000, 50, 300
James Stroud, 70, 135, 700, 25, 300
Sampson Rosser (Rossen), 200, 31, 2500,
250, 1000
Jas. C. Goodman, 70, 28, 400, 30, 350
William Rossen(Rosser), 45, -, 470, 25,
200
Holland Luter, 80, 60, 250, 25, 300
J. D. Luter, 50, 50, 600, 50, 300
Elisha Luter, 20, 30, 250, 25, 200
Richard Connel, 65, 30, 600, 50, 400
Robert Williams, 125, 85, 2000, 150,
1200
P. H. Williams, 125, 170, 2500, 150,
1200
Richard Bobo, 80, 44, 800, 40, 400
Marcy Drake, 100, 200, 2000, 125, 500
A. D. Cage, 200, 600, 2000, 20, 1000
F. P. Pennington, 100, 103, 1000, 100,
800
Isaac Robertson, 200, 700, 8000, 150,
1000
William Andrews, 300, 300, 7000, 150,
1000
Hartwell Husky, 80, 120, 400, 50, 300
James Darden, 400, 600, 4000, 400, 2750
R. E. Hughs, 200, 147, 2000, 75, 1000
Jas. T. Connel, 400, 300, 4000, 500, 3000
Geo. E. Draughan, 90, 72, 2000, 150,
1200
Joshua Elliott, 100, 107, 800, 100, 500
Jesse Darden, 200, 683, 3000, 200, 1000
R. D. Carr, 800, 700, 8000, 440, 5672
Edward H. Hudgens, 125, 475, 1500, 200,
1200
Joel Krantz, 30, 45, 260, 25, 125
Sarah Bobbett, 25, 15, 100, 28, 150
Robert Sanders, 60, 40, 500, 50, 300
Daniel Sanders, 100, 110, 600, 30, 250
Holloway Hudgens, 100, 100, 600, 30,
250
William Sanders, 70, 90, 400, 20, 500
J. M. Gent, 80, 116, 800, 30, 300
Ralls Maxey, 50, 50, 200, 15, 200
Hiram Lewis, 40, 65, 1000, 30, 300
Thomas Flintoff, 30, 270, 3500, 100, 500
Margaret Stewart, 100, 200, 2000, 100,
500

James Maxey, 300, 175, 2000, 100, 600
David Wall, 200, 150, 1200, 100, 1200
D. L. Stewart, 40, 40, 300, 30, 250
Jonathan Edwards, 40, 120, 640, 50, 300
James Hudgens, 65, 35, 150, 30, 250
William Read, 60, 41, 800, 50, 400
Geo. W. Hardeman, 100, 185, 1800, 75, 500
Mathew Hunt, 45, 255, 800, 50, 250
Jesse Sheron, 150, 190, 700, 50, 500
Hardridge Walker, 70, 530, 1500, 75, 800
J. F. Stack, 25, 26, 230, 15, 150
Nial Sheron, 75, 125, 700, 40, 300
Grenville Nichols, 100, 60, 800, 75, 1000
L. C. Harris, 50, -, 100, 15, 250
Jesse Nichols, 20, 15, 125, 15, 200
Harris Nichols, 70, 250, 800, 75, 300
James Nichols, 180, 140, 700, 50, 300
Zachariah Durham, 85, 300, 700, 75, 500
James Durham, 30, -, 300, 50, 300
John Durham, 10, 150, 400, 25, 200
James Walker, 30, 170, 400, 30, 200
Samuel Durham, 50, 50, 300, 30, 200
Wm. L. Hudgens, 30, 30, 250, 30, 300
John Hudgens, 25, 35, 250, 30, 300
Tabitha King, 80, 15, 400, 40, 300
Martha Hudgens, 80, 120, 600, 50, 250
Ephraim Simmons, 50, 160, 400, 50, 300
Elias Harris, 45, 255, 800, 50, 300
Joseph Nowlin, 70, 63, 300, 25, 200
Wm. L. Gower, 75, 40, 300, 30, 300
Levi Binkley, 100, 196, 800, 50, 500
William Hudgens, 100, 80, 400, 50, 500
Thomas Miles, 58, 100, 500, 40, 300
Eldridge Johnson, 35, 40, 400, 15, 100
Martha Cochran, 40, 110, 300, 50, 300
Geo. C. Binkley, 60, 65, 100, 50, 200
Henry Binkley, 40, 160, 600, 50, 300
Jeremiah Cochran, 40, 57, 160, 25, 150
Samuel Watson, 75, 250, 3000, 500, 1665
Thos. W. Harris, 250, 450, 2000, 200, 1000
J. J. Bradley, 80, 190, 2000, 100, 300
John Dowlin, 100, 162, 1000, 100, 300
Martha Bidwell, 40, 60, 400, 50, 400
Joseph Walker, 60, 40, 600, 50, 300
J. E. Walker, 55, 73, 500, 50, 200
M. A. Fountain, 15, 114, 1000, 50, 500
Ann Fountain, 100, 125, 500, 40, 200
A. B. Sawyer, 12, 88, 225, 50, 300
Isaac Naïve, 50, 68,m 350, 50, 200
Thos. W. Bracey, 40, 60, 300, 30, 200
Robert Williams, 180, 190, 1000, 75, 700
D. L. Alsbrook, 25, 75, 400, 60, 500
James Green, 50, 50, 400, 30, 200
W. C. Ralls, 40, 30, 250, 40, 200

Thomas Ledbetter, 30, 195, 700, 40, 200
George Murphy, 200, 400, 2500, 150, 600
Miles Carter, 50, 110, 800, 50, 300
Elizabeth Justice, 56, 100, 600, 50, 300
John J. Dunn, 80, 170, 1000, 50, 600
N. J. Cobb, 29, 76, 500, 40, 150
Martin Frey, 80, 150, 1000, 50, 500
Henderson Lipscomb, 42, 100, 500, 40, 200
Henry Carter, 40, 100, 900, 40, 50
Wiat Felts, 40, 100, 425, 40, 300
J. A. Holmes, 18, 180, 1500, 50, 500
Elijah Morgan, 18, 3, 150, 30, 400
Elizabeth Justice, 100, 238, 800, 40, 400
Hiram Head, 100, 225, 1200, 50, 400
J. H. Pentecost, 25, 59, 150, 25, 200
Samuel Bracey, 50, 50, 400, 20, 100
J. T. Webb, 18, 82, 300, 50, 150
James Venters, 70, 530, 2000, 50, 500
N. M. Felts, 80, 150, 700, 50, 600
Morris Felts, 60, 82, 500, 50, 300
B. P. Bracey, 15, 85, 600, 25, 150
M. D. Crockett, 300, 341, 1800, 150, 1000
J. M. Clark, 35, 62, 250, 40, 400
M. C. Banks, 65, 185, 1000, 50, 500
Thomas Crutcher, 18, 15, 129, 15, 150
B. W. Menees, 250, 41, 2000, 200, 1000
J. S. Parker, 60, 40, 500, 40, 300
Joseph Fuqua, 100, 167, 1000, 400, 500
John Culbertson, 60, 105, 500, 40, 300
H. A. Chambless, 50, 49, 300, 300, 150
Benj. Rawls, 100, 250, 700, 50, 400
William Hollis, 80, 140, 800, 50, 200
John Bainbridge, 160, 340, 2000, 100, 1000
Patterson Moore, 100, 203, 612, 50, 500
William Kiger, 8, 124, 264, 25, 200
Peter Hinkle, 60, 320, 1000, 50, 300
J. M. Pilant, 60, 40, 200, 40, 200
Thos. H. Farmer, 50, 65, 400, 30, 150
W. T. Hollis, 150, 850, 3000, 40, 500
William Street, 22, 78, 1000, 60, 400
Joseph Clinard, 10, 206, 700, 50, 500
Samuel Fuqua, 45, 68, 600, 40, 300
William Walker, 40, 85, 250, 40, 300
J. R. Reader, 60, 55, 300, 40, 200
Washington Clinard, 100, 208, 900, 40, 150
G. W. Frey, 69, 900, 1500, 50, 300
H. S. Frey, 120, 475, 4000, 50, 400
Henry Frey, 150, 563, 2600, 150, 600
J. C. Parker, 100, 145, 600, 50, 400
D. H. Parker, 100, 284, 1800, 50, 500
Andrew Clinard, 140, 108, 500, 50, 400
Samuel Alsbrook, 60, 40, 600, 40, 300

J. A. Pilant, 100, 297, 2000, 50, 400
John Miller, 100, 150, 1000, 50, 500
Peter Hollis, 100, 167, 700, 100, 800
Henry Green, 175, 192, 1800, 50, 400
William Woodard, 20, 25, 150, 30, 200
William Jamison, 80, 80, 1000, 50, 300
Nancy Martin, 100, 50, 200, 40, 300
Ira Dorris, 80, 100, 700, 40, 300
Alfred Reddin, 110, 300, 800, 50, 600
J. B. Pitts, 73, 100, 500, 50, 400
Thos. Martin, 80, 120, 300, 50, 300
H. S. Binkley, 50, 41, 400, 30, 200
Patrick Martin, 70, 110, 600, 50, 500
Joseph Rawls, 200, 175, 500, 50, 300
Samuel Farmer, 180, 100, 700, 50, 300
Marvel Lowe, 200, 415, 3600, 200, 1800
Caleb Keeler, 50, 146, 1000, 15, 300
Alexander Lowe, 150, 400, 4000, 150, 1500
W. E. Felts, 50, 150, 800, 50, 150
Whitsnell (Whitmell, Whitwell) Dowlin, 50, 46, 4000, 20, 150
Harris Dowlin, 70, 60, 600, 100, 600
Joseph McCormick, 50, 50, 300, 25, 200
Jno. B. Fiser, 400, 455, 5000, 350, 2000
B. W. Bradley, 250, 635, 3500, 150, 800
Lucy Harris, 40, 87, 200, 30, 300
Jno. C. Balthrop, 60, 200, 1000, 50, 300
W. H. Farmer, 60, 187, 650, 40, 150
James Head, 40, 58, 650, 40, 250
Mathew Woodruff, 75, 125, 325, 25, 300
James Gower, 20, 30, 150, 15, 250
Jacob Bell, 100, 800, 2000, 150, 40
Jas. O. Whites, 60, 80, 420, 20, 200
George Head, 60, 132, 150, 25, 200
David Alley, 40, 222, 200, 40, 200
Josiah Winters, 75, 107, 675, 100, 310
W. C. Head, 40, 60, 200, 25, 200
Jas. J. Wilson, 100, 163, 1000, 200, 500
James Elliott, 35, 15, 200, 25, 200
Thos. B. Williams, 60, 140, 600, 125, 600
Geo. W. Farmer, 30, 79, 500, 20, 250
M. B. Winters 77, 135, 700, 50, 300
Andrew J. Lipscomb, 100, 150, 825, 50, 400
Rolly Langford, 50, 96, 500, 40, 300
J. A. Justice, 75, 170, 600, 20, 300
William Elliott, 90, 130, 1000, 30, 400
D. J. Fort, 60, 100, 800, 10, 300
William Stroud, 80, 140, 600, 50, 300
A. J. Head, 70, 78, 350, 75, 250
Geo. W. Walker, 35, 67, 250, 15, 100
E. G. Murphey, 200, 47, 600, 50, 400
Agrippa Dickerson, 120, 84, 700, 50, 400
Joel Naïve, 50, 75, 700, 50, 300
Huey Head, 50, 139, 700, 50, 400

Mary Thompson, 300, 698, 5000, 150, 400
Celia Glover, 50, 50, 400, 40, 300
John Hulsey, 80, 87, 350, 50, 40
John Read, 40, 45, 450, 20, 200
William White Sr., 150, 209, 1100, 150, 1200
Lafayett Williams, 50, 550, 600, 50, 200
Soloman James, 200, 350, 2000, 50, 400
William Bernard, 100, 310, 2000, 50, 200
Robert Head, 50, 100, 400, 50, 200
Isaac Carter, 45, 100, 600, 50, 300
Henry Hide, 90, 134, 1300, 35, 300
Elizabeth Woodson, 200, 350, 1400, 50, 500
E. B. Harrison, 75, 725, 1500, 40, 300
Robert Moore, 40, 55, 300, 30, 200
Jas. W. Hunt, 150, 200, 10000, 100, 600
R. R. Felts, 30, 30, 200, 15, 150
B. L. Williams, 60, 150, 450, 50, 250
James Moore, 50, 47, 275, 50, 250
Willis Hide, 270, 330, 1200, 50, 500
John Hunt, 200, 435, 3000, 50, 600
Christopher Williams, 50, 50, 400, 40, 300
James Walker, 40, 160, 600, 40, 200
J. W. Pace, 75, 178, 340, 50, 200
Marsha Pace, 40, 120, 160, 20, 200
T. W. Pace, 40, 68, 200, 20, 240
Nathan Morris, 150, 275, 1200, 150, 600
Sarah Shaw, 40, 160, 400, 50, 200
David Felts, 100, 100, 1000, 50, 200
Jacob Stack, 40, 80, 500, 20, 200
J. J. Woodson, 8, 88, 210, 15, 150
Benj. Elliott, 300, 2000, 3000, 150, 1500
Sarah Ellis, 100, 2000, 600, 50, 300
James Nichols, 40, 53, 300, 40, 400
Dorothy Fort, 40, 60, 250, 30, 200
Levi Hunt, 50, 200, 500, 50, 200
J. E. Turner, 60, 200, 1200, 150, 1000
Robert Pennington, 200, 800, 2000, 100, 600
Jones Rossen, 65, 15, 150, 25, 400
Thomas Basford, 20, 40, 150, 20, 200
H. H. Harris, 35, 95, 400, 40, 300
Robert Alley, 25, 90, 400, 40, 150
Lorenzo Fox, 100, 150, 750, 100, 400
E. P. Morris, 80, 203, 700, 75, 400
Alex Williams, 510, 500, 1500, 100, 500
C. B. Binkley, 50, 252, 1200, 50, 500
N. H. Bugg, 30, 75, 400, 40, 350
Martin Choat, 16, 84, 400, 25, 150
Charles Crafford, 40, 171, 300, 40, 400
Peter Warren, 70, 540, 300, 40, 400
Hezekiah Warren, 30, 465, 750, 30, 400
John Crafford, 25, 25, 150, 30, 200

James Anderson, 80, 460, 800, 40, 400
Thomas Stanley, 50, 320, 500, 40, 500
William Hall, 30, 185, 500, 40, 600
John Agee, 50, 132, 300, 40, 500
Elizabeth Jones, 30, 183, 300, 40, 500
Francis Barns, 50, 140, 400, 30, 375
Bisho Boren, 15, 107, 125, 15, 300
James Culbertson, 64, 150, 400, 40, 350
Brown Clinard, 60, 134, 300, 40, 500
William Anderson, 100, 500, 400, 40, 400
Joel A. King, 44, 950, 1000, 40, 500
Lewis Robertson, 75, 75, 1000, 50, 400
Lewis Bromvale, 50, 50, 650, 40, 500
Jonathan Reader, 80, 270, 400, 40, 375
Hugh Smiley, 40, 260, 300, 40, 500
William Smiley, 50, 950, 400, 75, 750
James Amos, 60, 130, 200, 40, 250
David Smiley, 26, 174, 500, 40, 400

Jackson Warren, 35, 185, 150, 30, 300
John L. Oguime (Aguime), 40, 80, 400, 40, 500
William Mays, 30, 10, 101, 30, 400
William Ayrs, 11, 27, 150, 30, 300
Cobert Warren, 60, 50, 150, 20, 300
Samuel Webb, 80, 227, 800, 40, 600
Henry Jones, 35, 24, 170, 20, 250
Burwell Mays, 40, 65, 150, 40, 750
Andrewson Warren, 40, 68, 300, 40, 375
Walter Bell, 100, 500, 1250, 75, 1250
John Krisle, 125, 100, 800, 40, 500
Enoch Farthing, 60, 80, 500, 75, 500
William Morris, 110, 164, 2000, 150, 1000
Richard Roberts, 50, 390, 1000, 30, 350
David Henry, 200, 255, 2300, 75, 750

Rutherford County TN
1850 Agricultural Census

The Agricultural Census for 1850 was filmed for the University of North Carolina from original records in the Tennessee State Library and Archives.

The following are the items represented and separated by a comma: for example, John Doe, 25, 25, 10, 5, 100. This represents:

Column 1 Owner
Column 2 Acres of Improved Land
Column 3 Acres of Unimproved Land
Column 4 Cash Value of Farm
Column 5 Value of Farm Implements and Machinery
Column 13 Value of Livestock

The following symbol is used to maintain spacing where there are no numbers: (-)

Henry L. Schluler, -, -, -, -, 150
Archibald Jannaway, -, -, -, -, 60
Wilson Y. Jones, -, -, -, -, 320
John McDermot, -, -, -, -, 60
James O. Good, -, -, -, -, 110
Robert Bumpas, -, -, -, -, 10
Jane M. Brown, -, -, -, -, 10
Wm. D. Hick, -, -, -, -, 10
Mary Ellis, -, -, -, -, 10
James E. Wendel, -, -, -, -, 380
Wm. J. Lytte, -, -, -, -, 700
Moses G. Reeves, -, -, -, -, 10
Thomas Edwards, -, -, -, -, 135
G. T. Henderson, -, -, -, -, 17
John Lufer, -, -, -, -, 75
Daniel Linan (Lunan), -, -, -, -, 260
Wm. McFadden, -, -, -, -, 220
Rufus B. Jetton, -, -, -, -, 30
Joseph W. Nelson, -, -, -, -, 15
Wm. C. Duffer, -, -, -, -, 10
Wm. E. McLin, -, -, -, -, 85
Silas A. Bivens, -, -, -, -, 20
Edward J. Covington, -, -, -, -, 26
Wilson Thomas, -, -, -, -, 25
Fountain C. Mosby, -, -, -, -, 10
E. D. Wheeler, -, -, -, -, 130
Jesse J. Abernathy, -, -, -, -, 200
John C. Spence, -, -, -, -, 30
James Rude (Reede), -, -, -, -, 10
David D. Wendel, -, -, -, -, 380
E. B. McClam, -, -, -, -, 10
John Rather, -, -, -, -, 25
George Rather, -, -, -, -, 15
Newton C. Dill, -, -, -, -, 80
Mary D. Fletcher, -, -, -, -, 220

J. N. Ott, -, -, -, -, 10
G. W. Shanklin, -, -, -, -, 140
JohnWoods, -, -, -, -, 160
Charles Ready, 120, 80, 10000, 125, 1240
Nathaniel Burks(Banks), -, -, -, -, 10
Alfred Miller, -, -, -, -, 10
Daniel W. Taylor, -, -, -, -, 10
Reuben Boles, 5, -, 5000, 10, 140
George A. Sublett, -, -, -, -, 900
Grandison T. Fletcher, -, -, -, -, 20
David Travis, -, -, -, -, 130
James S. McLin, -, -, -, -, 180
Jackson Todd, -, -, -, -, 15
Samuel M. Brigs, -, -, -, -, 30
Edwin A. Kuble, -, -, -, -, 200
Horace P. Kuble, -, -, -, -, 135
Wm. Spence, -, -, -, -, 120
Harry Osbern, -, -, -, -, 20
Mathew B. Murfree, 100, 80, 18000, 100, 340
John T. Woman, -, -, -, -, 110
Daniel Eaks, -, -, -, -, 160
Wills Snell, -, -, -, -, 300
Robert W. January, -, -, -, -, 10
Wm. D. Fly, -, -, -, -, 120
James McDowel, -, -, -, -, 90
James McDowel, -, -, -, -, 80
John L. Huchinson, -, -, -, -, 10
Charles Watt, -, -, -, -, 10
J. G. Fellows, -, -, -, -, 80
Stubing B. Jones, -, -, -, -, 220
Tillford Allen, -, -, -, -, 10
Walace McDowel, -, -, -, -, 12
Wm. C. Fletcher, -, -, -, -, 600
Wm. S. Huggins, -, -, -, -, 100

Richard Saunders, -, -, -, -, 40
James Crichlow, -, -, -, -, 300
Edward A. Cochran, -, -, -, -, 90
F. Denny, 35, -, 1600, 150, 290
J. J. C. Haynes, -, -, -, -, 26
John D. Backster, -, -, -, -, 90
James A. Pitty, -, -, -, -, 110
Thos. Burchet, -, -, -, -, -
Benjamin Smith, 60, 20, 8000, 20, 360
Jonathan Huggins, -, -, -, -, 160
Green Clay, -, -, -, -, 200
Matthew Hillsman, -, -, -, -, 28
James Maney(Money), 200, 600, 32000, 200, 850
William Snell, 220, 190, 3300, 300, 1420
Logan _. Norman, 30, -, 500, 10, 250
Charles Featherton, 70, 143, 4000, 50, 310
Moses Swan, 70, 168, 3600, 125, 430
T. J. Canby, -, -, -, -, 20
D. M. Freeman, -, -, -, -, 320
Henry Norman, 150, 150, 700, 200, 670
Ebhugh Swan, 35, -, 300, 100, 455
Clement Wade, 27, -, 880, 10, 200
Nelson Allford, 60, -, 720, 10, 340
Joseph B. Rankin, 25, 58, 1660, -, 380
Richard Halliburton, 350, 130, 1200, 120, 1500
Henry J. Miller, -, -, -, -, 10
Wm. Rankin, 150, 150, 6500, 150, 560
Francis S. Maning, 80, 110, 5000, 120, 580
John T. Lawrence, 80, 190, 6000, 100, 460
Jackson Smith, -, -, -, -, 80
Harrison Lambert, 25, -, 650, 5, 60
Franklin Henderson, 400, 450, 20000, 350, 2000
Margaret E. Henderson, 200, 166, 8000, 50, 250
Isaac Rust, -, -, -, -, 60
Rebecca Philips, 25, -, 500, 5, 300
Joseph Philips, 400, 1100, 18000, 580, 3092
Alexander Tassy, -, -, -, -, 200
Arthur Woodfin, -, -, -, -, 100
Preston K., Davis, 130, 510, 8000, 200, 1900
Salina Bowman, 80, 280, 4800, 80, 280
Hugh Kirk, 225, 350, 8000, 350, 1215
John Kirk, 100, 220, 4000, 100, 370
Newton Fardly(Yeardly), 50, 73, 2600, 10, 450
John Wills, 30, -, 200, 5, 220
David B. Howman, -, -, -, -, 100

Wm. D. Nelson, 150, 105, 8000, 250, 1700
James Wilson, 50, 80, 5000, 80, 450
John Beller, 200, 200, 8000, 350, 625
L. H. Cornig, 650, 1450, 31500, 500, 1350
John Fleming, 50, 100, 1200, 80, 3500
A.Y. Slo__, 30, -, 500, 10, 175
Mary P. Nesbit, 40, 160, 800, 60, 570
Isaac Coleman, 35, 235, 1000, 80, 240
Sarah A. Coleman, -, -, -, -, 80
James Yearwood, 35, 60, 1500, 10, 180
Burrel Ward, 300, 145, 6000, 150, 2240
David Herald, 20, -, 100, 5, 150
Wm. Wilson, 50, 64, 3000, 100, 420
Richard Hughs, -, 40, 1000, 100, 470
Daniel Maberry, -, -, -, -, 300
James Keilough, 100, 130, 4000, 100, 400
Robert B. Jetton, 300, 300, 1000, 300, 2500
Nancy Jetton, 75, 125, 5000, 75, 230
James Lawrence, 75, 150, 5700, 70, 380
Alexander Lackey, 40, 170, 4000, 80, 280
Wm. E. Bella, 220, 460, 13000, 150, 800
John W. Childress, 400, 415, 18400, 400, 1970
Wm. Brock, 100, 90, 8000, 60, 5650
Wm. H. Kerr, -, -, -, -, 60
L. M. Bivins, -, -, -, -, 200
Wm. H. Halleburton, 100, 100, 2000, 100, 370
Nancy Newman, 29, -, 300, 5, 200
David Shockley, 45, 80, 1200, 60, 185
Sarah Brown, 16, -, 100, -, 150
John Johnson, 50, -, 500, 10, 220
John Snipes, 25, -, 250, 5, 210
Betsy Hughs, -, -, -, -, 70
Nancy M. Butler, 15, -, 150, 5, 350
Jefferson Horton, 35, -, 350, 10, 150
Isaac L. Miller, 175, 100, 60000, 100, 700
Robert Doke, 100, 100, 2500, 80, 465
Jerry Odle, 20, 20, 300, 5, 360
Beverly A. Cruse, -, -, -, -, 150
James Daniel, 150, 180, 5000, 100, 800
M. D. Ezell, -, -, -, -, 250
Elizabeth Miller, 100, 200, 2000, 200, 650
James L Nichols, 80, 50, 1000, 30, 400
Robert L. Sims, 170, 70, 3000, 100, 485
Ruleigh Morgan, 170, 176, 3700, 200, 1200
Lewis V. Young, -, -, -, -, 250
David M. McCulloch, -, -, -, -, 275
Adam Webb, 20, -, 300, 5, 170
John S. Shockley, -, -, -, -, 30
Abel Davis, 50, 225, 1000, 30, 150

John D. Button, 150, 113, 5000, 65, 310
John Murphey, 80, 70, 2100, 100, 350
Edward D. Drumgood, 43, 32, 1200, 100, 535
Blant Jordon, 250, 100, 7000, 150, 1300
Josiah Marshal, 80, 127, 2000, 50, 630
Thomas Fleming, 20, 10, 500, 20, 200
Jephthan Minter, 200, 200, 3000, 100, 790
Samuel Shockley, 10, 100, 800, 5, 85
Nicholas Welch, 70, 10, 1000, 80, 450
James Carrack, -, -, -, -, 175
Erasmus Lynah (Lynch), 40, 50, 250, 75, 470
Thomas P. Wills, -, -, -, -, 250
Samuel Boman, 50, 40, 1200, 80, 450
Andrew Edwards, 28, -, 200, 5, 400
Andrew McElroy, -, -, -, -, 200
Mary McElroy, -, -, -, -, 180
Esther Brown, -, -, -, -, 20
John Petty, -, -, -, -, 80
B. L. Coronahan, -, -, -, -, 400
Alfred Fleming, -, -, -, -, 10
Thomas A. Crichlow, -, -, -, -, 10
Mary Linster, -, -, -, -, 10
John J. Lowing, -, -, -, -, 110
Thomas Brewer, -, -, -, -, 120
Edmond G. Gringer (Guinage), -, -, -, -, 12
Philip D. McCulloch, -, -, -, -, 200
James M. Brown, -, -, -, -, 200
Allen T. Gooch, -, -, -, -, 230
Isabella Smith, -, -, -, -, 130
John m. Watson, -, -, -, -, 210
Mary Mitchell, -, -, -, -, 10
James Cauthern, -, -, -, -, 10
Wm. January (Janway), -, -, -, -, 450
Edmond Arnold, -, -, -, -, 35
John Smith, -, -, -, -, 80
Jordon Hooker, -, -, -, -, 10
Sarah Spencer, -, -, -, -, 250
Calvin Swancy, -, -, -, -, 75
Plesent W. Tucker, -, -, -, -, 10
James Bivins, 75, 41, 4640, 150, 680
Robert S. Cumin, -, -, -, -, 120
Elizabeth Cumin, 130, 350, 19000, 100, 1150
Wm. Eagleton, -, -, -, -, 110
Samuel Anderson, 120, 120, 9000, 100, 530
Radford G. Ellis, -, -, -, -, 27
Jeremiah Prichet, -, -, -, -, 65
Isaac Parker, -, -, -, -, 140
James F. Fletcher, 150, 125, 9000, 150, 6000
Thomas D. Kirby, 30, -, 1200, 10, 300

Elisha Williams 200, 132, 9000, 200, 850
Wm. L. Murfree, 900, 580, 45000, 1000, 4200
Wm. F. Lytte (Lytle), 750, 1730, 100000, 1300, 3390
Alfred Moss, 18, -, 250, 5, 175
Jacob Whitworth, -, -, -, -, 80
Stanford O'Kely, (O. Kely), 10, -, 100, 40, 100
Wm. Work, -, -, -, -, 400
W. H. Nailer (Nailen), 80, 20, 2000, 100, 550
Archer Johnson, 50, 70, 1200, 30, 390
G. W. C. Morton, -, -, -, -, 7
Eli C. Anderson, -, -, -, -, 130
Thomas Edwards, 25, 160, 1280, 60, 470
John S. Martin, 15, -, 150, 5, 165
Joseph Smith, 100, 300, 400, 200, 930
James F. Webb, 40, -, 300, 5, 300
A. J. Sublett, 40, 30, 500, 65, 330
Esther Smith, -, -, -, -, 220
Thomas Carrack, 100, 190, 1300, 100, 510
J. D. Gilmore, 200, 100,3 000, 150, 780
Nehemiah Parker, 120, 40, 1600, 80, 520
Wm. Vaghan, -, -, -, -, 250
Josephus Gregory, 45, 75, 1200, 5, 230
Benjamin T. Lamar, 14, 80, 900, 5, 30
Samuel G. Miller, 80, 220, 3000, 100, 770
James Taylor, 50, 80, 1200, 30, 370
Hiram Pearson, 250, 70, 2000, 100, 1880
John W. Glasco, -, -, -, -, 10
John D. Bigham, 70, 80, 1500, 100, 550
Harry Arnold, 30, 20, 500, 80, 260
Robt Lowing, 120, 110, 4000, 100, 520
Sarah P. Brothers, 200, 200, 2800, 80, 500
Josiah P. Miller, 100, 200, 2000, 80, 1100
Bennet G. Fields, 100, 40, 1500, 80, 730
Mary Parrrish, 30, 50, 800, 5, 240
John Ross, 20, 20, 80, 5, 100
Jon R. Miller, 16, 80, 400, 5, 200
Hardy Miller, 20, 120, 300, 5, 200
Jas. R. Farlis, -, -, -, -, 150
James C. Austin, -, -, -, -, 50
Champ Arnold, -, -, -, -, 200
Wm. Mayfield, -, -, -, -, 230
William Mayfield, 25, -, 250, 5, 230
Benjamin Thomas, 40, 120, 1000, 300, 240
Willis Vaughan, -, -, -, -, 110
Robert Denison, -, -, -, -, 150
Thomas S. Insel, 27, -, 270, 100, 200
John Adcock, -, -, -, -, 200
Stephen Perryman, -, -, -, -, 260

Levinia Underwood, -, -, -, -, 25
Jessee Perryman, 28, -, 280, 5, 60
Levi Anderson, -, -, -, -, 180
Morgan Adler, -, -, -, -, 275
Wm. Wilson, 25, -, 300, 5, 220
Wm. Sublett, 20, -, 150, 30, 375
James Rickets, -, -, -, -, 10
John Claxton, 15, -, 100, 5, 120
Bennet Smith, 60, 100, 1600, 80, 700
Hamilton McMurry, 150, 230, 2000, 25, 420
Wm. Faringer (Fringer), 125, 100, 2500, 75, 330
Milly Rouche, -, -, -, -, 140
Minus L. Fletcher, 180, 215, 8500, 250, 1035
Henry Hoover, 150, 200, 3500, 50, 500
Archibald Fulks, -, -, -, -, 150
Isaac Hoover, 50, 75, 875, 5, 245
Rufus S. McKee, 10, -, -, -, 140
John A. Stafford, 30, 5, 200, 5, 140
John L. Howland, 200, 125, 8120, 90, 1530
John Hoover, -, -, -, -, 110
Benjamin Hoover, 75, 225, 2000, 80, 1200
Andrew Hamilton, -, -, -, -, 20
Elizabeth Brooksher, -, -, -, -, 80
Paul Patton, -, -, -, -, 95
John A. Baro (Baw), 120, 205, 4850, 130, 735
Thomas Hoover, 15, 30, 450, 5, 130
Nathan Petty, 20, 1, 300, 5, 130
Wm. Armstrong, 7, -, 100 5, 100
Archibald Hays, 12, 5, 150, 5, 120
Wm. H. Perry, -, -, -, -, 40
Edwin Childress, 25, 100, 1200, 80, 210
James L. Lyons, 75, 60, 2000, 25, 330
Schoclate T. C. Goodlett, 150, 400, 6000, 100, 760
Lewis Garner, 350, 440, 15000, 400, 2325
Nathan E. Brady, -, -, -, -, 10
James Smith, 12, -, 240, 5, 130
Elijah Prater, -, -, -, -, 135
Claton Prater, 20, 5, 375, 5, -
Munroe Prater, 25, 25, 500, 5, 115
Philip Drake, 30, 30, 500, 5, 200
James H. Freeman, 22, -, 250, 5, 90
Chalres Talleforia, 16, -, 160, 5, 60
John Birdsong, -, -, -, -, 100
John Dobbins, 18, -, 150, 5, 220
Thomas Angling, -, -, -, -, 100
Bailey Pinkard, 75, 445, 4300, 70, 600
James Drake, 20, -, 300, 5, 175

Henry Williams, 200, 500, 8000, 100, 1125
John McGill, 150, 100, 3000, 100, 475
Lias E. Pinkard, 25, -, 250, 50, 310
Thomas Adkinson, 50, 50, 1000, 75, 220
James McGill, 400, 240, 9000, 100, 1160
Robert W. Brandon, 22, -, 200, 100, 180
George Avary, 20, -, 200, 5, 50
James D. Wootten, 35, 20, 600, 5, 200
David McGill, 200, 440, 7000, 200, 1150
B. W. Arent(Avent), 160, 400, 8500, 128, 520
Bailey Jones, 60, 20, 800, 5, 350
James Poindexter, 30, 34, 1000, 50, 330
Wm. R. Blackley, 35, -, 350, 125, 440
Joseph Nesbit, 90, 110, 4000, 75, 510
James Jones, 100, 100, 4000, 100, 900
Benjamin P. Norman, 35, 40, 1000, 5, 520
James Nelson, 30, 20, 900, 15, 350
Reuben Halliburton, 45,-, 500, 80, 390
Wm. Howland, 30, -, 150, 5, 260
James Howland, 25, -, 200, 25, 250
John Brown, 12, 88, 1000, 200, 380
Wm Walker, 30, -, 300, 5, 300
Nancy Morehead, -, -, -, -, 15
John Morehead, -, -, -, -, 100
Wm. H. Brown, -, -, -, -, 80
Henry L. Wootten, -, -, -, -, 15
John Ott, 50, 24, 800, 110, 160
Abner Bowen, 26, -, 200, 5, 100
Thomas Boyean (Boyeau), -, -, -, -, 50
Newton C. Miller, 250, 200, 5400, 100, 760
Jordon Brooks, 12, -, 120, 5, 67
John A. Newman, 10, -, 200, 60, 230
George W. Corn, 75, 100, 1000, 30, 150
M. T. L. Clemens, 30, 55, 900, 50, 375
Wm. Parker, 25, -, 250, 20, 200
Robert D. Smith, 25, 35, 300, 75, 375
Burrel Johnson, 70, 30, 800, 30, 400
L. D. Newman, 15, -, 150, 5, 340
D. H. Johnson, 200, 175, 6000, 100, 820
S. W. Jamison, 35, -, 400, 10, 220
Felix G. Miller, 90, 120, 2000, 40, 590
Richard Bailey, 20, -, 200, 5, 170
B. G. White, -, -, -, -, 380
Wm. T. McGrue, -, -, -, -, 145
U. F. English, 16, 4, 200, 50, 260
Littlebery English, 20, -, 200, 5, 150
Augustus H. White, 40, 300, 3400, 100, 580
Edward J. Hall, -, -, -, -, 25
Stokely White, 150, 170, 3500, 150, 850
Walter Clark, 15, -, 150, 5, 100
Norwood Cates, 15, -, 150, 5, 130

Isaiah Cates, 70, 80, 1500, 20, 345
Isaiah Kelton, -, -, -, -, 75
Joel Briles, 75, 60, 1200, 10, 265
Abner Marlin, 23, -, 200, 5, 280
Hiram Briles, 60, 100, 1200, 60, 330
John W. Rolins, 40, 80, 960, 80, 365
Joseph Pruitt, 40, 160, 1500, 5, 300
L. A. Pruit, -, -, -, -, 35
Nehemiah Taylor, 12, -, 70, 15, 180
Felix Miller, 16, 25, 400, 5, 75
Thomas T. Clark, -, -, -, -, 35
John Powel, 50, 50, 1000, 125, 500
Thomas Richarson, 95, 115, 2000, 125, 500
Wm, Booker, -, -, -, -, 75
Wm. Miller, 65, 135, 2000, 40, 330
John Osment, 25, -, 260, 4, 175
Francis M. Pruit, 50, 150, 2000, 25, 300
Henry Pruit 130, 230, 3500, 25, 800
Boker Rolins, -, -, -, -, 70
Alexander Majors, 50, 150, 2000,3 0, 340
Joel Johnson, -, -, -, -, 60
M. B. Albie, 25, -, 250, 5, 250
Richard Gother, -, -, -, -, 180
Wm. Clark, 18, 17, 400, 5, 100
Wm. Clark, 40, 80, 1200, 80, 500
John Asby, 70, 70, 1200, 30, 200
Elihugh Bigdon, 100, 100, 2000, 80, 1200
Yandle Clark, 75, 25, 1500, 20, 200
John Brothers, -, -, -, -, 70
Henry Wigs, 35, 75, 600, 40, 350
Rebecca Epps, 20, 50, 750, 25, 430
John M. Clark, 25, 70, 1500, 10, 190
Matilda Waller, -, -, -, -, 70
Jane Clark, 50, 50, 1000, 20, 550
Robert J. Kelton, 50, 55, 1500, 25, 250
Wm. Jacobs, 35, 10, 450, 15, 150
Crede T. Briant, 20, -, 80, 5, 100
George McMurry, 100, 250, 3000, 15, 400
Nancy Jemison, 100, 110, 2000, 100, 425
Mary Miller, 30, 40, 1500, 10, 270
Catharine Miller, 60, 57, 1100, 25, 365
Ann Simpson, -, -, -, -, 100
Champion Bailey, 15, -, 150, 5, 150
Edward Johnson, 45, 55, 700, 40, 300
Mathew Hoover, -, -, -, -, 50
Angaline Richerson, -, -, -, -, 20
Martin L. Alexander, 40, 40, 2000, 100, 460
Wm Rushing, -, -, -, -, 60
Daniel Gober, -, -, -, -, 150
S. B. Martin, -, -, -, -, 80
Goodman Segiorus, -, -, -, -, 70
John Woods, -, -, -, -, 100
John W. Bird, 15, -, 100, 5, 220

Richard Fulks, 40, 40, 400, 25, 550
Daniel Duncan, -, -, -, -, 60
Reason Jacobs, -, -, -, -, 20
Wm. Smith, 30, 30, 420, 5, 250
Elizabeth Erwin, 30, -, 300, 5, 120
Alfred P. Gowen, 25, 25, 400, 10, 110
Robert Lowe, 40, 60, 400, 5, 220
Mary Lowe, 40, 15, 1000, 110, 320
Samuel Lowe, 28, 95, 400, 210, 665
G. W. Robinson, 25, 60, 600, 5, 185
Wm. S. Lowe, 40, 10, 800, 80, 630
Calvin Lowe, 60, 130, 500, 60, 280
Reubin Todd, 70, 120, 500, 60, 280
Aaron Todd, 80, 163, 700, 100, 320
Fielding Todd, 70, 55, 1200, 30, 290
Alfred P. Lowe, 45, -, 1400, 135, 450
Jerry Todd, -, -, -, -, 90
Calvin Reynolds, 13, -, 130, 5, 65
Lewis Howland, 30, -, 160, 5, 200
Wm. F. Asby, 25, -, 100, 5, 300
Peter Saddler, -, -, -, -, 10
Thomas Prater, 18, -, 180, 5, 270
Jerry Jacobs, 80, 200, 1600, 120, 440
Charles Markins, 40, -, 2400, 25, 250
John Brinkley, -, -, -, -, 50
John Mankins (Markins), 165, 500, 3990, 75, 1645
Joseph Armstrong, 30, -, 180, 5, 265
Celia Mankins, -, -, -, 75, 75
Michael Borman, 50, 100, 1000, -, 230
George B. Painter, -, -, -, -, 100
Thomas Summers, 70, 55, 1000, 25, 110
Wm. D. Markins, 40, 100, 600, 30, 400
John Jacobs, 60, 4, 800, 30, 395
John W. Yardley, -, -, -, -, 110
U. T. Summers, 18, -, 270, 30, 268
David Summers, 24, 30, 500, 5, 160
Wm. Daughtery, -, -, -, -, 110
Tyler Daughtery, -, -, -, -, 70
Jerry Daughtery, 16, -, 80, 5, 140
Laura Belt, 12, -, 60, 5, 120
Wm. Morgan, -, -, -, -, 40
Davidson Summers, 20, -, 200, 5, 80
Epiritas Carlock, -, -, -, -, 180
Wm. Hazelwood, -, -, -, -, 60
James H. Kelton, 40, 60, 800, 100, 210
Bazel Jacobs, 25, 15, 320, 30, 175
George Asby, 10, -, 100, 5, 30
Robert G. White, 70, 80, 1500, 140, 840
Alexander Locite, 40, -, 400, 30, 230
James Lowe, 50, 80, 130, 25, 600
Abner Newman, 60, 80, 1400, 10, 310
A. J. McNoble, -, -, -, -, 100
John S. Hazlewood, -, -, -, -, 50
Lewis Herald, -, -, -, -, 150
Hiram Elliott, -, -, -, -, 225

James Marchbanks, 16, -, 80, 5, 180
Ambrose Cobb, 30, 100, 1600, 10 250
Thomas Allman, -, -, -, -, 10
Jivary Summers, -, -, -, -, 125
Alvin Summers, -, -, -, -, 10
Samuel Kelton, 30, 10, 400, 5, 180
Solomon Sanders, -, -, -, -, 18
Altheas Cates, 23, -, 230, 50, 110
Samuel Robinson, 12, -, 125, 5, 120
E. R. Bowen, 30, 80, 250, 5, 160
Mathew Hoover, 70, 230, 4000, 10, 420
Mary Zumbo, 30, -, 150, 5, 180
John Williams, 160, 540, 14000, 100, 570
John Gum, 30, 70, 1000, 5, 260
Virginia Darel, 25, 75, 300, 35, 210
Cam___Marlin, 35, -, 500, 10,2 00
James G. Wootten, 16, -, 160, 70, 180
Coral Wootten, 20, -, 200, 50, 180
Edward Alfred, -, -, -, -, 115
Wm. Kelton, 35, 100, 1300, 200, 240
Wm. T. Knox, 25, -, 250, -, 150
Tilford Pennywell, 25, -, 240, 5, 135
George D. Summers, 75, 75, 1300, 5, 150
Philip Prater, 60, 100, 1500, 50, 350
Clinton Jacobs, 100, 112, 2000, 90, 560
Elizabeth Ellison, -, -, -, -, 80
Plesant Jacobs, 70, 40, 800, 50, 360
Allen Serot, 18, -, 150, 5, 210
Wm. Pilkington, -, -, -, -, 19
Sarah Kelton, 20, 16, 300, 5, 170
Mary Brothers, 20, 5, 250, 5, 150
Wm. Jacobs, 15, -, 150, 5, 70
Joseph Rolins, -, -, -, -, 150
Wm. Pearson, -, -, -, -, 140
Wm. P. McKee, 40, 194, 900, 30, 150
Saloman Cates, 35, -, 350, 5, 210
Wm. Mayfield, 12, 100, -, 5, 110
Joseph Pearson, -, -, -, -, 140
Abner Summers, 90, 140, 2000, 80, 450
Jonathan Ireland, 15, -, 150, 5, 305
Robert Stephenson, 16, -, 160, 5, 135
Bartly Rushing, 30, 40, 400, 5, 140
Acy S. Lee, 20, -, 200, 5, 100
John Painter, 50, 25, 600, 30, 260
Westly Fox, 20, -, 150, 25, 230
Elizabeth Fox, 35, 45, 800, 20, 220
Wm. Rollins, 13, -, 100, 65, 180
Jackson Fox, 30, 150, 900, 20, 275
Kirchen Janican (Ganican), 15, -, 100, 5, 150
John L. Hoover, 100, 130, 2000,3 0, 815
Mathius Hoover, 100, 600, 3000, 100, 710
Julius Hoover, 50, 70, 2000, 60, 560
Ephraim B. Hoover, -, -, -, -, -
Mathew Fox, 100, 50, 4000, 50, 500

Mary A. Hoover, 110, 200, 3500, 75, 850
Thomas Marlin, 60, 74, 1400, 10, 320
William Belt, 30, -, 250, 5, 100
Dodson Belt, 15, -, 100, 5, 150
James Caldwell, 14, -, 100, 5, 75
Frederich Rushing, 80, 90, 1200, 10, 350
Mathius B. Miles, -, -, -, -, 300
Malvina Stafford, -, -, -, -, 15
John Eaton, 40, 60, 800, 30, 400
Susanna McKee, 25, 85, 600, 10, 130
James King, 20, 45, 300, 5, 120
John King, 20, 70, 300, 5, 140
Rebecca Brown, -, -, -, -, 800
Washington Gibson, 70, 120, 2500, 50, 470
Peter Fleming, 34, -, 270, 125, 520
Munroe Burnet, 15, -, 150, 5, -
Washington Benson, 30, 100, 450, 70, 180
Letty Renchar, 16, 37, 200, 5, 170
Walker Peak, 30, 10, 300, 60, 330
J. P. Hoover, 15, -, 105, 5, 155
Wm. K. Herod, 25, -, 750, 5, 180
Lewis D. Ships, 12, -, 70, 5, 105
Newton A. McElroy, 30, 95, 500, 135, 310
John Kelton, 20, -, 150, 2, 150
Doctoin Parker, 10, -, 80, 5, 135
Mabry Parker, 12, -, 120, 5, 280
Wm. Pitts, 25, 15, 400, 65, -
Mariah Bush, -, -, -, -, 60
Thomas Yeardly, 12, -, 120, 5, 100
James Yeardly, 60, 340, 1100, 190, 285
Mathew Bolin, 15, -, 150, 5, 295
Robert Brown, 2, 116, 1200, 5, 260
Frederick Fatherby, 50, 250, 3000, 5, 108
Samson Mather, -, -, -, -, 146
Byran Nichol, 45, 155, 1000, 115, 237
Jessee Thompson, 40, 300, 2500, 80, 275
George Hooper, 4, -, 40, 10, 57
Elijah Hickinlotte, 100, 250, 3000, 50, 240
John Benson, 15, -, 150, 5, 130
Merit Shelton, 20, -, 200, 5, 120
Willis Jones, 100, 500, 1500, 160, 300
Elizabeth Evans, 155, 100, 500, 5, 360
Aaron Pilkington, 19, -, 190, 5, 25
Thomas Bevin, 6, -, 60, 5, 185
Thomas W. Harry (Harny), 30, 100, 1000, 5, 300
Robt. M. Good, 10, 56, 400, 5, 140
John C. McElroy, 30, 75, 500, 5, 300
Edmond Lambert, 20, 49, 200, 5, 50
Dean Rogers, 20, 30, 150, 5, 60
Sarah Crowder, -, -, -, -, 70
Mathew Jones, 15, 5, 100, 5, 45

Wm. Harris, 1, -, -, -, 25
Dabney Lancaster, 50, 120, 700, 60, 300
Joseph Evans, 18, -, 180, 5, 85
Mathias Hoover, 100, 150, 2000, 40, 460
Benjamin McFarland, 30, -, 350, 5, 200
Pruit Dun, 70, 130, 2000, 100, 705
Hesakiah Garner, 8, -, 40, 45, 160
Frances Youree, 100, 400, 3000, 130, 1115
John W. Hoover, 17, -, 85, 5, 155
Wm. Dun, 50, 50, 500, 5, 640
Christina Laughlin, 40, 100, 700, 38, 300
Francis O. Youree, 50, 50, 600, 5, 385
Elizabeth Elder, 40, -, 240, 5, 320
Lindy Moore, 10, -, 60, 3, 90
Mathew L. McElroy, 40, 75, 1450, 20, 265
Mary Matz, 35, 10, 500, 50, 320
John D. Good, 40, 110, 500, 5, 250
Adam McElroy, 40, 30, 5, 330
Joseph Youree, 20, -, 200, 5, 35
G. W. McCulloch, 5, -, 25, 35, 145
Wm. W. Davel, 85, 115, 1500, 35, 655
Mary McFarland, 74, 200, 1500, 70, 730
Japhtha Goodman, 40, 60, 500, 5, 310
Petre Reed, 40, 60, 500, 5, 270
Sarah Reed, 25, 10, 200, 5, 190
Wm. Carnohan, 30, 40, 400, 55, 235
Aaron Stacy, 30, 30, 500, 20, 100
Peterson Gilly 70, 90, 800, 5, 300
Preston Carnohan, 42, 34, 600, 30, 170
Andrew Carnohan, 30, 60, 600, 5, 210
James Carnohan, 25, 25, 300, 30, 290
John Gordon, 40, 60, 500, 5, 330
Robert Cocke, 60, 320, 1800, 60, 400
Wm. S. Davel, 160, 173, 1600, 60, 460
Armstead Carter, 100, 130, 1000, 30, 400
Samuel Lusk, 35, 95, 800, 10, 390
Burton Lusk, 35, 150, 150, 30, 370
Charles Jones, 10, 15, 800, 35, 65
Nelson Greer, 40, 60, 250, 30, 2054
John Prater, 11, 38, -, 5, 100
James M. Newman, -, -, -, -, 74
Right Herald, 12, -, 60, 5, 80
Thomas Herald, 17, 6, 160, 6, 63
Herod Burks, 40, 160, 1400, 30, 345
Henry Herald, -, -, -, -, -
Wm. Herald, 30, 170, 800, 35, 175
Wm. Brown, -, -, -, -, 20
Reuben Herald, -, -, -, -, 100
Reuben Herald, 45, 100, 500, 25, 210
Miles Herald, 25, 100, 800, 30, 225
Reuben S. Herald, 25, 25, 150, 45, 115
Franklin Herald, -, -, -, -, 100
Arther McCrary, 29, -, 300, 10, 175
Jessee Williford, -, -, -, -, 45

Thomas W. Bruce, 5, -, 15, 25, 100
John _. Bruce, 6, 70, 100, 20, 20
Isaac Jetton, 95, 86, 2700, 130, 815
Ephraim Jetton, 40, 110, 750, 30, 275
Nancy Bruce, -, -, -, -, 10
Alvin Lowery, 4, -, 12, 5, 130
Edward Brown, 10, 40, 150, 5, 80
William Lowe, 100, 200, 1500, 100, 740
William Keath, 15, -, 75, 5, 175
Dorothy Youree, 200, 240, 2000, 80, 1400
Elizabeth Brandon, 50, -, 250, 5, 250
Mary L. Loving, 25, -, 125, 5, 120
Andrew Lewis, 30, 40, 400, 20, 300
Thomas Smoot, 50, 50, 600, 25, 410
Wm. Patrick, 65, 150, 1000, 10, 500
Wm. Hill, -, -, -, -, 200
Daniel Bradford, 70, 80, 1026, 30, 375
Garland Anderson, 35, -, 210, 5, 270
Johnson Lyons, 60, 20, 600, 100, 530
Thomas Lyons, 50, 60, 1000, 10, 350
Arther McCrary, 90, 65, 1500, 30, 765
Eligah Lyons, 40, 85, 500, 60, 425
Nathan Lyons, 250, 200, 2500, 100, 1170
Betsy Lyons, -, -, -, -, 240
Thomas Youree, 75, 80, 2000, 130, 865
Wm. Hall, 70, 100, 1100, 100, 660
Isaac Herald, 40, 22, 250, 85, 350
Robert Todd, 30, 65, 250, 10, 280
John W. Brewer, 30, -, 150, 5, 45
Thomas Carter, -, -, -, 25, 100
Wm. Jacobs, 85, 140, 1000, 30, 470
Wm. Todd, 30, -, 150, 10, 220
Wm. Todd Sr., 100, 375, 1500, 150, 700
Walker M. Todd, 20, -, 100, 5, 190
Levi Todd, 25, -, 125, 5, 220
Benjamin Todd, 60, 87, 600, 60, 140
John McCrary, 110, 255, 3000, 80, 500
George McCrary, 100, 160, 1800, 30, 520
Burrel Brown, 12, -, 60, 5, 526
Martin Elliott, -, -, -, -, 50
Houston Jacobs, 15, 110, 400, 5, 80
Medford Coffey, 100, 230, 3000, 100, 885
Daniel Bowman, 40, 80, 1200, 80, 440
Henry Bowman, -, -, -, -, 125
Benjamin Bowman, 75, 96, 1500, 100, 430
T. P. Hall, 15, -, 150, 5, 85
Hiram Murry, 120, 280, 2000, 10, 400
John Fulks, 80, 250, 3300, 100, 630
Wm. Murry, 200, 300, 2000, 150, 980
Albert M. Fleming, 15, -, 180, 5, 250
James Crawford, 110, 115, 3000, 110, 750
Thomas Pully, 50, -, 1000, 65, 370

James P. Merit, 150, 87, 4000, 80, 720
Isaiah Robertston, -, -, -, 85, 365
E. L. Mathers, 200, 220, 4220, 220, 940
John E. Vaughan, 5, 45, 600, 500, 430
Stephen A. Hill, 125, 191, 3000, 50, 290
Peter T. Vaughan, 60, 40, 2200, 75, 490
Thomas Owen, 60, 70, 1800, 100, 670
Nathaniel Owen, 100, 70, 1170, 10, 310
Stephen Owen, 15, -, 150, 5, 150
Richard D. Saunders, 35, -, 350, 25, 350
Samuel Rucker, 300, 300, 8000, 640, 1200
John Miller, -, -, -, -, 10
James Jones, 75, 15, 900, 15, 170
Cloa Walch, -, -, -, -, 80
Wm. Mullins, 30, -, 300, 10, 130
Robert W. Gardener, 100, 126, 3500, 170, 710
James Bour, 150, 350, 3000, 100, 270
A. C. Sublete, 170, 174, 6800, 120, 595
Thomas Dill, 11, -, 80, 5, 200
Samuel McAdoo, 220, 323, 6000, 120, 850
Aaron McCrary, -, -, -, -, 10
Nancy Arnold, 30, 50, 450, 5, 250
Silas M. Ragsdale, -, -, -, -, 80
Samuel Wade, 100, 113, 1200, 50, 345
John Owen, 11, -, 100, 5, 100
D. T. Hill, -, -, -, -, 60
Susan Rolinson, 300, 340, 3200, 270, 1030
Lin Martha Rolinson, -, -, -, -, 300
Linas Rather, 30, -, 300, 38, 185
Wm. S. Rather, 35, -, 350, 40, 215
James Alexander, 1, 49, -, -, 10
John H. Alexander, -, -, 250, 2, 20
Thomas Lofly (Tofly), 50, 30, 800, 30, 305
Ezekial Rollins, 7, -, 50, 5, 70
R. L. Hazelwood, 35, 161, 1000, 25, 125
T. J. Swain, 1, 19, 100, -, 75
John Oliver, -, -, -, -, 115
Isaac Winston, 50, -, 250, 10, 205
Henry Hurt (Hunt), 20, 55, 300, 5, 140
James T. Leach, 15, 270, 180, 12, 155
Joseph Johnson, 100, 12, 3384, 150, 465
Joseph B. Arnold, 12, 60, 300, 5, 210
Thomas Cotton, 3, -, 600, 55, 70
Wilson Edwards, 25, 70, 250, 10, 140
Wm. D. Harris (Faris), 30, -, 500, 70, 130
Carly Cox, -, -, -, -, 3
Jeremiah Barrot (Burnet), -, -, -, -, 10
John B. Edwards, 3, 7, 150, -, 120
Milly Moon, -, -, -, -, 10
Elmodum Barrot (Barnet), 7, 20, 320, 5, 160

John P. Stewart, 45, 70, 370, 20, 246
Soloman Bonds, 100, 170, 850, 60, 230
Paul V. Johns, 100, 124, 2000, 120, 680
Hiram Hunt, 35, 165, 1000, 30, 340
Isaac Hall, 30, 70, 600, 10, 110
Jonathan Hall, 45, 50, 600, 75, 345
Hinton Barlow, 10, -, 200, 5, 115
Stephen Arnold, 1, -, 10, 1, 65
Hugh Hearry, 25, 15, 600, 10, 195
Thomas Dunaway, 50, 90, 420, 30, 323
Jacob Dunaway, -, -, -, -, 80
Thomas Pearcy, 40, 45, 400, 10, 175
Josiah Haw, 12, 26, 170, 25, 55
Jacob Johns, 40, 60, 1000, 25, 206
Sterling C. Edwards, -, -, -, 5, 90
Wm. Leath, 200, -, 2000, 100, 500
Suth Hall, -, -, -, -, 50
Nancy Dunaway, 75, 125, 1500, 30, 415
Wm. Johns, 150, 100, 3000, 120, 800
Wm. A. Vaughan, 150, 180, 590, 95, 350
Moserly Hill, 20, 20, 300, 5, 175
Mary Smith, 8, -, 40, 3, 90
John Mckee, 15, 26, 250, 185, 515
James McDanel, 18, -, 40, -, 175
Thomas Pearcy, -, -, -, -, 60
Wm. Dunaway, 60, 30, 2500, 25, 400
Joel Hall, 100, 60, 2000, 10, 310
Wm. S. Turner, 50, 80, 1040, 30, 240
Nathan Thurman, 30, 39, 300, 5, 65
Wm. H. McDanel, 12, -, 160, 5, 60
Wm. McDanel, 50, 60, 600, 5, 310
John Pearcy, 35, 35, 400, 5, 200
Algermine Pearcy, 75, 85, 800, 10, 410
Ambrose McKee, 100, 180, 1200, 10, 365
N. H. Johns, 50, 80, 720, 50, 250
Martha Marshall, 40, 85, 400, 28, 193
Peter Petterson, -, -, -, -, 65
Rebecca Pully, -, -, -, -, -
Rebecca Lewis, 40, -, 320, -, 310
Eliga Allen, 50, 40, 1000, 30, 380
Abner Upchurch, 20, -, 200, 5, 270
W.M. Childers, -, -, -, -, 250
B. H. McAdoo, 300, 217, 6000, 200, 1775
Mary McAdoo, 110, 290, 4000, 110, 550
Robert W. Martin, 100, 290, 4000, 40, 475
Kendel Barlow, 40, 40, 900, 10, 190
Plesant White, 60, 30, 1000, 100, 500
S. A. S. Ivy, 45, 36, 1500, 15, 580
Elizabeth Davis, 50, 53, 1500, 120, 240
Spencer S. Slaughter, 25, -, 400, -, 100
Lunsford P. Black, 325, 475, 1600, 250, 1120
Hardy M. Burton (Barton), 175, 375, 9000, 200, 1120

Benjamin Rucker, 400, 400, 16000, 350, 1600
Robert P. Pearcy, -, -, -, 2, 132
Jessee Brashere, 200, 300, 5000, 100, 1020
Jacob Strups, 20, -, 200, 5, 170
Jams B. Huchinson, 25, -, 120, 30, 230
Arthur Lewis, 15, -, 50, 5, 100
James C. Fartherby, 100, 350, 800, 50, 420
Sarah Burnet, -, -, -, -, -
Samuel Burnet, -, -, -, -, 70
Turner Patterson, 16, 28, 120, 5, 55
Thomas Price, 15, -, 45, 5, 70
James Jemison, 20, -, 40, 5, 320
Wm. J. McDanel, 15, 45, 250, 5, 180
Chalres Demart (Dement), 45, 75, 440, 30, 200
Elizabeth Fannin (Fornin), 25, -, 115, 55, 250
Elbert J. Allen, 70, 180, 4000, 35, 500
Armisted Hartwell, 150, 165, 4700, 150, 910
Warren Moore, 120, 150, 3500, 80, 760
James A. Tofly, 80, 75, 2000, 120, 5000
James Fuller, 30, -, 500, 50, 210
Isaac M. Hicks, 150, -, 2250, 250, 330
James Sanford, 100, 125, 4000, 40, 550
Wm. Dunn, -, -, -, -, 20
James Nichol, -, -, -, -, 10
John Thompson, -, -, -, -, 300
Wm. P. Sharp, 120, 62, 3500, 100, 535
Mary Sharp, 120, 55, 2500, 75, 400
Robert Jones, 125, 115, 3100, 125, 380
Wm. H. Guthery, 50, 40, 1800, 40, 130
Anderson Pitts, 13, -, 360, 5, 190
Theofilas Pitts, 16, -, 320, 5, 190
Henry C.Clayton, 80, 90, 3000, 35, 155
Nancy Herendon, 22, -, 100, 5, -
Lucinda Snider, -, -, -, -, 75
John Strupe, 100, 300, 3000, 560, 770
Wm. Zumbro, 30, -, 240, 5, 185
Wm. Yearwood, 60, 250, 9000, 100, 40
John H. Keilough, 30, 270, 1000, 80, 385
Jas. R. McClannahan, 40, 180, 650, 15, 300
James M. Anderson, 40, 60, 500, 70, 290
Wm. Hill, 12, 48, 120, -, 65
James M. Yearwood, 15, -, 90, -, 20
Wm. A. Maxwell, 5, 10, 100, 5, -
Adam Hope, 20, 116, 800, 5, 280
Clara Clark, 10, -, 30, 5, 75
James Richardson, 40, 150, 500, 5, 280
John Crumpton, 30, 117, 335, 5, 155
Lemuel M. Baird, 65, 65, 10000, 40, 620
Richard Wasson, 45, 80, 12000, 10, 210

David M. Jarrot, 50, 70, 5000, 100, 400
James P. Baird, 36, 118, 3500, 75, 325
Benjamin Lillard, 470, 800, 24500, 150, 1300
J. M. Baird, 90, 80, 6800, 100, 658
George Lillard, 30, -, 450, 5, 365
Wm. A. Keilough, 150, 86, 4300, 10, 275
Joel Woods, -, -, -, -, 40
George Zumbro, -, -, -, -, 220
James Duglas, -, -, -, -, 120
Ivin Harris, 9, 27, 108, 5, 120
Kasiah Arbuckle, 25, 25, 200, 2, 10
Samuel Smith, 40, 20, 1000, 70, 290
Jackson Walace, 60, -, 1800, 5, 390
John Bradley, 4, 350, 10700, 10, 160
Alsia Harris, 15, -, 450, 35, 420
Jeremiah Kirby, 100, 100, 3000, 78, 430
Absalom Crumpton, -, -, -, -, 60
Lucy Vaughan, -, -, -, -, 150
Benjamin Johnson, 400, 250, 13000, 700, 1275
James Fleming, 21, 24, 1350, 110, 445
David Lillard, 65, 35, 2025, 25, 350
Mordakai Lillard, 80, 60, 2600, 100, 375
John Johnson, 10, 40, 2500, 60, 145
Wm. J. Philips, 120, 93, 5300, 75, 465
John Baird, 100, 65, 4000, 60, 380
Benjamin Clayton, 150, 184, 3000, 88, 650
Mary Wills, -, -, -, -, 25
Stephen Dove, -, -, -, -, 30
Benjamin Moore, 30, -, 600, 60, 145
Thomas Midloff, 20, -, 340, 18, 200
Joanna T. Lawrence, 30, -, 300, 5, 200
John M. Caldwell, 50, 60, 2000, 100, 400
Henry Kirby, 150, 150, 6500, 500, 680
James Rucker, 340, 200, 10800, 350, 2400
Andrew J. Olipant, 40, -, 300, -, 100
Nancy Thompson, 60, 70, 2600, 10, 300
Lunsford D. Yondle, 75, 225, 6000, 65, 1270
Martha Brashere, 25, 25, 750, 55, 180
Joseph Rucker, 140, 100, 4800, 75, 435
John W. Qualls, 100, 50, 3000, 150, 430
David Mitchel, 110, 155, 5000, 100, 600
Daniel Dejarnett, 80, 85, 3500, 75, 600
Mary Dejarnett, 70, 30, 2000, 35, 160
Mary House, -, -, -, -, 100
Wm. Picket, -, -, -, -, 115
Wm. Burchet,-, -, -, -, 80
Wm. Harrison, 110, 120, 400, 85, 455
Anderson Burnet, 40, 10, 2175, 10, 370
Mary Harrison, 50, 60, 2000, 5, 360
Noble Moon, 13, -, 530, 5, 68
George Sanford, 100, 60, 9500, 140, 800

Samuel Watkins, 125, 55, 3600, 170, 555
Owen E. Austin, 18, 11, 1200, 80, 350
John Jones, 135, 95, 7500, 100, 320
Wm. R. Rucker, 200, 175, 11250, 100, 426
Isaac McCulloch, 75, 20, 250, 65, 245
John L. Jetton, 150, 110, 4500, 180, 750
Allen Cotton, 60, -, 600, 30, 260
John Brown, 250, 150, 9000, 320, 1980
Wm. H. Smith, 200, 180, 5600, 90, 940
Patrick Ryan, -, -, -, -, 60
Michael Gallaher, -, -, -, -, 100
Abraham Ford, 40, -, 600, 10, 57
Margaret Chestnut, -, -, -, -, 20
Thomas Brown, -, -, -, -, 240
John Thompson, -, -, -, -, 85
James B. Cavender, -, -, -, -, 60
Thomas Brown, 100, 215, 3000, 115, 550
Thomas Wetherford, -, -, -, -, 120
Franklin Brown, 40, -, 240, 95, 260
Tobias Coonts, 10, -, 30, 5, 120
Spencer Course, 60, 60, 600, 35, 360
Mariah Greer, 10, -, 60, -, 113
John Grear, 20, 60, 600, 10, 310
Stephen Grear, 10, -, 60, 5, -
A. S. Butler, 100, 185, 1400, 114, 440
Silas McHenry, 150, 250, 4500, 75, 540
Josiah Jordan, 15, 25, 215, 5, 120
James Orerall (Overall), 70, 150, 2000, 40, 560
William Thomas, 12, -, 120, 5, 133
Nace Overall, 40, 60, 600, 365, 460
N. S. Overall, 60, 60, 800, 115, 450
Elizabeth Arnold, 12, -, 100, 5, 110
Catharine Ivy, 18, -, 70, 3, 125
Robert C. Pearce, 35, 70, 600, 35, 360
Wm. Mathers, -, -, -, -, 80
Z. C. Bell, 20, -, 80, -, 70
John Bell, -, -, -, -, 20
E. M. Lawrence, 50, 72, 550, 50, 255
Esther Bivins, -, -, -, -, 50
Richard W. Bivins, 30, 110, 550, 5, 300
Leonard Bains, -, -, -, -, 15
Thomas Huchinson, 200, 250, 5000, 95, 2375
Edward Ford, 30, 28, 300, 5, 125
R. S. Hunt, -, -, -, -, 130
Robert Simpson, 65, 60, 1000, 35, 420
Elizabeth Barton, 50, -, 500, 5, 140
Henry Bains, 80, 80, 2600, 65, 700
Hosea Northcut, 60, 50, 1000, 88, 300
H. C. Crouse, 20, -, 200, 25, 150
James Northcut, 12, -, 120, 5, 145
Michael Swink, 30, 40, 400, 4, 145
Benjamin Roland, -, -, -, -, 80
Hugh Walace, 10, 40, 200, 2, 150

Wm. Henry Smith, 150, 126, 2760, 35, 740
Mathew Pitts, 30, -, 300, 30, 155
Charles E. Owen, 100, 90, 1600, 50, 110
Robert Thompson, 20, -, 100, 5, 250
Sarah Neal, 50, 10, 350, 5, 216
John A. Reeves, 30, 30, 700, 5, 265
James McCulloch, 95, 80, 2000, 85, 358
John R. Dun, 14, 56, 215, 5, 130
Ann Thompson, 70, 255, 3000, 60, 400
Alexander McCulloch, 50, -, 800, 50, 160
Samuel J. Rucker, 90, 90, 2000, 85, 475
J. C. Reeves, 200, 300, 6000, 250, 750
Wilson Kerr, -, -, -, -, 250
Wm. Arnet, 40, -, 300, 20, 220
John Arnet, -, -, -, -, 160
Marshall Saunders, 100, 150, 1200, 75, 470
Andrew M. Fort, 16, -, 80, 5, 75
Marvel Dill, 40, 85, 800, 10, 500
Wm. Hunt, 75, 225, 1500, 85, 560
Andrew J. Hunt, -, -, -, -, 110
Josiah Clark, 5, 95, 500, 5, 127
Francis S. Slaton, 10, 30, 100, 5, 70
George Lawrence, 12, 28, 150, 55, 220
Redford Barton, 20, -, 200, 5, 185
Surinfield Barton, 12, 220, 1000, 45, 260
Hill Barton, 15, -, 150, 5, 115
Ezekiel Pitts, 15, -, 150, 5, 270
Ellis Davis, 50, -, 200, 110, 330
Nathan Hall, 30, 100, 700, 40, 170
E. F. Smith, 250, 300, 5000, 800, 910
Caroline Gilliam, 150, 60, 4000, 85, 520
William Gilliam, -, -, -, -, 70
Richard Brown, 30, 50, 700, 35, 185
James Mires (Mins, Mims), 10, -, 150, -, 10
James L. McKnight, 30, 47, 600, 10, 260
David M. McKnight, 30, 82, 1250, 50, 325
Richard Sevaner, 35, -, 350, 15, 335
George Peoples (Probles), 150, 150, 4000, 75, 609
Thomas Cragner (Crayner), 50, 60, 1000, 15, 630
Wm. G. Morrison, 33, 17, 600, 10, 375
Shadrack Kelly, 20, 30, 300, 5, 215
Robert Black, 60, 60, 800, 85, 510
P. C. Talley, 160, 267, 500, 170, 1285
John Selvage, 150, 150, 1800, 78, 906
Edward Donoho, -, -, -, -, 95
Wm. V. Thompson, -, -, -, -, 80
James Bell, -, -, -, -, 105
Jesse Rayney, -, -, -, -, 125
John E. Newman, -, -, -, -, 175
A. B. Witherspoon, -, -, -, -, 120

Robert F. Marshal, 50, 50, 1200, 200, 580
B. W. White, -, -, -, -, 95
B. H. Brilbo, -, -, -, -, 165
Sterling H. Bottoms, -, -, -, -, 110
Jesse Johns, -, -, -, -, 30
Jordon Patterson, -, -, -, -, 70
Joseph Fear (Fan), 6, -, 60, 8, 25
Jesse Alexander, -, -, 2000, 315, 700
Wm. Ray, 150, 50, -, -, 45
Robert Church, -, -, -, -, 95
James Wooldrigee, 60, 45, 1000, 40, 265
Dennis Smith, 100, 130, 2000, 135, 570
Thomas Vaught, 70, 30, 1000, 10, 310
James Blackwood, 30, 98, 1200, 10, 235
Henderson Cole, 50, 50, 1000, 80, 210
James Vaught, -, -, -, -, 350
John C. Hood, 150, 90, 2000, 150, 1215
Joseph Knox, 50, 40, 670, 85, 1745
Mathew (Mathias) Crowly, 75, 92, 2100, 40, 420
Parthenia Donoho, 150, 200, 3000, 150, 1640
John S. Lacitee, 100, 93, 2500, 100, 1755
Calvin Dillen, 40, 30, 500, 40, 265
Wm. Miller, 6, 24, 150, 5, 40
Wm. Gormany, 32, 100, 600, 10, 170
Wm. Dillen, 65, 60, 800, 35, 380
Jesse Jennings, 75, 93, 1000, 700, 500
Arns__, Patterson, 60, 70, 1400, 10, 485
Sarah Moss, -, -, -, -, 17
Amos Hays, 12, 15, 300, 25, 170
Adam Taylor, 13, 15, 300, 10, 190
John Vaught, 30, 40, 500, 450, 170
Thomas Dillen, 40, 43, 500, 5, 240
James Jordon (Jordorn), 25, 30, 700, 10, 240
Thomas Lacitee, 30, -, 300, 4, 165
Wm. M. Wilson, 13, -, 130, 5, 135
Thomas Wilson, 59, 95, 900, 110, 175
Alexander Jordon, 50, 40, 1300, 10, 665
Nancy Jordon, -, -, -, -, 140
David Jordon, 95, 180, 3000, 320, 730
Thomas Cole, 115, 138, 1250, 50, 775
Wm. L. Fan, 34, 36, 550, 10, 260
Reuben Adams, -, -, -, -, 16
John Smith, -, -, -, -, 15
George Bell, -, -, -, -, 20
John Ragner(Rayner), -, -, -, -, 36
Sarah Huchinson, 20, 20, 60, -, 75
Hardy Parker, 12, -, 120, 3, 35
James K. Mathers, 40, 60, 1000, 5, 135
Wm. Bell, 45, 45, 1000, 10, 135
Wm. J. Ball, -, -, -, -, 250
Wm. B. Jordon, -, -, -, -, 40
Thomas T. Hays, 25, -, 250, 5, 365
Wm. L. Mathers, 50, 80, 1000, 50, 515

John Doil, -, -, -, -, 45
Robert J. Allen, 45, 50, 850, 10, 145
James Hill, 15, -, 150, 5, 260
Sarah Jones, -, -, -, -, 120
James Lahigh, -, -, -, -, 80
Eli__ Jennings, 7, -, 50, 5, 188
Robert Pilon, 25, 10, 200, 5, 300
Wm. Hill, 60, 73, 1300, 30, 460
John Coonts, 5, -, 50, -, 44
Mary Anderon, -, -, -, -, 15
Nathan Harris, 80, 120, 1000, 115, 535
Horace Patterson, 64, 107, 1300, 15, 500
Amos Jarman, 95, 155, 1500, 20, 550
Granville Midling, 85, 27, 1660, 50, 340
Catharine Murry, -, -, -, -, 65
Wm. Adams, -, -, -, -, 65
Willeba Coonts, -, -, -, -, 90
Henry Jones, 40, 145, 1200, 75, 290
Joseph Dill, 70, 70, 2000, 85, 475
Coty Stephens, -, -, -, -, 25
Stephen Grear, 20, -, 50, 30, 160
Jos. Grear, 16, -, 160, 5, 100
Henry Crouse, 70, 70, 1000, 25, 300
Nathan Grear, 100, 50, 1500, 30, 675
David Dement, 75, 90, 2500, 85, 575
Ann B. Donal ,180, 220, 4300, 110, 820
Peyton Mcadoo, 105, 128, -, 85, 675
Lidia Hays, 15, 10, 100, -, 100
James Hays, -, -, -, -, 50
Lemuel Murry, -, -, -, -, 35
James Swink, -, -, -, -, 190
George Parks, -, -, -, -, 240
James D. Oore (Dore), 30, -, 450, 10, 115
Dolison Barker, 50, 140, 1500, 30, 410
D. W. Barr, 20, 20, 275, 10, 135
Isaac Crocker, -, -, -, -, 110
Wm. Sullivan, -, -, -, -, 110
S. M. Elrod, 60, -, 500, 25, 417
Jacob Wright, 750, 1200, 17000, 250, 2400
Andrew Alexander, 150, -, 2500, 250, 1550
John D. Smith, 250, 50, 2000, 40, 600
Daniel Wright, 70,6 0, 1200, 50, 543
Thurstain Daniel, 300, 800, 500, 75, 1027
Cobb Martin, 16, 29, 200, 5, 327
Hampton Sullivan, 25, -, 120, 75, 500
James C. Elrod, 40, 160, 1200, 60, 380
John Dennis, 14, -, 140, 10, 160
Stephen Mitchel, 25, -, 200, 5, 95
Robert Mitchel, 27, 7, 100, 30, 200
Robert Gallaher, -, -, -, -, 70
Martha Davis, 45, 55, 650, 5, 215
James A. McErvin, -, -, -, -, 300
Lucinda McErvin (McEwen), -, -, -, -, 30
David F. Tassy, 30, 60, 540, 85, 405

John M. Tassy, 25, 25, 300, 5, 215
John D. Alexander, -, -, 3000, 60, 665
Samuel A. McKnight, 50, 50, 800, 40, 650
Samuel C. McQuister, 25, -, 250, 10, 397
Henry Fagan, 50, 52, 100, 15, 275
Henry Barkley, 50, 4, 500, 60, 68
John Maberry, 45, 80, 900, 60, 200
Thomas C. Higden, 15, -, 150, 5, 105
Enos McKnight, 100, 130, 1600, 60, 545
James McKnight, 80, 300, 2000, 150, 1040
Charlotte Cook, 30, -, 300, 10, 385
Stephen Cook, 40, -, 300, 10, 218
Andrew Barkley, 40, 40, 1000, 35, 500
Samuel Knox, 50, 50, 1000, 40, 200
Dennis Hagwood, 45, 55, 1000, 55, 600
Wm. McKnight, 150, 35, 2500, 150, 910
Gilly Dell, 65, 115, 2000, 35, 595
Samuel Vaught, 40, 95, 1000, 10, 185
Benjamin Knox, 80, 120, 2500, 115, 783
Alfred Martin, 3, -, 10, -, 52
James Vaught, 40, -, 60, 55, 265
Fanny Barker, 35, 15, 600, 10, 147
George Vaught, -, -, -, 110, 575
Wm. Crawford, 5, -, 200, 5, 115
Gilbert Moss, -, -, -, -, 20
John B. McGee, 45, 100, 750, 60, 290
Wm. Thomas, 25, -, 250, 10, 275
Frances Thomas. 90, 70, 1100, 60, 2385
J. J. Wordfin, -, -, -, -, 142
Abraham Overall, 100, 125, 2500, 70, 515
Nancy Overall, 100, 100, 2000, 65, 550
Richard Floid, 90, 210, 2500, 65, 420
Thomas A. Floid, 50, 20, 600, 5, 190
Backster D. Overall, 65, 75, 2000, 40, 245
Robert Summers, 10, -, 100, 5, 145
Wm. McComes, 35, 30, 300, 25, 345
Francis R. Ryan, 125, 240, 2200, 115, 490
Margaret Jones, 55, 145, 1000, 78, 610
Anderson Jones, 50, 50, 800,100, 650
Robert Overall, 100, 200, 2400, 75, 800
Asberry Overall, 40, 40, 800, 10, 140
Thomas Woods, 15, 85, 300, 65, 400
Wm. Northcut, 46, -, 60, -, 81
Hosea Northcut, -, -, -, -, 130
A. J. Kerl, 15, -, 105, 10, 80
Reason Phelps, 10, 20, 60, 5, 75
Samuel Williford, 30, -, 240, 10, 125
Robert Williford, 40, 120, 1500, -, 75
Lidia Saunders, 12, 10, 75, -, 20
Robert Saunders, 50, 180, 800, 30, 395
Caroline Wright, -, -, -, -, 35

John S. Wright, 112, 24, 3500, 135, 85
Thomas Lewis, 16, -, 80, 10, 200
Thomas L. Saunders, -, -, -, -, 115
John King, -, -, -, -, 20
Samuel P. McKnight, 50, 50, 800, 10, 40
William McGee, 12, -, 100, 5, 70
James B. Bell, 8, -, 40, 5, 75
Robert McGill, 12, -, 60, 2, 65
Wm. Barker (Booker), 20, 100, 800, 10, 290
George Cook, 16, -, 48, 10, 55
Robert Boyd, 30, 90, 600, 10, 220
Isaac McGill, -, -, -, -, 70
Thomas Elrod, -, -, -, -, 85
Ezekial Beaty, 6, -, 60, 5, 6
Thomas Beaty, 12, -, 60, 5, 135
Nathaniel Beaty, -, -, -, -, 150
Obadiah Bell, -, -, -, -, 50
Wm. Beaty, 50, 250, 1200, 90, 540
Samuel Herendon, -, -, -, -, 140
Wm. C. Lewis, 25, 20, 415, 10, 265
Wm. E. Watts, 6, -, 60, 5, 90
Winfrey Witherspoon, 70, 80, 1200, 90, 640
Stewart McElhotten, 6, 19, 150, 5, 100
Caroline McKnight, 6, 19, 125, 5, 140
Jam__ James, 65, 40, 750, 116, 640
Joseph Trimbles, 300, 500, 3000, 165, 1273
Nancy Palmer, 8, -, 80, 5, 210
Andrew Palmer, 12, -, 60, 5, 139
James McKee Jr., 30, 50, 400, 60, 165
James McKee Sr., 100, 200, 4000, 60, 410
James Northcut, -, -, -, -, 110
Robert Sulivan, 15, -, 160, 10, 175
John Sneed, 20, 250, 1200, 40, 260
Green Palmer, 12, -, 60, 5, 90
John Patrick, 40, -, 200, 5, 150
James Barker, 10, -, 50, -, 160
A. M. McKnight, 50, 70, 1600, 30, 370
Joseph Morton, 200, 153, 5000, 200, 1000
Simmons Peak, 100, 200, 3000, 75, 235
Joseph R. Thompson, 4, -, 40, 60, 420
Nancy Peak, 40, 25, 800, 78, 350
Wm. N. Moore, 45, -, 450, 30, 230
Wm. J. Wolhup, 60, 90, 800, 50, 333
Charles J. Grie, 100, 100, 2000, 40, 360
John W. Luke, 30, -, 270, 10, 240
James Wolhup, 100, 60, 2000, 50, 570
Peyton Sheppard, 6, -, 100, 10, 75
Joseph Bolin, 6, 29, 95, 45, 130
Wm. L. Bradly, 12, -, 120, 5, 260
Mahala Beaty, 200, 300, 4000, 100, 850
Franklin L. Hall, 65, 40, 1000, 65, 320

Willis Sanford, -, -, -, -, 115
Sarah Cornohan, 35, 65, 500, 10, 228
Wm. M. McCulloch, 30, 70, 1000, 45, 360
G. W. Brandon, 100, 40, 2000, 200, 310
Chales Read, 200, 300, 15000, 1000, 1230
L. L. Peay , 70, 80, 3000, 100, 435
John Davidson, 70, 60, 1000, 100, 225
Elizabeth P. Tinch, 60, 120, 1000, 45, 430
David Herald, 50, 200, 1700, 50, 490
Wm. D. Smith, 30, 70, 1000, 60, 285
Caleb Early, 40, 60, 1000, 40, 245
John W. Beasley, 31, 150, 250, 20, 65
Wyley Ballard, 100, 12, 2500, 40, 240
Elihugh Jones, 100, 300, 4000, 70, 690
Elizabeth Moore, 12, -, 130, 50, 143
John A. Yearwood, 65, 110, 900, 40, 650
Wm. Brown, 93, 120, 1800, 80, 427
Wm. Johnson, -, -, -, -, 65
James Ballard, 9, -, 90, -, 35
Wm. Yearwood, -, -, -, -, 155
James Pace, 15, -, 150, -, 24
Wm. C. Cross, 15, 80, 500, 65, 175
Elizabeth Hoover, 30, 70, 850, 5, 145
James Holmes, -, -, -, -, 130
Jesse Gilliam, 70, 130, 1200, 55, 235
Henry Gilliam -, -, -, -, 30
Stephen Cantrel, -, -, -, -, 48
Reuben Rex, 45, 45, 600, 65, 440
Allen Jemison, 15, -, 150, 10, 68
Samuel Shelton, 25, 20, 300, 5, 172
Samuel Fulks, 70, 30, 1500, 70, 283
Wm. Huchinson, 25, 50, 600, 60, 295
Joseph McCrackin, 75, 25, 250, 45, 438
James Yearwood, 60, 90, 1500, 5, 155
Randolph Hill, 30, 20, 400, 25, 240
John E. Beasley, -, -, -, 3, 140
Joshua Helton, -, -, -, 2, 42
Rachael Wilson, 4, 12, 100, 5, 15
Carrol Pace, 50, 60, 600, 4, 325
Daniel G. Hoover, 15, 35, 500, 5, 148
J. N. Thompson, 10, -, 100, 5, 150
James E. Daniel 12, 18, 150, 65, 214
Thomas Burnet, 30, 10, 160, 80, 265
Edward Adams, 130, 200, 1200, 50, 185
B. R. Bivins, -, -, -, -, 165
James Mitchel, 20, -, 30, 5, 190
James L. Bowman, 65, 75, 1800, 75, 580
Rebecca Goodloe, 60, 148, 1700, 35, 345
Isaac Wright, 15, 10, 550, 10, 540
Nicholas Cornohan, 28, -, 280, 60, 230
Harnet McEwen, 30, 85, 300, 60, 190
Zenas Saunders, 75, 65, 1000, 100, 445
Margaret Todd, 10, 30, 80, 5, 30
Thomas Covington, 25, 25, 175, 5, 172

Wm. Pace, 25, 25, 300, 5, 75
Dolison Barker, 15, 50, 500, 10, 160
Wm. Lowing, 30, 30, 400, 10, 230
Mima Taylor, 8, 6, 30, -, 19
James McKnight, 35, 40, 400, 60, 145
John _. Smith, 35, 40, 400, 10, 130
Ramsey Wetherford, -, -, -, -, 22
Frederick A. Hoover, 20, 55, 300, 10, 160
Levi Johnson, -, -, -, -, 42
James. M. Wetherly, 70, 155, 2500, 50, 505
Edward Croslin, -, -, -, -, 95
Elizabeth Hughs, 15, 35, 300, 10, 180
Rolston Arbuckle, 40, 70, 632, 110, 415
Charles N. Wetherford, 6, 19, 86, 5, 40
Wm. S. Huchinson, -, -, -, -, 122
Morris A. Goodloe, 75, 75, 2000, 60, 210
Thomas Brandon, 20, -, 100, 55, 165
Ezekiel Ivins, 65, 130, 2500, 30, 846
R___ Ivins, 20, -, 200, 10, 129
Jenet Cook, 140, 136, 5000, 195, 1245
Beverly M. Miller, -, -, -, -, 10
James E. Jones, -, -, -, -, 105
Enoch Jones, 150, 150, 3000, 75, 1400
John H. Frie, 75, 187, 1000, 75, 270
Stephen Leroy, -, -, -, -, 50
John W. Hall, 180, 300, 6000, 200, 1075
G. B. Hall, -, -, -, -, 600
Joel B. Northcut, -, -, -, -, -
Robert E. Richardson, -, -, -, -, 110
Livina Posy, -, -, -, -, 65
Martha McCrag, -, -, -, -, 35
John Burnett, 150, 106, 2500, 150, 545
J. J. Hoberry, -, -, -, -, 12
Wm. Burnett, -, -, -, -, 10
Wilson Shelton, -, -, -, -, 67
W. G. Bishop, 70, 80, 800, 80, 277
Wm. Burnett, 7, 10, 80, 55, 227
J. H. Williams, -, -, -, 5, 16
Elizabeth Higden, -, -, -, -, 40
Stepney Montgomery, -, -, -, 5, 55
Wm. Hollingsworth, 35, 65, 550, 15, 65
Jno. R. Eskridge, 30, 70, 600, 40, 217
Jno. Mullins, 140, 90, 2750, 300, 1050
G. W. Ivey, 50, 50, 1000, 88, 295
Jno. W. Walker, 60, 68, 1000, 80, 340
Mush Luck, -, -, -, 10, 261
Jno. W. Fletcher, -, -, -, -, 60
Joshua Phelps, 60, 70, 780, 6, 160
Jno. S. Vaughn, -, -, -, -, 10
Asa R. Phelps, 40, 56, 500, 120, 477
Wm Walder (Walden) Sr., 50, 138, 1800, 40, 260
Jno. L. Bell, 4, 7, 50, 8, 135
Judith Covington, -, -, -, -, 32
E. S. Walden, -, -, -, -, 91

Duberry Cowthern, 15, 18, 900, 5, 142

Thomas Latimer, -, -, -, 10, 263

Jno. Martin, 60, 91, 3000, 140, 339

Thos. J. Mabry, 171, 229, 6400, 60, 760

Thos. W. Shelton, 70, 30, 600, 80, 760

Lewis G. Burnett, 100, 70, 1200, 100, 474

Wm. N. Mason, 70, 39, 1000, 20, 300

Nathan L. Norvell, 80, 20, 1000, 100, 463

Thos. McNeal, -, -, -, 5, 90

Eli Sinclair, -, -, -, 5, 96

Leml. R. Mullins, 135, 135, 3500, 300, 605

Hardy Tawns, -, -, -, 6, 84

Nathan W Carter, 65, 150, 2200, 130, 578

Thos. Fuller, -, -, -, 5, 40

Martha Sparrow, -, -, -, -, 20

Wm. Goodman, 45, 51, 900, 100, 370

Thos. Neely, -, -, -, 7, 297

Jas. W. Ight, -, -, -, 7, 130

Jno. D. Neely, -, -, -, -, 12

Jno. N. Balentine, 60, 40, 800, 140, 320

Wm. St. Clair, -, -, -, -, 40

Charles Balentine, 100, 126, 1800, 30, 280

Jas. Crutchfield, -, -, -, -, 10

Amiga C. Martin, 110, 190, 4800, 150, 220

Wm. Martin, 60, 140, 3200, 125, 661

Wm. Whitmore, -, -, -, -, 8

Jno. Z. Morton, -, -, -, 5, 251

Lewis Tune, -, -, -, 5, 96

Wm. H. Davis, 199, 81, 3500, 60, 580

Benjamin Furguson, 453, 592, 19400, 4710, 2420

Jno. Edmonson, 160, 188, 6645, 130, 1200

Wm. Robb, 120, 135, 4650, 110, 740

Jas. H. Ralston, 80, 139, 4000, 150, 602

Saml. Williams, -, -, -, -, 16

Hiram Dobson, 70, 98, 2000, 145, 375

Mary Thompson, 100, 70, 2000, 70, 409

Timothy D. Sample, -, -, -, 20, 425

Moser R. Buchanan, 400, 780, 16800, 220, 1819

Robt. M. Hunter-, -, -, -, 85

Levi B. White, 275, 177, 7072, 288, 1263

Wm. Finney, 140, 90, 3000, 55, 607

Jas. Traylor, -, -, -, -, 29

Henry Grayson, 190, 145, 4800, 110, 795

Allenson Cannon, 200, 133, 5940, 270, 624

Jas. Cannon, 250, 173, 6700, 90, 1042

Wm. M. Thompson, -, -, -, 90, 850

Jno. C. Gavet, 400, 926, 23600, 300, 2750

Adeson H. Williams, -, -, -, 5, 12

R. H. Mason, 200, 300, 4500, 150, 910

Robt. H. Hunter, -, -, -, -, 85

Sarah O. White, 150, 50, 3200, 130, 643

C. G. Perry -, -, -, 10, 177

Turner Perry, 75, 125, 3000, 65, 585

Jno. Reese, -, -, -, 10, 55

Wm. G. Pugh, 15, 175, 500, 8, 128

Jas. McDaniel, -, -, -, 5, 40

Moses Brown, 5, 45, 200, 5, 60

Jno. B. Goodwin, 120, 195, 4800, 180, 855

Julia Morris, -, -, -, -, 36

Jas. T. Pugh, 5, 55, 200, -, 65

Geo. W. Castleman, 125, 170, 1000, 70, 253

Cyntha Begerly, -, -, -, 5, 118

Ann Pugh, 35, 142, 850, 45, 195

Elizabeth Bradford, 140, 160, 2500, 80, 247

A. J. Bradford, -, -, -, 12, 167

Bryant B. McDearmon, -, -, -, 5, 156

Wm. Bryant, -, -, -, 10, 40

Henderson Bryant, 50, 290, 1200, 50, 426

Thos. Lantany, -, -, -, 5, 94

Hartwell Smith, 70, 130, 2000, 15, 200

Major Hedgpeth, 25, 103, 300, 125, 185

Stephen C. Sanders, -, -, -, -, 105

Jas. McMenerway, 30, 65, 285, 12, 242

Jas. G. Hamilton, 55, 90, 900, 45, 453

Wm. Sanders, 60, 166, 1000, 100, 443

Cornelius Sanders Jr., -, -, -, 60, 490

Jno. Sanders, 130, 175, 1500, 70, 560

Wm. R. Sanders, -, -, -, 5, 140

Cornelius Sanders Sr., 75, 65, 800, 5, 189

Isaac Sanders Jr., 30, 142, 750, 55, 312

Wm. Cox, -, -, -, 5, 93

Wm. Spann, -, -, -, -, 30

Margaret Sanders, -, -, -, -, 15

Isaac Sanders, 40, 81, 605, 80, 336

Frederick Leonard, -, -, -, -, 10

Nathaniel Courtney, -, -, -, 5, 80

Isaac Sanders Sen., 100, 100, 1000, 55, 345

Jas. B. Smith, 50, 100, 600, 10, 191

Micajah Robertson, 11, 13, 100, 5, 89

Joshua Underwood, -, -, -, 10, 154

H. B. Gally, -, -, -, 10, 60

A. I. Spickard, 40, 100, 800, 90, 325

Arther Nichol, -, -, -, 5, 159

Wm. M. Sanders, 109, 80, 1000, 75, 589

Wiley Pafford, -, -, -, 5, 174

Geo. E. Baker, -, -, -, 10, 60,

Paskel Ford, -, -, -, 10, 75

Phillip Smart, 45, 95, 600, 40, 260

Saml. Freeman, 50, 67, 800, 80, 350

Robt B. Chandler, -, -, -, 5, 30

Jno. Wilkinson, -, -, -, 5, 40
Jas. M. Sanders, 65, 35, 500, 110, 255
Jarrett Sanders, 40, 79, 600, 3, 174
Saml. C. Caraway, -, -, -, -, 83
Wm. C. Eaks, -, -, -, -, 20
Edward Childress, -, -, -, 10, 25
Alfred Childress, -, -, -, 10, 90
Jesse W. Sulivaan, -, -, -, 10, 106
Cynthae Flowers, -, -, -, 5, 54
Ambrose Burnett, -, -, -, -, 10, 132
Mary Sanders, 110, 58, 1680 65, 635
Wiley Caraway, -, -, -, 6, 160
Jas. Sanders, -, -, -, 5, 87
Smith Sinclair, -, -, -, 60, 210
Thos. Thorn, 75, 75, 1800, 10, 466
John Mills, -, -, -, -, 75
W,. Thorn, 80, 160, 2700, 125, 345
Jane Underwood, 18, 96, 400, 5, 163
Thos. S. Sanders, 100, 70, 2500, 65, 752
Marcy Maxwell, 30, 72, 500, 5, 116
Daniel B. Bonus, 17, 50, 350, 8, 160
Alexander Carter, 40, 110, 550, 8, 183
Laban Carter, -, -, -, 5, 125
Jno. N. Lannon, 3, 34, 111, 80, 295
Wm. M. Welch, 50, 55, 1000, 85, 275
Wm. Lannon, 65, 45, 1000, 90, 412
Mary Hancock, 60, 59, 1000, 60, 408
Thos Barker, 80, 90, 1700, 50, 432
Wm. D. Barber, -, -, -, 5, 157
Thos. K. Welch, -, 38, 225, 10, 248
Wm. S. Lannon, 45, 59, 1000, 15, 202
Nathan Lannon, 50, 125, 1000, 60, 443
Eliga (Eliza), Kirk, 35, 60, 1000, 25, 300
Jas. Lannon, -, -, -, -, 13
Robt. Roggers, 3, 32, 100, 5, 55
Wm. D. McCulloch, -, -, -, -, 32
Tilman Lannons, 14, 35, 50, 10, 160
Jas. G. Arnold, 23, 128, 450, 75, 434
Thos. Rose, 47, 53, 550, 50, 406
Wm. Rose, -, -, -, p, 80
Phillip Batson, -, -, -, 5, 43
Sarah D. Sneed, 115, 85, 3000, 100, 101
Wm. Arnold, 100, 150, 1700, 12, 280
Preson Lockhart, -, -, -, 5, 62
Azebuland Harthen (Horthen), -, -, -, -, 98
Calab Swane, 20, 107, 639, 20, 185
Elijah Arnold, 80, 100, 3000, 20, 386
Wiley Sanders, 125, 75, 300, 70, 910
Jas E. Adkinson, 70, 80, 2200, 130, 470
Elias Lockhart, 2, 37, 25, 57, 80
M. G. Jones, 10, 20, 500, 7, 205
Frances D. Cockran, 96, 74, 2000, 50, 210
Jas Adkinson, 200, 400, 9000, 430, 1121
Ann E. Tucker, -, -, -, -, 50
Saml. Adkisson, -, -, -, -, 103

Young Thompson, -, -, -, 7, -
Sturling Brewer, -, -, -, 6, 34
Robt. P. Morrow, 40, 110, 900, 10, 285
Saml. A. Jopling, -, -, -, 5, 56
Kiziah Fleming, -, -, -, -, -
Thos Burk, 125, 134, 5000, 70, 650
B. L. Woodall, -, -, -, -, 68
Wm. Arnold, 100, 369, 1950, 100, 615
Andrew Northcut, -, -, -, -, 114
James Miller, -, -, -, 6, 150
Patton A. McPeak, -, -, -, 5, 163
Jno. McPeak, 90, 110, 1000, -, 151
Wm. Jones, 160, 150, 27000, 270, 840
Juliet Hannah, 160, 310, 2500, 25, 430
Richard Patterick, -, -, -, 10, 53
Geo. W. McPeak, -, -, -, 10, 320
Jas. Semple, -, -, -, 5, 92
Mary McCullough, 100, 140, 1900, 75, 381
Saml Archay, -, -, -, 5, 80
Miciel Archey, -, -, -, 6, 80
Thos. S. Ward, 170, 230, 3800, 150, 615
Jno. M. Peyton, 160, 151, 3200, 150, 744
Albert Jones, 110, 73, 2000, 165, 903
Thos. Donald, 125, 225, 4000, 70, 535
Jas. Brothers, -, -, -, 40, 323
Henry Jones, -, -, -, 55, 162
Randel Barnet, -, -, -, 35, 265
Henry Miller, -, -, -, -, 70
Thos. Miller, 50, 25, 500, 15, 285
Jane Weatherly, -, -, -, -, 56
E. I. Sims, -, -, -, -, 10
Abram George, -, -, -, 7, 31
Wm. Hart, -, -, -, 5, 446
Jno. C. Farris, 80, 80, 2200, 90, 567
Jno. W. Morrow, 15, 35, 350, 6, 165
Pinkney G. Sanders, -, -, -, 5, 46
Jas. Bennett, -, -, -, -, 10
Jas. E. McIntire, -, -, -, -, -
Wm. McIntire, -, -, -, -, 18
Ransford McGregor, 9, 100, 1000, 200, 992
Thos. G. Nevil, -, -, -, 10, 109
Jno. C. Harris, 500, 400, 18000, 150, 6700
David Abbott, -, -, -, 5, 640
Albert Alexander, 400, 400, 18000, 340, 1060
Joshua Freeman, -, -, -, -, 76
Beverly Randolph, 250, 150, 7000, 350, 1230
Hardy Boothe, -, -, -, -, 170
Wm Alford, 300, 150, 6000, 210, 950
Wm. M. Alford, -, -, -, -, 95
Adward A. Rowlett, 30, 30, 700, 12, 175

Mariah Malone, 250, 350, 9000, 240, 1094

Anderson Short, 80, 35, 1000, 110, 496

Geo. Collins, -, -, -, 5, 35

Wm. Collins, -, -, -, 5, 118

Sudwell Evans, -, -, -, 40, 241

Jno. Dement, -, -, -, -, 137

Smith Oliver, -, -, -, 5, 10

Baker Rather, 205, 500, 6000, 135, 1370

Samuel Hunt, 300, 500, 5000, 150, 1010

Alfred Pearce, 150, 130, 4000, 200, 580

M. M. Drake, 125, 121, 3250, 70, 738

Hary L. Conally, -, -, -, 15, 273

Jno. Robinson, -, -, -, 10, 344

Wm. Bains, -, -, -, 10, 160

James Evans, -, -, -, -, 30

Gideon M. Alsop, 50, 80, 1700, 65, 421

Granodle L. Pearce, -, -, -, 10, 250

Jas. H. Barkley, -, -, -, -, 50

Fanny Black, 75, 105, 4000, 20, 490

Charles M. Thacker, 100, 200, 3600, 120, 705

Henry Mason, 70, 30, 1200, 110, 568

Jas. M. Green, 100, 200, 4200, 120, 565

Drury Dunce, 180, 150, 4700, 115, 694

Jas. A. Reed, -, -, -, -, 177

Thos. Rowlett, 50, 50,4 50, 10, 268

Travis H. Tune, -, -, -, 10, 63

Sylvia Midlens, -, -, -, 5, 50

Wm. N. Lenoir, 90, 243, 4000, 60, 450

Geo. _. Cane, -, -, -, 10, 76

Peyton Rowton, 80, 130, 1400, 70, 552

Jas. H. Short, -, -, -, 15, 144

Mathew Pitts, 130, 200, 3000, 70, 610

Crawford McDaniel, -, -, -, 5, 62

Isham Traylor, -, -, -, -, 50

Wm. Meredith, -, -, -, -, 30

David D. Newgent, -, -, -, -, 75

Wm. N. Guram, 50, 75, 1200, 55, 350

Martha Ward, 75, 75, 2400, 100, 500

Basyell Ward, -, -, -, -, 30

Taylor _. Beadley (Bradley), -, -, -, 8, 125

Jno. B. Hicks, 200, 182, 3800, 110, 330

Thos. B. Miles, 50, 25, 1300, 100, 365

Jno. Seward Jr., -, -, -, 15, 272

Wm. B. Halowell, 15, 25, 250, 20, 30

Jas. Mabry, 25, 20, 1200, 8, 210

Jno. Bowman, 110, 90, 2000, 75, 470

David C. Hutcherdson, 20, -, 300, 20, 239

Frances McGowen, 225, 15, 2800, 75, 561

Jas. E. Stockard, 40, 40, 800, 50, 336

Wm. Corble, -, -, -, 5, 262

Jno. James, -, -, -, 5, 105

Geo. N. Taylor, -, -, -, 5, 150

Saml. G. McGowen, 100, 150, 2400, 55, 240

Martha _. McGowen, 75, 175, 2400, 50, 242

Enoch Wrather (Wraither), 30, 23, 530, 50, 337

Jno. S. Rass__ann, -, -, -, 85, 526

Wm. A. Smith, 70, -, 1500, 15, 221

Thos. C Black, 120, 330, 6750, 85, 725

Wilson S. Wadkins, 175, 115, 7200, 205, 657

David Baxtor, -, -, -, -, 28

Susan Wheeler, -, -, -, 10, 265

Rebecca Elam, 140, 175, 3900, 100, 498

Simeon Taylor, -, -, -, -, 16

Jno. C. Wade, 400, 300, 10500, 210, 1077

O. H. Wade, 150, 60, 3200, 100, 560

Daniel McColester, -, -, -, 10, 144

Mordecai D. Wade, 235, 265, 7500, 380, 910

S. A. Kincanon, -, -, -, 150, 343

Wm. C. J. Burras, 280, 220, 10000, 315, 1520

Thos. R. Peak, 13, -, 325, -, 281

Josiah Peak, -, -, -, -, 85

Bradley Burgess, 3, -, 100, -, 25

Enoch M. Adkison, 100, 150, 4000, 100, 460

Randolph V. Johns, 110, 139, 3824, 85, 580

Susan D. Wade, 60, 40, 1200, 112, 255

Joseph Lindsey, 250, 125, 6600, 120, 690

Andrew McGinnis, -, -, -, 80, 810

Jas. H. Greene, 150, 160, 6200, 55, 622

Wm. A. Rucker, -, -, -, 50, 364

Jas. M. Tompkins, 200, 300, 4500, 120, 635

Henry D. Smith, -, -, -, -, 50

Geo. C. Smith, -, -, -, -, 70

Thos. Hagwood, -, -, -, -, 11

James Vernon, 25, 12, 715, 6, 106

Anderson D. Sott (Scott), 55, 9, 1600, 25, 195

Nancy Gun, 10, -, 400, -, 68

Addison Mitchell, 140, 130, 6000, 100, 751

Jas. B. Rucker, -, -, -, -, 10

Calvin G. Mitchell, 150, 150, 6000, 100, 880

Sarah C. Hodge, 60, 90, 1200, 10, 116

Benj. F. Pitts, -, -, -, 5, 233

Wm. Wm. Ross, 112, 92, 2800, 120, 690

Wm. Denton, -, -, -, -, 51

Richard W. Wade, 300, 350, 1300, 300, 900

Wm. C. Seward, -, -, -, 60, 345

Saml. Foster, -, -, -, 5, 191
John Elliott, 120, 80, 6000, 20, 360
Thos. Hoard, 500, 500, 20000, 500, 2135
Wm. H. Cayce, 4, 1, 1000, -, 40
Benja. Lewis, 160, 40, 6000, 100, 480
Saml. Davis, -, -, -, -, 250
Wm. Major, 250, 216, 10000, 330, 1160
Hally McFadden, 40, 16, 1400, 20, 350
Geo. F. Banks, - -, -, 10, 150
Agnes Peak, 45, 5, 1000, 5, 140
Jas. Miller, 60, 10, 1400, 10, 160
Jno. Tune, 48, 05, 280, 45, 353
Wm. C. Oliphint, -, -, -, -, 127
Wm. G. Tune, 12, 15, 600, -, 436
A. S. Davis, -, -, -, -, 77
Robt. S. Northcutt, -, -, -, 15, 55
Benja. F. Church, -, -, -, 5, 72
Varner D. Cowen, 300, 200, 20000, 280,
1785
Allen James, 159, 48, 3700, 120, 1290
Edward Burgess, -, -, -, 10, 174
Rachiel Powell, -, -, -, -, 235
Benja. W. McCulloch, 130, 120, 6200,
165, 1470
Sarah McCulloch, 300, 150, 14000, 300,
790
Jno. A. Maxwell, -, -, -, -, 28
Wm. Warran, 200, 175, 6500, 115, 1355
Benj. Blanton, 65, 80, 2800, 105, 608
Hiram Jenkins, 200, 1700, 25000, 120,
920
Edward M. Rucker, -, -, -, 80, 216
J. R. Husbands, -, -, -, -, 190
Lafayett Burrus, 400, 220, 930, 200, 1960
Nelson Parish, -, -, -, -, 50
Wm. S. Overall, -, -, -, 140, 778
Jas. P. Todd, -, -, -, -, 194
Wm. Daniel, -, -, -, -, 62
Joseph Wadkins, 260, 45, 6500, 380, 900
Jennings H. Rooker, 8, 2, 250, 10, 130
Nathaniel Miller, 180, 60, 2000 60, 808
Jeremiah Hunt, -, -, -, -, 103
Jno. W. Richardson, 150, 96, 6000, 190,
1685
David F. Hunter, -, -, -, -, 26
Mary H. Bowman, 45, 58, 2060, 65, 553
Jessee Sikes, 600, 190, 24000, 260, 2425
Jacob S. Hasburg, -, -, -, -, 110
Richard Hazelwood, 175, 45, 8000, 350,
960
Jas. _. Ward, 170, 230, 8000, 100, 622
Richard Woodruff, -, 100, 300, -, 105
Jno. E. Smith, -, -, -, 31, 273
Bill Ward, 75, 75, 3000, 155, 414
Jno. Etter, 300, 450, 15000, 150, 1262
Joshua Elder, 37, 12, 1100, 40, 909

James McDowell, -, -, -, 10, 110
Elizabeth Ralston, 150, 150, 7200, 315,
1460
Robert L. Ralston, 70, 36, 2200, -, -
Eveline B. Weakley, 500, 1150, 32000,
325, 1465
Lucy Muse, 360, 340, 15000, 300, 1470
Lewis Martin, -, -, -, 15, 172
Jas. H. Hunter, -, -, -, 7, 83
Thos. Lannon, 28, 22, 1000, 10, 145
Jas. M. Tucker, 20, 30, 750, 5, 130
Jno. H. Harrison, 75, 61, 2200, 100, 258
Drury Wood, -, -, -, -, 40
O. G. Tucker, 55, 60, 2300, 88, 300
Mary Wright, 80, 65, 2900, 20, 401
Pheba Tucker, 100, 80, 3600, 48, 330
Reuben O. Johnson, -, -, -, -, 15
Thos. C. Wright, 150, 52, 3000, 100, 670
Thos. Johns, 210, 132, 10000, 330, 1085
Alexander B. Rather, -, -, -, 15, 180
Bena. H. Ward, -, -, -, -, 40
Marcus H. Leath, 100, 20, 1300, 100, 663
Geo. Thompson, 300, 233, 16000, 325,
1855
Wm. Neely, -, -, -, -, 8
Robt. S. James, -, -, -, -, 83
Edmond Lively, 7, -, 500, -, 77
Wm. H. Wilson, 3, -, 600, -, 224
Joel Pinson, ¾, -, 50, -, 15
Jno. Jones, 70, 86, 3600, 115, 95
G. B. Lannon, -, -, -, -, 660
Wilie Waller, 2 ½, -, 700, 40, 280
Wilson S. Bone, -, -, -, -, 140
Wm. G. Morrow, -, -, -, 75, 547
Saml. Tucker, -, -, -, 8, 96
Thos. R. Mullins, 3,-, 1000, 100, 300
Jacob Batson, -, -, -, -, 15
Edmon Traylor, -, -, -, -, 65
E. S. Seward, 80, 86, 2500, 90, 556
Wm. Rooker, 100, 66, 2500, 80, 415
Martha Traylor, 1, -, 35, -, 85
Wm. Ward, 90, 93, 3660, 100, 295
Nancy Wade, 2, -, 250, 5, 75
Broomfield, L. Ridley, 400, 500, 20000,
360, 2190
Archible Meredith, -, -, -, -, 17
Wm. H. Crosthwait, -, -, -, 5, 168
Wm. Jarrell, -, -, -, -, 70
Alexander Hester, -, -, -, -, 50
Wm. Parton, -, -, -, -, 160
Jno. Nevil, -, -, -, -, 235
Edmon Jarrall, -, -, -, -, 75
Walter Keeble, 287, 80, 9175, 90, 954
Mary Reed, 185, 90, 4500, 68, 910
Benja. Ward, 90, 21, 3300, 75, 418
Mary Allen, -, -, -, 20, 366

Elizabeth Ridley, 300, 285, 14250, 100, 1240

Geo. Finch, -, -, -, 80, 250

Jno. R. Newson, 180, 177, 13000, 275, 397

Jas. B. Sneed, 100, 200, 6000, 275, 1950

Jas. M. Collier, 100, 16, 3500, 90, 622

Albert _. Henderson, 150, 90, 6000, 270, 745

Peter F. Hagan, -, -, -, -, 115

Nicholas G. Ward, -, -, -, 22, 257

John Walden, 190, 81, 5500, 60, 918

Fanny Henderson, 50, 30, 1500, -, 720

As. Avant, 300,180, 11700, 390, 1650

Wm. D. Neal, 500, 230, 14600, 681, 1378

Elizabeth Thurman, 59, 61, 1800, 10, 179

Eliza E. Beasley, -, -, -, 155, 300

Elizbaeth McClanahan, 50, 40, 1900, 15, 328

Nathaniel B. Reed, 130, 221, 10500, 475, 1051

Constant Hardeman, 200, 100, 12000, -, -

Robt. Esprey, 190, 240, 10750, 250, 651

Alford Goodman, 140, 80, 1760, 80, 770

Wm. Goodman Sr., 50, 60, 3000, 65, 560

Thos. H. Goodman, 40, 35, 460, 125, 478

Jno. K. Kirkpatric, 1365, 75, 2100, 80, 445

Isaac N. Oliphint, -, -, -, -, 232

Jno. M. Hart, 80, 76, 1248, 90, 288

A. R. Fasacett, 40, 39, 650, 10, 102

Jas. F. Richards, -, -, -, 8, 148

Thos. N. Crutchfield, -, -, -, -, 12

Martha James, 75, 112, 1870, 38, 290

Mary A. Mathews, 80, 120, 4000, 60, 395

Robertson Forgis, -, -, -, 10, 46

Delila Beavers, 30, 20, 400, 8, 137

Jas. C. Bell, 90, 53, 800, 10, 165

Isaac M. Marable, 2, 1, 50, -, 5

Jno. R. Goodman, 130, 105, 2000, 40, 280

Jas. B. Buchanan, 300, 700, 2500, 155, 1514

Francis Stegar, 130, 140, 2900, 60, 444

Mathew Nelson, 300, 50, 10500, 70, 555

Jno. W. Walden, -, -, -, 6, 233

Frederick Mays, 100, 100, 2000, 65, 405

John Noe, 20, 30, 600, 10, 225

J. H. Crutchfield, 12, 13, 250, 10, 144

Beverly Nelson, 120, 100, 3300, 130, 660

Charles H. Walder (Walden), 125, 125, 4000, 100, 750

Drury D. Nelson, 100, 130, 5000, 40, 375

Abner W. Nelson, 100, 110, 3500, 350, 435

Jno. Hill, 150, 150, 6000, 100, 1100

Booker Dove (Dore), -, -, -, 15, 75

Jno. W. Waldron, -, -, -, 10, 250

Collins C. Leonard, -, -, -, -, 30

Jno. H. Hill, 80, 45, 1600, 115, 370

Orphey Clay, -, -, -, -, 12

Joseph Kimbro, 300, 160, 8500, 100, 3294

EdmonTodd, -, -, -, 5, 75

Jno. L. Haynes, 250, 240, 10000, 460, 1623

Hazel Singleton, -, -, -, 5, 280

N. S. Haynes, -, -, -, 10, 238

James House, -, -, -, 10, 56

James H. Baldridge, -, -, -, 140, 630

Wm. Wm. Nance, -, -, -, 100, 505

Thos Gainer (Garner), 50, 11, 1000, 150, 302

Geo. Patts, 100, 41, 2800, 80, 445

Jas. G. Gambell, 35, 25, 720, 80, 287

James Nivin, 60, 120, 2000, 50, 625

Wm. Nivin, 50, 69, 1400, 15, 362

Jno. C. McSwain (McLuesovin?) 60, 40, 900, 10, 231

Jno. Britton, 150, 50, 2500, 155, 944

Jane Colewell, 90, 164, 3500, 45, 222

Raph Neal, 100, 38, 1100, 25, 358

Jackson Brothers, 150, 100, 4000, 75, 606

Jno. Neel, 35, 29, 1800, 150, 465

Benj. Buffil, -, -, -, -, 20

Talifura Benjamin, -, -, -, 70, 210

Prestly W. Oliphint, 50, 77, 762, 10, 113

Allen J. Mason, -, -, -, 50, 538

Simeon Smith, -, -, -, -, 215

Thos. Neel, 250, 170, 4000, 85, 105

Jas. S. Smith, -, -, -, 150, 1875

Jno. F. Blair, 55, 65, 1500, 52, 352

Sarah Finch, 120, 180, 4000, 10, 279

Charles H. Walpole, 90, 10, 650, 40, 457

Jas. W. Blair, 30, 10, 600, 15, 310

Thos. M. Hart, 100, 169, 2964, 60, 455

Wm. B. Vaughter, -, -, -, 125, 274

H. G. Williamson, -, -, -, -, 8

O. M. Crutchfield, 60, 59, 1200, 80, 473

Henry Harris, -, -, -, 8, 125

Jas. Harris, -, -, -, 5, 216

Lucy Gambrell, 42, 118, 2400, 50, 206

Samuel Filpot, 50, 38, 712, 5, 243

Wm. S. J. Blair, 60, 120, 1200, 50, 330

Ralph A. Blair, 60, 41, 1000, 110, 345

Wm. Thompson, -, -, -, 5, 55

Noah Martin, -, -, -, 10, 175

David (Daniel) N. Tune, -, -, -, 5, 16

Henry White, 400, 480, 18660, 150, 1540

Nelson Mullins, -, -, -, 35, 131

Wm. R. James, 60, 47, 2000, 60, 273

Thos. James, 65, 42, 2000, 30, 285

Thos. D. Walpoole, -, -, -, -, 85
Eli Smith, 230, 55, 5800, 105, 776
Geo. W. Allen, -, -, -, -, -
Martha Smith, 60, 22, 1500, 8, 80
John P. Beasley, 382, 25, 9000, 250, 1063
Wm. White, -, -, -, -, 10
Obediah Biles, 32, -, 480, 55, 208
Wilie Brown, -, -, -, 150, 565
N. G. Garner, -, -, -, -, 115
R. H. White, 200, 177, 900, 315, 1267
Jas. Herndon, -, -, -, 5, 60
Jno. Mullins, 30, 120, 1200, 65, 180
Charles L. Davis, 300, 425, 12400, 200, 1290
Jane V. Grisham, 85, 62, 3000, 75, 620
Geo V. Ridley, 175, 77, 6300, 125, 919
Jas. Taylor, -, -, -, 19, 300
Jno. Fuller, 75, 75, 3750, 100, 615
Christopher Beasley, 50, -, 625, 40, 605
Jno. W. Lewis, -, -, -, 10, 195
Nancy Posey, 120, 63, 1200, 50, 250
Patterson Miles, 200, 48, 8000, 200, 1200
John Seward, 170, 50, 8000, 200, 394
Warren Seward, -, -, -, -, 170
Isaac H. Overall, 300, 231, 8115, 300, 1029
Thos. Rideout, 100, 85, 4500, 50, 454
Cleburn Howse, 200, 100, 7500, 130, 735
Wm. Anderson, 100, 130, 5000, 275, 764
Joseph Hallowell, -, -, -, 40, 366
Jas. Beaty, 50, -, 1200, 20, 258
Julia A. House, 67, 20, 1740, 40, 327
Alford Blackman 600, 200, 20000, 525, 1900
Raiford Blackman, 150, 50, 3200, 40, 320
James Hale, -, -, -, 8, 89
Salome Beasley, 200, 200, 5000, 15, 190
Survant (Suvant) Beasly, -, -, -, 40, 458
John Payne, -, -, -, 10, 75
Charles Puckett (Duckett), 270, 105, 5625, 165, 1620
Wm. A. Puckett (Duckett), 150, 100, 3750, 115, 1958
Wm. Vauly(Vanly), 200, 105, 4575, 225, 144
Wm. H. Smith, 600, 600, 20000, 500, 2000
Frances W. Washington, 120, 145, 7000, 200, 405
G. W. Smith, 250, 220, 1200, 200, 1615
C. M. Smith, 220, 80, 7500, 380, 1260
Wm. T. Banks, -, -, -, 50, 460
Mary Harrison, -, -, -, 55, 255
Stephen Holloway, -, -, -, 15, 200
Lazarus Blackman, 90,58, 2900, 100, 465
Jas. Buss, 500, 500, 18000, 475, 1779

Ambrose Howse, 500, 650, 37000, 600, 2710
Stephen C. Wright, -, -, -, -, 20
Benja. Marable, 300, 150, 10000, 120, 690
Isaac Burkson, 200, 150, 700, 175, 1095
John Clark, 100, 32, 3300, 90, 395
Mary Hutson, -, -, -, -, 20
Levi Wade, 700, 350, 22900, 550, 2085
Thos. W. Buss, 100, 50, 1500, 415, 348
John Pope, 100, 100, 5000, 50, 510
Sarah Griffin, 53, -, 1000, 40, 375
J. P. Griffin, -, -, -, -, 50
Wm. Adkesson Jr., 70,35, 1260, 50, 284
Wm. Pope, 80, 26, 2100, 55, 530
Theophilas Revil, -, -, -, 50, 348
Wm. G. Howell, -, -, -, -, 15
Peter Rowlett, -, -, -, 8, 180
Wm. Adkinson Sr., 200, 219, 5000, 70, 618
Matilda Babit, -, -, -, -, 20
Benj. W. Rowlett, -, -, -, 5, 30
Leonard Rowlett, 60, 47, 850, 40, 240
Peter R. Foster, -, -, -, 10, 100
Daniel (David) Williamson, -, -, -, 50, 175
Benj. Patten, -, -, -, 15, 145
G. W. White, -, -, -, 4, 70
H. P. Blackman, 100, 6 0, 2000, 50, 325
G. W. Beaty, 270, 215, 6000, 100, 960
Ann Beaty, 200, 38, 3000, -, 650
John Haynes, 250, 250, 3400, 60, 633
J. M. Haynes, -, -, -, 10, 222
Everett Haynes, 210, 216, 3000, 300, 395
Barnett Elliott, 75, 198, 1365, 300, 395
H. W. Vaughan, -, -, -, -, 84
Narcissa Vaughan, 200, 260, 5000, 100, 1230
R. M. Vaughan, -, -, -, 60, 378
Thos. G. Vaughan, -, -, -, -, 140
Wm. Wood, 60, 47, 700, 80, 377
Elizabeth Hayse, -, -, -, 5, 112
A. P. Vaughan, -, -, -, 10, 75
Jas. A. Edwards, -, -, -, 125, 455
Geo. B. Johnson, -, -, -, 75, 345
Silas Tucker, 900, 510, 24000, 500, 2885
Nelson Farm, 400, 168, 12000, 200, 803
Hugh B. Hill, -, -, -, -, 400
Jas. Vaughan, -, -, -, -, 10
Elizabeth Seavey, -, -, -, -, 70
Jno. Reed, -, -, -, -, 85
Pleasant A. Watson, -, 3, 60, -, 145
Jackson Smith, 400, 409, 24000, 450, 2176
Francis James, 78, 25, 1250, 15, 330
Jno. Finch, -, -, -, 15, 306

Jas. D. Howell, -, -, -, 10, 85
Peter Barkhart, -, -, -, 15, 158
Mathew Baldridge, -, -, -, 10, 110
Hilas F. Traylor, -, -, -, 60, 289
Jno. R. Rowlett, -, -, -, 5, 70
Nancy Ross, 140, 40, 3600, 300, 1195
Felix G. Ross, 400, 390, 1120, -, -
Wilson Phelps, -, -, -, -, 14
Henry Lee, 80, 20, 700, 35, 346
Wm. Willie Harmon, 100, 700, 2000, 30, 278
Jas. S. Payne, 85, 85, 1700, 40, 486
Wm. H. Lawrence, -, -, -, 10, 282
Thos. Nelson, 240, 330, 7000, 380, 1036
Wm. A. McRae, -, -, -, 135, 180
Susan Delbridge, 126, 74, 2000, 15, 443
Allen C. McClary, 55, 75, 1700, 110, 418
Richard B. Vaughan, 300, 200, 5400, 100, 973
Sutton Coleman, -, -, -, 5, 60
Charles Spann, 35, 40, 900, 10, 117
Wm. A Lewis, 50, 48, 600, 60, 230
Wm. M. Deason, -, -, -, -, 10
Charles Howse, 70, 50, 700, 30, 249
Andrew Heath, -, -, -, 10, 75
Kenneth McRae, -, -, -, 30, 150
Thos. C. Edmons, -, -, -, 10, 11
Henry Beaty, -, -, -, -, 18
Jas. J. Jones, 250, 215, 2325, 52, 825
E. I. Jordan, 80, 70, 1500, 75, 710
Jas. R. Lanier, -, -, -, -, 20
Jas. N. Nance, 150, 50, 150, 100, 249
Wm. McRae, 160, 140, 3600, 50, 304
Ann Lewis, 70, 62, 1056, 40, 355
Daniel Coleman, -, -, -, 15, 140
Joseph Coleman, -, -, -, 10, 75
Abdias Mosley, -, -, -, 10, 70
Wm. Lewis, 65, 55, 460, 80, 450
Thos. Christopher, 20, 15, 300, 25, 180
Mary Rullage, 25, 18, 300, 25, 357
Jas. M. Haynes, 80, 70, 1200, 45, 390
Balam Newson, -, -, -, 8, 180
Richard H. Lewis, -, -, -, 10, 200
Josh__ Christopher, -, -, -, 10, 83
Jno. S. Curry, -, -, -, -, 10
Wm. S. Posey, 80, 57, 2500, 700, 475
Spencer Hardy, 12, -, 50, 10, 83
David Beaty, -, -, -, 5, 40
Wm. Colewell, 30, 20, 1000, 75, 266
E. C. John, 60, 98, 800, 40, 349
Reubin Smithey, -, -, -, -, 50
Wm. Forbs, -, -, -, 10, 60
Benj. S. Talum, -, -, -, -, 4
Benj. H. Nelson, -, -, -, -, 170
Jno. Vardell, -, -, -, -, 10
Jessee C. Robinson, 35, 15, 700, 150, 319

Reubin R. Peach, -, -, -, 8, 100
Wm. Dickey, 30, 47, 770, 10, 260
Benj. P. Jobe, 20, 30, 512, 8, 207
Joshua Tucker, -, -, -, 50, 80
Ann Taylor, -, -, -, -, 40
Tabitha Allen, -, -, -, 10, 263
Aaron Boyd, -, -, -, 5, 66
Jas. Robberds, -, -, -, 10, 65
Saml. Newson, 80, 107, 1800, 42, 225
Tinsley Vernon, 200, 225, 4250, 200, 731
Jas. _. Smith, 200, 250, 3000, 50, 386
Jno. Smith, -, -, -, 5, 160
Lodwick Puckett, 50, 20, 350, 20, 228
Saloman Newsom, 50, 66, 600, 35, 358
James Hodge, -, -, -, 20, 230
Thos. Lee, 40, 27, 500, 10, 195
Hardin Eskew, -, -, -, 10, 130
Isaac Williams, 65, 60, 1250, 30, 220
Benja. Beaty, 350, 110, 9000, 400, 1450
Aguilla Davis, 130, 10, 2800, 328, 545
Jas. W. Martin, 350, 4000, 13000, 328, 1260
Leonard Davis, 120, 10, 2800, 100, 710
Isham R. Peebles, 300, 240, 14000, 270, 986
Thos. Cook, 60, 40, 2000, 20, 245
Jas. Cook, -, -, -, 5, 126
Wm. B. Beasley, 250, 110, 7000, 200, 690
Joseph Mason, 350, 460, 12000, 100, 833
Robt. Cook, -, -, -, 15, 235
Geo. Beaty, 150, 30, 2500, 150, 665
Luch Wade, 15, 18, 400, 5, 130
Jesse Mullins, -, -, -, 6, 230
Lafayett Eppes, -, -, -, 5, 54
Jno. D. Cook, 250, 180, 8000, 50, 354
Richard Cook, 30, 27, 1140, 38, 230
Luraney Cook, 58, 57, 2200, 38, 260
Richard D. Cook, -, -, -, 10, 60
Luckett Davis, 150, 110, 6800, 325, 1300
John Carter, -, -, -, -, 50
Coleman H. Vaughan, - -, -, 10, 120
Alfred Ross, 101, 101, 6000, 100, 526
Rebecca Garver, -, -, -, 5, 134
John D. Cook, Jr., -, -, 1, 15, 277
Unity H. Mullins, -, -, -, -, 85
Wilson Y. Posey, 50, 56, 1000, 15, 234
Nancy Corder, -, -, -, -, 10
Constant Jordan, 75, 75, 1500, 100, 618
Andrew J. Covington, 27, 7, 320, 10, 270
Jacob Ray, 60, 53, -, 10, 75
Joseph Ray, 50, 63, 1000, 10, 340
Jesse Coleman, 30, 30, 400, 10, 220
Isaac Johnson, 60, 50, 800, 10, 170
Jas. E. Coleman, -, -, -, 10, 150
John McCluran, -, -, -, 150, 1036

Josiah Ellis, 100, 60, 1120, 50, 317
John Tucker, -, -, -, 5, 90
Hannah Gambrell, 65, 47, 2000, 50, 364
Dennis Lusk, 80, 81, 3000, 40, 280
Thos. A. Bennett, -, -, -, 10, 410
Jno. E. Bennett, -, -, -, -, 90
Jno. T. Neal, 12, 12, 288, 8, 129
Armstead R. Neal, 2, -, 50, 5, 46
Jas. H. Coleman, 18, 6, 288, 8, 145
Wm. A. Coleman, 100, 36, 1500, 120, 394
Thos. Bennett, 500, 200, 8400, 250, 2560
Wm. E. Haly, 40, 10, 500, 10, 90
Henry Allen, -, -, -, -, 105
Wm. Lawrence, 20, 4, 480, 10, 197
Edwin Coleman, -, -, -,10, 115
Jas. Coleman, 60, 79, 600, 75, 305
Mary H. Coleman, 50, 50, 800, 10, 190
Wm. C. Coleman, 25, 32, 500, 8, 135
Jas. A. Williams, 30, 26, 300, 10, 191
John Tombs, 130, 129, 1800, 75, 286
Hardin Tombs, -, -, -, 10, 137
Jno. H. Tombs, 40, 60, 1000, 15, 300
Wesley Tombs, -, -, -, 8, 84
Wm. F. Foster, -, -, -, 10, 108
Jas. McCanless, -, -, -, 10, 100
Wm. Lovel, 30, 30, 600, 80, 306
John Shelton, 60, 30, 800, 100, 580
Wm. H. Allen, 140, 190, 3300, 150, 1290
Jno. A. Clay, -, -, -, -, 10
Isham Coleman, 65, 69, 1900, 100, 342
Branch Jordan, -, -, -, 8,1 09
Lucinda Coleman, 100, 100,2000, 15, 240
David Barnwell, -, -, -, 10, 100
Martha Lewis, 80, 16, 600, 200, 165
Jno. T. Dickey, -, -, -, -, 130
Wm. F. T. Coleman, 120, 48, 1500, 290, 589
David L. Prewett, 45, 60, 1000, 50, 291
Wm. N. Jones, 75, 48, 1000, 125, 350
Wm. Spann, 60, 80, 1350, 100, 527
Richard H. Spann, 40, 60, 3000, 50, 253
Wm. Hutson, -, -, -, 5, 72
Jas. Spann, 23, 41, 744, 10, 184
Burge Spann, 50,25, 750, 75, 238
Benj. Lewis, 34, 23, 425, 10, 182
Richd. Spann, 2, 13, 75, 5, 38
Benj. Spann, 10, 40, 500, 5, 70
Wm. R. Spann, 45, 40, 500, 10, 159
John Ryan, 60, 100, 800, 50, 322
Joseph Gates, -, -, -, 6, 75
John B. Miles, 35, 83, 520, 15, 490
Nancy Lane, 40, 83, 400, 40, 210
Wm. H. Lee, 60, 40, 450, 10, 139
Whitfield Sanders, -, -, -, 10, 110
Wm. Glimph, 28, 36, 500, 100, 309

David Blankenship, -, -, -, -, 26
Labun Blankenship, 66, 21, 450, 20, 200
Jas. B. Glipms, -, -, -, 10, 134
Charles Laster, 100, 61, 1600, 50, 280
Jas. E. Fleming, -, -, -, 10, 60
David Glenn, 200,1 89, 4000, 100, 565
Abram Osbern, 55, 82, 909, 55, 630
Edmon Webb, -, -, -, 5, 45
Jos. Vaughan, 50, 137, 1000, 65, 455
John M. Lanier, -, -, -, 5, 45
Wm. Hickman, 30, 20, 500, 10, 80
Harvy J. Haynes, 40, 10, 350, 6, 123
Jasper T. Hayne, 30, 45, 600, 50, 205
Jas. Anderson, 100, 120, 1500, 50, 318
Nathan A. Boyd, -, -, -, 10, 190
Mc. W. Haynes, 36, 33, 600, 10, 125
Wm. Grogan, 50, 45, 600, 10, 50
Abel Rushing, 200, 140, 9000, 90, 780
Jemmima A. Cannon, 200, -, 4000, -, -
Alfred Elliott, -, -, -, -, 133
Aather M. Edward, 525, 527, 21000, 285, 1785
Nancy Taylor, 30, 75, 800, 10, 105
Joseph A. Gates, -, -, -, 10, 80
Wilson Hale, -, -, -, 10, 60
Miles P. Murphy, 15, 85, 500, 15, 260
Jno. C. Vaughan, -, -, -, 10, 59
Henry Vaughan, -, -, -, 60, 240
James Vaughan, -, -, -, 12, 166
Charles _. Elliott, -, -, -, -, 105
Jas. Blake, 25, 37, 210, 30, 346
Wm. P. Stephens, -, -, -, -, 40
Geo. E. Cenedy, 35, 40, 450, 10, 178
Jas. Polk, 37, 30, 400, 10, 120
D. M. Maxwell, -, -, -, -, 166
Jane D. Covington, 80, 200, 4200, 80, 347
Rebecca Coleman, 16, 20, 180, 10, 127
R. D. Snell, 130, 80, 4000, 250, 1378
Harvy Haynes, -, -, -, 5,80
Jas. E. Webb, 155, 72, 4000, 150, 765
Jno. F. Webb, -, -, -, -, 183
Jno. Lytle, 400, 500, 13500, 400, 1860
Jas. M. King, 600, 1700, 35000, 425, 2800
Theodorick North, 90, 40, 1500, 30, 415
Widner Ransom, -, -, -, 100, 700
Robt. Baty, -, -, -, 10, 122
H. H. Batey, -, -, -, 10, 190
Martin Rucker, -, -, -, 10, 225
Moses Hill, -, -, -, 10, 50
John Mabry, -, -, -, 10, 113
Benha. H. Jarrett, -, -, -, 140, 430
Micajah Benson, -, -, -, 5, 48
Jas. W. Mallard, -, -, -, 20, 378
Wm. A. Ranson, 220,58, 6900, 75, 628

Jas. A. Floyd, -, -, -, 10, 263
Jane W. Snell, 125, 175, 2500, 75, 390
D. S. Mason(Manor), 75, 100, 1750, 50, 1181
J. G. Prinom, 85, 60, 1700, 130, 713
Jas. Morris, -, -, -, 65, 135
Travis Windrow, 150, 100, 2000, 90
Thos. Wm. Beasley, -, -, -, 10, 75
Sarah Bendley, 40, 95, 800, 15, 219
M. B. Jordan, 300, 248, 3288, 50, 607
Jas. M. Haynes Jr., -, -, -, 50, 430
Andrew J. Haynes, 90, 110, 1720, 10, 147
Geo. D. Wilson, -, -, -, -, 67
Thos. C. Parsley, -, -, -, 15, 195
Wm. A. Ray, -, -, -, 10, 106
Elizabeth Bobett, 60, 59, 700, 10, 105
David R. Owen, 40, 43, 800, 8, 185
Liney M. Ray, 50, 43, 800, 8, 185
Edward Thomas, 100, 150, 1500, 30, 345
Wm. Licett, 40, 10, 300, 10, 85
David Watson, 50, 70, 850, 35, 307
Thos. K. Haynes, 85, 102, 1200, 45, 329
Jas. Morris, -, -, -, 10, 62
Wm. A. Haynes, -, -, -, 100, 448
Wm. P. Regan, -, -, -, 2, 10
Wm. Floid, 90, 70, 1000, 50, 495
Jno. H. Floyd, -, -, -, 5, 106
Chaney Prince, 56, 50, 600, 10, 93
Beyers Windroud, 80, 185, 1800, 40, 290
Jno. Windrow, 150, 159, 2500, 25, 470
Jno. P. Harris, 100, 50, 3000, 40, 566
Anthony North, 140, 70, 3000, 100, 580
Elizabeth Ransom, 150, 50, 5000, 300, 820
Jno. S. Peacock, -, -, -, 70, 290
Mary Gowen, 40, 10, 200, 5, 105
Jacob Blesing, -, -, -, 60, 93
Saml. B. Robinson, 7, -, 300, -, 235
Jno. A. Crockett, 180, 201, 6500, 50, 760
Robt. Robison, -, -, -, 3, 86
E. H. Dean, -, -, -, -, 128
H. D. Ransom, 80, 79, 2000, 40, 355
Temperance Mathews, -, -, -, 8, 261
Jno. Smith, 450, 450, 14000, 300, 1430
Jno. Merrett, -, -, -, 6, 75
Robt. H. Wood, -, -, -, 30, 349
Edmon G. Wood, 65, 49, 800, 30, 150
Eveline Martin, -, -, -, 10, 120
H. D. Jameson, 240, 320, 5600, 100, 928
Leml. Ransom, 70, 80, 1500, 150, 353
Elijah Crowder, 28, 44, 800, 10, 236
Wm. Robbertson, -, -, -, 10, 50
Wm. Bracy, 40, 35, 400, 10, 177
Meek Boyd, 30, 325, 350, 10, 106
Wm. C. Dunn, 200, 50, 1000, 8, 302
Robt. Boyd, 85, 78, 2400, 55, 336

Jno. M. Sudberry, 30, 30, 600, 40, 89
Asuria Kimbro, 210, 315, 7800, 340, 1653
Isaac J. Frazer, 120, 146, 4000, 90, 700
Wm. W. Kimbro, 20, 250, 8000, 11, 1840
T. B. Snell, 55, 250, 8000, 11, 1840
Thos. Rowland, -, -, -, 10, 135
Mary Smotherman, -, -, -, 10, 135
Wm. Neal, -, -, -, 60, 630
Joseph Green 40, 40, 800, 50, 200
Robt. Maxwell, -, -, -, -, 75
Edmond Loving, 26, 23, 124, 10, 70
Jno. Smotherman, 47, 60, 500, 60, 190
Bart Smotherman, 45, 55, 500, 20, 200
P. H. Sudberry, 27, 31, 210, 5, 111
Thos. G. Stegall, 15, 5, 100, 25, 94
Alson Spence, 100, 100, 1000, 90, 259
Jno. Holden, -, -, -, 8, 104
Valentine Trail, -, -, -, -, 66
Abra Douglass, -, -, -, 10, 180
E.D. Ballard, -, -, -, -, 220
Charles Coursey, -, -, -, 5, 208
Younger Douglass, -, -, -, 10, 191
Cimson West, -, -, -, 8, 69
Prestley Featherston, -, -, -, 10, 263
E. Robertson, -, -, -, -, 10
Devereaux Masthor, -, -, -, 8, 193
Jno. Steprem, -, -, -, 10, 116
Thos. May, 55, 47, 1300, 70, 316
Benja. Penington, -, -, -, 10, 61
Bowling King, -, -, -, 50, 306
Wm. W. May, 100, 100, 2500, 30, 680
Blake Carlton, 50, 90, 1300, 100, 340
Kinion Carlton, 100, 150, 2000, 125, 720
Emely Carlton, 7, -, 75, 10, 133
Thos. A. Lyle, -, -, -, 10, 160
Wm. H. McGowen, -, -, -, 40, 99
G. W. Davis, 20, 10, 300, 15, 93
Pleasant Rutledge. -, -, -, 100, 332
Wm. Earthman, -, -, -, 75, 328
Geo. G. Elam, -, -, -, 35, 275
Jno. J. Jarrett, 350, 750, 10000, 300, 1753
Thos. S. Jarrett, 600, 400, 8000, 150, 548
Wm. Woodson, 75, 45, 1500, 15, 171
Robt. May, 200, 200, 8000, 300, 770
Henry B. Taylor, -, -, -, 10, 210
Wm. Rowland, -, -, -, , 40
Littlebery Rowland, -, -, -, 6, 263
Hardy Wintel, 50, 150, 1000, 90, 279
Lent Bowman, 200, 80, 3000, 75, 661
Jno. Rowland, -, -, -, 10,38
Roberta A. Baines, 40, 68, 1000, 45, 275
Jas. B. W. Beasley, -, -, -, -, 100
Wm. H. Crawford, -, -, -, 15, 164
Jarrett Simmons, -, -, -, 15, 183
Henry Floyd, -, -,-, 10, 70

Ives P. Burns, 33, 15, 300, 15, 278
Wm. Burton, -, -, -, -, 112
Isiah Dyer, 150, 150, 2500, 190, 467
Robt. Morris, -, -, -, 10, 174
Kinion Thornton, 17, 26, 250, 8, 196
Daniel Winset, 35, 80, 475, 15, 176
Davis Graves, 40, 100, 500, 15, 171
Thos. _. Vaughan, -, -, -, 10, 241
Jno. _. Winset, 10, 39, 200, 5, 50
Thos. J. Heath, -, -, -, 5, 105
Geo. Crick, 20, 29, 300, 5, 37
Gilbert Brasheares, -, -, -, 4, 123
Green B. Mangnam, 15, 72, 600, 25, 232
Benja. Floyd, 50, 60, 900, 45, 400
Nat. Haynes, 40, 80, 650, 35, 163
Velden Brashears, 2, -, 40, 5, 45
Richard Heath, 35, 34, 300, 35, 124
Robt. Jarrett, 65, 40, 1300, 20, 214
Jas. _. King, 40, 35, 550, 10, 296
O. Wm. Crockett Jr., 50, 60, 1000, 40, 413
Devereaux Jarratt, 500, 250, 8000, 120, 1140
Joseph Spence, -, -, -, 10, 135
Wm. Rucher, 25, -, 500, 10, 213
Aaron Patterson, -, -, -, 5, 75
Cloe Rucker, 35, 15, 600, 20, 205
Sarah Ranson, 350, 100, 8000, 200, 840
Jas. E. Wilson, -, -, -, 10, 70
Geo. W. Anderson, -, -, -, 60, 170
Lewis M. Grigg(Crigg), 20, -, 1500, 120, 250
O. W. Crockett Sr., 200, 50, 6000, 120, 1010
Thos. O. Butler, 400, 474, 16400, 630, 2005
A. E. Alexander, -, -, -, 30, 200
Jno. Vaughan, -, -, -, -, 34
Hiram Jenkins, 49, 11, 1500, 300, 670
Margarett Henderson, 100, 120, 4400, 75, 422
Geo. W. Beckton, -, -, -, 200, 574
J. W. Hargett, 600, 250, 21200, 480, 4925
M. H. Brady, 15, -, 600, 10, 250
Giles S. Harden, 80, 20, 2000, 50, 750
Elias King, 275, 184, 11500, 340, 1345
Jas. Whiless, -, -, -, 10, 110
Thos. B. Turner, 600, 670, 27000, 400, 2458
Lewis M. Maney, 350, 650, 20000, 180, 1225
Jno. Hubbard, 180, 180,3 060, 50, 489
C. M. Brooks, 44, 50, 1800, 35, 510
Thos. Oden, 35, 15, 1000, 30, 225
John Malloy, 200, 130, 6600, 250, 1175

Paschal Zayer (Yayer), 100, 130, 3000, 200, 395
Saml. Campbell, 120, 230, 7000, 100, 693
Jas. W. Binford, 250, 316, 8000, 100, 960
Edward Zagur, 100, 150, 10000, 100, 199
Wm. Sowell (Lowell), -, -, -, 10, 220
Burrell Janaway, 320, 200, 12000, 400, 1080
Francis M. Malloy, 80, 20, 1500, 50, 650
Elisha Cox, 8,7, 400, 25, 100
Hiram Young, 220, 155, 5000, 240, 1435
Jno. M. Wade, 200, 280, 9600, 350, 1033
Charles Anderson, 230, 170, 10000, 350, 1340
Henderson Anderson, -, -, -, -, 270
J. C. Hallerburton, 152, 188, 3800, 390, 751
Pettis Norman, 33, 82, 2300, 20, 242
E. A. C. Norman, 20, 90, 2300, 265, 425
P, M. M. Alexander, -, -, -, 120, 258
Prichett Alexander, 200, 100, 6000, 60, 500
R. D. McCullough, 120, 164, 2580, 360, 850
Thos Dutton (Dalton), 35, 40, 500, 70, 225
Wm. N. Wooten, 40, 50, 600, 12, 368
Jas. Horton, -, -, -, -, 305
Jas. E. Fowler, -, -, -, -, 175
Thos. Zaurs (Yours), -, -, -, 10, 217
Wm. S. Butler, 400, 800, 16000, 500, 1670
Benja. Brothers, -, -, -, 20, 450
Cummilly Patterson, 200, 120, 3000, 60, 404
Stephen A. Smith, -, -, -, 15, 102
Young Davis, 100, 228, 4500, 70, 821
Isaac Hardy, -, -, -, -, 136
Leonard H. Sims, -, -, -, 10, 320
Henry Hall, 450, 500, 20000, 370, 1290
B. Wm. Henry, 340, 400, 16000, 350, 1610
Isaac Ledbetter, -, -, -, 25, 335
Wm. Ledbetter, 300, 360, 30000, 300, 2000
Wm. Hall, 66, 34, 2000, -, 900
Jas. Warren, -, -, -, -, 185
Wm. Hubbard, -, -, -, 35, 278
Thos. Sims, 300, 270, 600, 75, 716
Sweston Sims, 75, 50, 2000, 40, 234
Milton Birdwell, 100, 169, 2500, 30, 665
E. C. Hallowell, -, -, -, 10, 145
E. B. Ruby, -, -, -, 8, 127
Thompson Jarrett, 500, 500, 7300, 250, 970

H___ H. Yeagar, 5, 125, 700, 10, 280
Edward A. McNeal, 40, 70, 1600,15, 360
Susanah Thompson, 40, 110, 900, 35, 256
Jno. E. Drumgavle, 100, 200, 5000, 150, 927
Wm. Featherston, -, -, -, 30, 220
Alfred M. Jacobs, -, -, -, -, 20
Benja Wallis, 5, -, 150, 10, 164
Thos. D. Harrison, 80, 20, 200, 15, 275
Aaron Webb, 150, 50, 6000, 275, 912
Wm. H. McCabe, 60, 50, 1250, 50, 320
Alexander Nisbett, 90, 60, 2400, 125, 1177
Andrew Hall (Hull), 80, 110, 4000, 100, 734
Anderson Todd, -, -, -, -, 55
G. B. Jacobs, -, -, -, 10, 163
Uphram F. Lytle, 300, 500, 20000, 375, 1580
Mathew Jacobs, -, -, -, 5, 208
Jacob Mathews, -, -, -, 10, 120
Saml. Bowman, 40, 50, 1000, 100, 407
Harriett Bell, -, -, -, 100, 446
Nathaniel Winston, 80, 45, 2500, 40, 570
Saml. Winston, 2150, 243, 15700, 220, 3344
Wiley Huff, 200, 105, 5500, 150, 685
J. M. Leatherman, 100, 85, 4000, 45, 374
Littleton Averett, 66, 67, 2000, 50, 650
Jno. D. Lawrence, 100, 100, 2600, 100, 461
Elizabeth Colter (Cotter), 40, 58, 500, 60, 184
Daniel Alexander, 225, 287, 5374, 140, 970
Mary Beasley, 46, 12, 400, 10, 175
D. M. Crockett, 100, 30, 2000, 50, 4000
Jas. Wood, -, -, -, 10, 190
Wm. Smith, 350, 210, 11000, 200, 1140
Wm. D. Lillard, 300, 170, 11700, 325, 1344
A. C. Rutledge, -, -, -, -, 90
Edmond G. Cock, -, -, -, -, 239
Jas. S. Faucett, 30, 19, 490, -, 20
Mary Collins, -, -, -, -, 18
Alfred Miller, 350, 350, 11000, 300, 711
Henry W. Wilson, 35, -, 1000, 15, 325
Saml. Wadley, 200, 100, 3000, 65, 502
M. B. Wadley, -, -, -, 10, 261
Elijah Horton, -, -, -, 5, 113
Adam Comer, 35, 17, 400, 60, 170
William Williams, -, -, -, 6, 147
Nathan A. F. Yeargar, 150, 60, 2500, 95, 456
Lewis Cousins, -, -, -, 5, 143

M. H. Alexander, 300, 665, 12165, 300, 945
Nancy Nash, -, -, -, 4, 55
Geo. W. Hutton, 168, 97, 3900, 65, 869
E. H. White, -, -, -, 5, 105
Elizbaeth Grimses, 120, 89, 1900, 50, 239
W. W. White, 100, 115, 2580, 15, 169
Benj. _. Crocker, -, -, -, -, 30
Benja. Webb, 15, 10, 250, 5, 135
Jas. M. Holden (Holder), 50, 10, 250, 5, 135
Richard Spence, 200, 230, 2200, 120, 690
Nelson Horton, 50, 230, 2200, 120, 690
Alford Mallard, 80, 89, 1890, 70, 612
Charles Holden (Holder), 100, 75, 2500, 95, 741
Edmon Rowse, -, -, -, 7, 121
Younger Wiett, -, -, -, 40, 340
Greenwood Wadkins, -, -, -, -, 10
Jno. Gorden, 65, 15, 1000, 265, 535
Simson Harris, 80, 196, 3000, 27, 304
John Winston, 75, 75, 1200, 40, 553
Baens E. Patterson, -, -, -, 5, 170
Benshaw Spence, 130, 320, 9000, 80, 1280
Lewis Harrison, -, -, -, 2, 40
William Holden, -, -, -, 6, 183
William Oakly, -, -, -, 8, 90
W. H. Jackson, 25, 21, 322, 5, 121
H. G. Lune(Tune), 55, 86, 2200, 40, 208
W. C. Lune (Tune), 35, 65, 1200, 20, 111
Saml. M. McKey, -, -, -, 55, 119
John M. Wadkins, 120, 140, 2000, 75, 705
Jas. W. Oakly, -, -, -, -, 104
Stephen M. Mankin, -, -, -, -, 76
W. G. Crockett, 100, 70, 1150, 80, 487
John Modrall, -, -, -, 10, 216
C. E. Modrall, 60, 72, 1300, 30, 343
Kenton Tucker, 115, 65, 1800, 70, 561
James H. Clark, -, -, -, 10, 18
Geo. N. Edwards, 25, 25, 400, 40, 240
Martin Edwards, 25, 75, 600, 100, 400
Burton Acree, -, -, -, 3, 54
John Smith, -, -, -, 2, 65
Morgan Smith, -, -, -, -, 10
Benja. Crocker, 60, 98, 1000, 40, 267
R. H. Powell, 65, 46, 1200, 5, 269
Lewis Tucker, 165, 338, 5000, 200, 1633
William Morgan, 150, 100, 2500, 50, 675
R. Cooper, 110, 156, 2300, 15, 269
Martin Turner, 60, 30, 1000, 150, 421
Ephram Turner, -, -, -, 5, 255
William Taylor, -, -, -, 5, 278
James Hicks, -, -, -, 5, 74
Nathan W. Landers, -, -, -, 5, 88

Thos. Sanders, 90, 10, 800, 50, 210
John Harris, -, -, -, 10, 235
Edmon Wiett, -, -, -, 8, 70
Francis M. Webb, -, -, -, 2, 142
James Douglass, -, -, -, 5, 90
Alford West, -, -, -, 5, 100
Jno. M. Elliott, -, -, -, 5, 92
Jno. Patterson, 180, 6, 3000, 100, 884
Hicks Ellis, 65, 40, 1000, 15, 346
Rebeckah Filpipps, 65 135, 2000, 20, 333
Hiram H. Wood, 40, 90, 1000, 125, 268
Sarah Clanton, -, -, -, -, 10
Jno. Wilson, 80, 80, 1200, 20, 246
J. N. Holden, -, -, -, 65, 465
Thos. C. Price, 8, 118, 1000, -, 155
Adam Comer, 120, 30, 2000, 125, 425
A. A. Vinson, 22, 48, 8000, 40, 319
J. J. Taylor, -, -, -, -, 198
Allen W. Senters, 20, 18, 578, 6, 89
Wm. Vinson, 75, 140, 1500, 35, 345
Jno. N. Webb, 100, 212, 4000, 128, 755
Jas. M. Cambrell, 1, -, 300, -, 92
Jno. A. Reed, -, -, -, -, 51
William H. Barksdale, 5, -, 800, 7, 94
Jno. W. Wadley, ¼, -, 100, -, 100
Benja. Williams, -, -, -, 7, 72
Robt. B. Rucker, 200, 75, 2750, 50, 455
Robert B. McClune(McClure), 1, -, 400, 65, 283
C. G. McClune, 300, 340, 6400, 150, 1270
Hugh McGear, -, -, -, -, 20
Polly Holden, 35, 24, 300, 45, 232
Wm. L. Baskett, 140, 170, 6000, 150, 928
H. V. Alexander, -, -, -, 7, 150
A. H. McClune, 70, 30, 1500, 75, 257
Miles Underwood, -, -, -, -, 70
Lewis Smotherman, 300, 100, 3000, 50, -
Liney Moore, 85, 10, 600, 30, 222
C. F. Hickman, -, -, -, 1, 15
Martha Burge, 45, 100, 800, -, 75
Thos. C. Reed, -, -, -, 5, 65
Rebeckah Chery, -, -, -, -, 228
W. Senthers, 75, 135, 1200, 100, 302
G. W. Holden, 85, 115, 2000, 12, 508
Jno. R. Smotherman, -, -, -, 5, 136
Alfred Smotherman, -, -, -, 20, 69
Franklin Nash, -, -, -, 6, 131
Mary Grimes, -, -, -, -, 125
C. G. Crocker, -, -, -, 5, 22
Thos. N. Suge, 50, 43, 350, 20, 168
Thos. D. Dunn, 30, 76, 800, 5, 70
T. H. Leathers, 40, 47, 400, 10, 257
W. M. Smotherman, 100, 166, 1400, 8, 322
P. W. Underwood, -, -, -, 2, 94

H. D. Smotherman, -, -, -, -, 78
Jno. A. Wood, -, -, -, 5, 41
Saml. J. Holden, 100, 170, 2500, 150, 432
E. Smotherman, 50, 50, 1000, 5, 70
Burton Smotherman, -, -, -, 6, 149
E. Smotherman, -, -, -, 6, 100
J. G. Smotherman, 50, 75, 700, 100, 83
Milton Garratt, 90, 70, 1500, 50, 377
Wm. Grinage, -, -, -, 75, 251
Sarah C. Holden, 120, 200, 3000, 30, 400
C. W. Holden, -, -, -, -, 145
Geo. Robbertson, 15, 5, 130, 6, 125
Abram Maxwell, -, -, -, 15
H. Smotherman, 65, 50, 1200, 60, 605
Francis Smotherman, -, -, -, 5, 54
Jno. R. Holton, -, -, -, -, 63
Thos. M. Primm, 54, 6, 750, 15, 924
Williams Jackson, 400, 100, 4000, 130, 725
J. C. Hopkins, -, -, -, -, 90
Elizabeth Covington, 76, 20, 1000, 45, 547
Jno. N. Clark, 70, 103, 2000, 100, 421
Silas Winset, 80, 100, 800, 15, 268
W. G. Smith, 60, 145, 1100, 260, 476
Hallace Cooper, -, -, -, 5, 102
David W. Patterson, -, -, -, 25, 135
Aron Hall, -, -, -, 4, 34
J. G. Crick, -, 40, 150, 30, 210
Jas. L. Brashears, -, -, -, -, 18
Martha A. Simmons, 20, 50, 300, 10, 260
Thos. S. Taylor, -, -, -, 15, 237
Alfred Hatson, 17, 63, 400, 10, 263
Jas. C. Brooks, 75, 85, 1200, 1 00, 352
John Gillaspie, -, -, -, 105, 250
Thos. Hendrix, 75, 60, 1864, 50, 343
David Hendrix, -, -, -, 5, 297
B. B. Taylor, 145, 145, 2500, 60, 731
Nathan Jackson, 200, 309, 4000, 150, 1435
F. I. Hendrix, -, -, -, 10, 20
Mary F. Hendrix, 35, 15, 500, 15, 297
John Jones, 70, 47, 1000, 75, 757
Wm. Smotherman, -, -, -, 5, 57
Saml. M. Hopkins, 15, 16, 425, 5, 139
James O'Neal, -, -, -, 2, 67
J. F. Taylor, 25, 14, 400, 5, 137
R. M. Taylor, 40, 45, 700, 15, 152
Robt. Taylor, 43, 107, 1000, 10, 251
Wm. White, 60, 127, 1100, 40, 455
Jas. Gillaspie, 40, 127, 800, 5, 259
Robt. Reed, 100, 120, 1600, 75, 494
Mary Reed, -, -, -, -, 120
Vinson Taylor, 70, 200, 2500, 140, 930
L. A. Covington, 73, 60, 1000, 350, 791
Wm. Walker, -, -, -, 3, 15

Jas. Patman, -, -, -, 5, 52
Wm. L. Woodliff, -, -, -, 10, 40
Jacob D. Crick, 57, 57, 1000, 10, 154
Willis B. Crick, - -, -, 3, 50
John Buncom, -, -, -, -, 13
Austin Walker, -, -, -, 7, 38
E. F. Manine, -, -, -, 10, 95
Geo. Wright, -, -, -, 15, 125
R. B. May, 70, 30, 1200, 6, 219
Thos. Lamb, -, -, -, 10, 206
Saml. Murry, -, -, -, 8, 186
Jno. T. Seay, 30, 35, 550, 20, 200
W. Westbrooks, -, -, -, 7, 133
S. R. Tutor, -, -, -, -, 10
Thos. I. Taylor, -, -, -, 5, 13
Eli A. Suy, 110, 340, 3000, 50, 520
Jas. C. Taylor, -, -, -, 80, 350
Josiah Hewett, -, -, -, 10, 60
Willis Jackson, 17, 13, 400, 90, 191
A. L. Casterman, -, -, -, -, 20
Jno. E. Starber (Sharber), 150, 185, 2250, 300, 1222
Jas. Holstead, -, -, -, 2, -
Susan Holstead, 35, 20, 445, 3, 91
Miles Holsead, -, -, -, 4, 69
Wm. Trail, -, -, -, 3, 81
Wiley Trail, 25, 15, 250, 5, 102
R. Ranson, 75, 65, 800, 100, 483
Jehu Sharber, 35, 65, 650, 45, 392
Thos. Jackson, 50, 126, 1100, 140, 821
Thos. L. Hendrix, -, -, -, 12, 100
A. P. Darrell, -, -, -, 3, 220
C. B. Farris, 150, 150, 2500, 125, 668
Wm. H. Crick, 60, 103, 912, 15, 268
Caswell Puckett (Duckett), 100, 90, 1575, 50, 626
Jesse H. Carson, 1, -, 50, 20, 160
John Furgison, -, -, -, 3, 65
Elizabeth Ray, 40, 40, 500, 10, 227
Robt. D. King, -, 6, 400, -, 192
W. B. King, 2, 72, 200, 10, 108
Jno. C. Welk(Wink), -, -, -, 10, 84
Thos. Garner (Jarner), -, -, -, -, 111
Thos. Hogan, -, -, -, 5, 20
A. J. Crafton, 45, 100, 800, 10, 156
Gideon Coul, 45, 45, 1000, 120, 197
Nancy Coul, 34, 6, 400, 5, 106
Anderson Tombs, -, -, -, 5, 20
PeterRregan, -, -, -, 5, 65
Green B. Smotherman, -, -, -, 10, 97
Jno. Landron, 150, 200, 1850, 50, 353
Jonas _. Winset, -, -, -, 90, 240
David Young, 40, 52, 500, 60, 431
Thos. Lamb, 300, 500, 2700, 50, 955
Alfred S. Little, 45, 55, 400, 40, 107
Jno. Crick, 25, 40, 300, 25, 425

Charles Pope, 90, 40, 720, 40, 581
Edmon C. Crick, 50, 88, 700, 50, 230
C. G. Reed, -, -, -, 5, 199
King W. Patterson, 89, 41, 800, 80, 403
Wm. Pope, 49, 100, 950, 50, 401
E. W. Hendrix, 250, 107, 1500, 150, 588
W, T. Lenss (Leuss, Seuss), 40, 25, 769, 125, 409
Wm. Davis, 100, 25, 1500, 15, 440
Jno. Dunn, 88, 85, 1250, 40, 447
Richard Nance, 150, 80, 1800, 50, 737
Jas. Smotherman, -, -, -, 20, 223
David Lamb, 60, 40, 1000, 45, 266
Richard Jackson, 80, 170, 1500, 50, 386
Jas. G. Williams, 70, 80, 1500, 50, 410
Wm. T. Spence, -, -, -, 5, 130
Benj. Williams, -, -, -, 10, 189
W. Corsey (Cassey), -, -, -, 5, 35
Elijah Smotherman, 150, 387, 3000, 50, 617
Francis Jackson, 200, 322, 3654, 700, 1540
C. B. Hailey, 27, 18, 360, 10, 122
Berry J. Lamb, 28, 12, 450, 8, 65
Cassander Comer, 60, 40, 750, 10, 209
G. W. Hutcheson, 2, -, 100, -, 85
F. G. Trail, 30, 20, 250, 40, 199
Geo. Willis, 25, 25, 150, 8, 47
Abner Bishop, -, -, -, 15, 120

The following names appear on what shows as Rutherford Co. but Scott Co. is also written on the page and the handwriting is very different. Many of the names are different. Therefore, these last names will appear in both counties. This census taker also uses the ZERO.

Calvin Cooper, 10 ¼, 9 ¾, 200, 0, 250
John L. Smith, 45, 1955, 100, 50, 535
Emanuel Phillips, 25, 40, 500, 50, 120
James Crabtree, 100, 241, 800, 25, 120
Jesse Crabtree, -, -, -, -, 50
Robert Smith, -, -, -, 25, 100
Stephen Thomas, 30, 40, 400, 100, 400
James Sacton, 6, 294, 100, 5, 115
James Reed, 50, 200, 800, 300, 255
Stephen Gibson, 40, 10, 200, 25, 250
Thomas Lawson, 45, 130, 500, 100, 200
Martha Leuallen, 12, 488, 150, 10, 125
Nathan Boling, 8, 200, 100, 5, 30
Mary Loyd, 95, 100, 10, 85
Lourdan Owen, 20, -, 300, 10, 60
Anna Marcum, 60, 100, 300, 20, 100
Wm. Jeffers, 40, 63, 100, 40, 60
Enoch Robertson, 75, 100, 400, 100, 300

Champain Duncain, 40, 100, 400, 20, 100
John Adkins, 5, 113, 375, 12, 60
John Duncain, 40, 10, 350, 20, 175
Lewis Thompson, 100, 1300, 600, 50, 400
Wm. Smither, 30, 170, 200, 25, 300
Joshua Duncain, 90, 5710, 2000, 200, 1000
Steven Jeffers, 25, 10, 350, 20, 175
Wm. Cross (Crap), 15, 75, 50, 20, 100
Wm. Jeffers, 15, 0, 45, 10, 50
G. B. Duncain, 12, -, 35, 10, 60
Wm. Loyd, 11, 0, 100, 12, 200

Thomas Loyd, 16, 0, 10, 10, 50
Wm. Childers, 20, 0, 200, 50, 200
Lavinia Marcum, 25, 50, 150, 20, 150
H. C. Marcum, 68, 1758, 1000, 100, 200
Herman Thompson, 25, 425, 450, 50, 228
Jesse Boling, 15, 85, 100, 25, 100
Riley Chambers, 50, 580, 500, 50, 150
Wm. Marcum 10, 0, 50, 5, 10
Ale Hatfield, 80, 400, 300, 100, 400
David Shoopman, 75, 1972, 600, 20, 200
James Ceall, 45, 305, 500, 20, 250
Drury Smith, 20, 0, 20, 30, 1000

Scott County TN
1850 Agricultural Census

The Agricultural Census for 1850 was filmed for the University of North Carolina from original records in the Tennessee State Library and Archives.

The following are the items represented and separated by a comma: for example, John Doe, 25, 25, 10, 5, 100. This represents:

Column 1 Owner
Column 2 Acres of Improved Land
Column 3 Acres of Unimproved Land
Column 4 Cash Value of Farm
Column 5 Value of Farm Implements and Machinery
Column 13 Value of Livestock

Calvin Cooper, 10 ¼, 9 ¾, 200, 0, 250
John L. Smith, 45, 1955, 100, 50, 535
Emanuel Phillips, 25, 40, 500, 50, 120
James Crabtree, 100, 241, 800, 25, 120
Jesse Crabtree, 0, 0, 0, 0, 50
Robert Smith, 0, 0, 0, 25, 100
Stephen Thomas, 30, 40, 400, 100, 400
James Sacton, 6, 294, 100, 5, 115
James Reed, 50, 200, 800, 300, 255
Stephen Gibson, 40, 10, 200, 25, 250
Thomas Lawson, 45, 130, 500, 100, 200
Martha Leuallen, 12, 488, 150, 10, 125
Nathan Boling, 8, 200, 100, 5, 30
Mary Loyd, 5, 95, 100, 10, 85
Lourden Owen, 20 0, 300, 10, 60
Anna Marcum, 60, 100, 300, 20, 100
Wm. Jeffers, 40, 63, 100, 40, 60
Enoch Robertson, 75, 100, 400, 100, 300
Champion Duncain, 40, 100, 400, 20, 100
John Adkins, 5, 113, 375, 12, 60
John Duncain, 40, 10, 350, 20, 175
Lewis Thompson, 100, 1300, 600, 50, 300
Wm. Smither, 30, 170, 200, 25, 300
Joshua Duncain, 90, 5710, 2000, 200, 1000
Steven Jeffers, 25, 10, 350, 20, 175
Wm. Cross (Crap), 15, 75, 50, 20, 100
Wm. Jeffers, 15, 0, 45, 10, 50
G. B. Duncain, 12, 0, 36, 10, 60
Wm. Loyd, 11, 0, 100, 12, 200
Thomas Loyd, 16, 0, 10, 10, 50
Wm. Childers, 20, 0, 200, 50, 200
Lavinia Marcum, 25, 50, 150, 20, 150
H. C. Marcum, 68, 1758, 1000, 100, 200
Herman Thompson, 25, 425, 450, 50, 228
Jesse Boling, 15, 85, 100, 25, 100
Riley Chambers, 50, 580, 500, 50, 150

Wm. Marcum, 10, 0, 50, 5, 10
Ale Hatfield, 80, 400, 300, 100, 400
David Shoopman, 75, 1971, 600, 20, 200
James Ceall, 45, 305, 500, 20, 250
Drury Smith, 20, 0, 20, 30, 1000

The preceeding names are either on the first page of the Scott Co. census or the last page of the Rutherford Co. census and therefore, are shown in both counties. Both county names appear at the top of this particular page.

Hiram Baker, 0, 5, 8, 10, 4
John Carson, 60, 602, 401, 50, 500
Isaac Smith, 50, 700, 300, 150, 400
Riley La__her, 0, 15, 2331, 30, 10
Obediah Adkins, 0, 20, 6550, 40, 6
Isaac Reed, 0, 0, 0, 0, 0
Jane Richardson, 2, 0, 10, 0, 1
Daniel Vougone, 20, 0, 10, 0, 1
Isaac Reed Jr., 0, 0, 0, 0, 225
Isaac Parker, 50, 50, 50, 25,25
Nancy Reed, 30, 70, 400, 50, 100
Allen Reed, 40, 500, 1000, 25, 75
Elijah Terry, 35, 300, 600, 50, 150
Robert Jeffers, 0, 0, 0, 25, 200
Wm. Massengille, 30, 220, 600, 20, 200
James Litton, 50, 200, 300, 50, 200
Wm. W. Cotton, 30, 7500, 300, 75, 500
Joel Chitwood, 22, 273, 400, 25, 300
R. M. Bennett, 30, 7500, 300, 75, 500
Leander King, 0, 0, 0, 0, 500
Wm. R. Chitwood, 0, 0, 0, 0, 50
Hamilton Brown, 10, 20, 100, 25, 100
Thomas Angel, 4, 46, 100, 25, 100
George McDonold, 20, 70, 300, 25, 155
Joshua Good, 0, 0, 0, 20, 300

A. M. Cross, 150, 300, 250, 400, 800
Ruben Bridges, 19, 31, 100, 6, 1500
John Smith, 15, 0, 50, 10, 200
H. Hunnycutt, 100, 200, 600, 150, 90
H. Adkins, 25, 0, 100, 15, 150
Thomas Chambers, 55, 152, 300, 25, 220
Fealden Penington, 50, 255, 300, 15, 30
Janrex Fox, 50, 150, 150, 5, 50
George Adkins, 55, 255, 300, 3, 0
Henry Co_elm, 18, 150, 150, 0, 0
Elizabeth Write, 8, 0, 100, 0, 0
John Cook, 18, 0, 150, 0, 0
David Harness, 25, 45, 250, 25, 350
G. Penington, 25, 250, 130, 40, 30
Wm. Bird, 30, 270, 150, 30, 100
G. W. Marcum, -, 5, 8, 10, 50
Benjamin Dagly, 20, 300, 300, 23, 600
Isaac Roisden, 10, 200, 500, 25, 300
Joseph Ryan, 700, 385, 450, 100, 500
Robert Ross, 90, 471, 700, 100, 300
James Sharp, 2, 0, 0, 0, 0
Peter Tuttle, 4, 70, 100, 25, 120
James Wilson, 20, 10, 0, 50, 120
Nicholas Sharp, 30, 320, 500, 100, 350
Henry Duncan Jr., 30, 50, 300, 23, 150
Henry Duncan Sr., 15, 0, 100, 25, 200
Johnathan Phillips, 40, 160, 200, 50, 1218
Elijah Phillips, 40, 110, 500, 10, 100
Jacob Lawson, 18, 38, 60, 20, 100
Andrew Leuallen, 15, 100, 100, 15, 85
Samuel Lawson, 125, 460, 1200, 100, 800
John Leuallen, 60, 300, 300, 100, 300
John Chambers, 90, 580, 1000, 100, 300
Andrew Griffis, 80, 125, 50, 25, 300
Steven Caudle, 170, 500, 115, 40, 230
David Trammel, 60, 140, 550, 25, 3000
Dauswell (Danswell), Trammel, 8, 20, 50,
12, 300
Holaday Moses, 50, 149, 600, 50, 200
Owen Adkins, 25, 60, 200, 25, 200
Henry Ross, 25, 25, 75, 15, 200
James Angel, 25, 30, 125, 25, 300
Denis Angel, 30, 25, 25, 25, 300
Daniel McClung, 55, 495, 500, 600, 400
Wm. Chitwood, 30, 100, 140, 15, 500
Richmond Taylor, 30, 30, 400, 25, 400
J. S. Chitwood, 30, 195, 400, 15, 400
Drewry Ryan, 5, 150, 100, 15, 300
J. H. Chitwood, 75, 500, 600, 75, 200
Isaac M. Hamby, 30, 209, 300, 75, 300
F. Bell, 80, 785, 800, 500, 400
Andrew Wilson, 90, 1610, 1500, 100,
1500
S. D. Lay, 15, 35, 150, 20, 160
J. L. Chitwood, 100, 200, 250, 50, 100
Daniel Chitwood, 50, 100, 30, 80, 400

James Chitwood, 20, 20, 40, 50, 400
Andrew Chitwood, 30, 100, 100, 30, 3000
Abner Thomas, 30, 410, 300, 100, 300
Joseph Phillips, 60, 200, 500, 100, 600
Alfred Brown, 50, 500, 350, 100, 300
Jesse Bats, 18, 0, 50, 10, 50
Oliver Litton, 25, 125, 150, 50, 300
Wm. Carrol, 10, 10, 100, 12, 100
Isham Sharp, 15, 210, 332, 1, 0
Frederick Smith Sr., 50, 8000, 600, 50,
300
Reuben West, 40, 210, 500, 100, 500
Charles West, 12, 200, 200, 100, 150
Wm. Marcum, 40, 228, 300, 40, 300
Edmond Stevens, 18, 630, 100, 15, 300
Andrew Boling, 50, 28, 600, 50, 300
C. C. Reed, 10, 4000, 50, 10, 100
John Sexton, 15, 0, 200, 50, 150
John Phillips, 15, 285, 150, 50, 30
John Thomas, 30, 245, 150, 20, 100
Wm. Buttrum, 20, 45, 100, 200, 400
Richard _. Newport, 2, 5030, 100, 15, 50
Plephant Chambers, 100, 198, 800, 50,
200
W. S. Hamby, 10, 1012, 55, 10, 100
James Barker, 4, 100, 50, 15, 100
Wm. Newport, 10, 26, 50, 20, 50
Joseph Burnett, 30, 750, 150, 25, 60
Andrew Reed, 10, 120, 200, 25, 100
Wesley Buttrum, 10, 490, 50, 15, 50
Rubin Smither, 0, 25, 10, 0, 100
David Overton, 22, 10, 200, 30, 100
Berry Boling, 20, 3, 300, 200, 100
Shadrach Sexton, 8, 80, 50, 100, 100
Calvin Thomas, 15, 300, 200, 20, 60
Isaac Hill, 30, 55, 200, 20, 200
John Thompson, 30, 470, 100, 10, 100
Wm. R. Phillips, 0, 760, 200, 10, 100
A. McDonald, 10, 0, 200, 10, 100
Wm. Buttrum, 8, 780, 100, 25, 200
Reason West, 35, 345, 200, 20, 100
Herod Leuallen, 10, 490, 100, 10, 200
Rubin Smither, 5, 200, 200, 20, 100
Andrew Reed, 10, 100, 100, 20, 100
Wm. Griffis, 0, 50, 300, 30, 50
James Carson, 5, 50, 100, 40, 100
Joseph Newport, 20, 0, 100, 15, 100
B. S. Newport, 60, 195, 300, 25, 200
Roads Stanley, 20, 480, 250, 50, 200
David Stevens, 5, 1000, 50, 15, 300
Daniel Acres, 50, 100, 600, 5, 100
James Acres, 25, 25, 100, 12, 200
Briant Honnycut, 30, 70, 150, 10, 50
T. M. Cross, 15, 35, 150, 10, 100
Isham Sharp, 30, 220, 100, 25, 33
John Stevens, 15, 110, 100, 15, 65

L. W. Cross, 70,3 20, 1500, 25, 400
Caswell Cross, 3, 47, 50, 10, 25
Louis Cross, 6, 94, 50, 15, 50
A. D. Loyd, 8, 0, 40, 40, 75
Samuel Newport, 15, 100, 25, 150, 100
Joel Looper, 10, 50, 200, 25, 20
Michael Rolins, 50, 100, 1000, 50, 300
James Whollaway, 10, 150, 150, 20, 50
Aaron Good, 13, 100, 200, 25, 80
Sary Good, 0, 0, 0, 10, 30
Mary Griffis, 0, 0, 0, 15, 40
Culberth Webb, 20, 40, 200, 25, 60
A. H. Cross, 30, 60, 500, 30, 150
A. D. Elliott, 10, 90, 100, 20, 100
_. Triplett, 0, 0, 0, 0, 100
A. R. Leuallen, 80, 1840, 100, 200, 500
Andrew Leuallen, 30, 1000, 500, 100, 250
Walter Leuallen, 20, 100, 250, 300, 240
Joel Leuallen, 50, 300, 500, 250, 350
James Bruten, 10, 100, 200, 150, 250
Ezekiel Newport, 8, 200, 300, 125, 150
John Jeffers, 5, 100, 200, 50, 125
Wm. Riche, 30, 100, 500, 75, 200
Jame Hughett, 30, 50, 300, 20, 200
Wesly Owen, 10, 100, 150, 20, 250
Joseph Low, 25, 175, 300, 30, 200
R. B. Embry, 20, 100, 200, 20, 300
Thomas Griffis, 25, 100, 100, 30, 100
Wm. Hughett, 30, 75, 80, 75, 200
Asahel Eeds, 10, 25, 100, 50, 100
Caswell Hoe, 60, 195, 300, 25, 200
Ruthy Stanly, 20, 30, 200, 20, 50
Mary Stanly, 0, 0, 0, 10, 20
Eliza Stanly, 0, 0, 0, 10, 20
Joshua Good, 10, 90, 100, 20, 100
Joel Hamby, 50, 100, 600, 5, 100
A. S. Griffith, 10, 50, 200, 20, 100
Richard Griffis, 30, 70, 150, 10, 50
Timothy Sexton, 15, 35, 150, 10, 100
Manuel Sexton, 30, 220, 100, 25, 33
Lahew Phillips, 15, 110, 100, 15, 65
Mathew Young, 10, 90, 100, 25, 50
Phebe Bigley, 20, 480, 200, 50, 100
Fountain Sexton, 25, 1000, 50, 50, 50
H. W. Pemberton, 2, 100, 50, 50, 100
Thomas Richards, 25, 25, 100, 12, 200
_. S. Lackey, 30, 70, 150, 10, 50
Learner Sexton, 15, 35, 150, 10, 100
Jesse Bird, 15, 20, 100, 10, 100
John Bird, 20, 100, 200, 10, 100
John Potter, 70, 320, 1500, 25, 500
A. R. Jeffers, 6, 94, 50, 15, 50
Jas. Cove, 8, 0, 0, 15, 50
Jesse Hix, 8, 0, 0, 40, 30
Samuel Harness, 15, 1025, 1500, 15, 75

Joseph Delk, 75, 300, 200, 100, 200
John Good, 50, 1800, 200, 50, 400
Wm. R. Bashears, 25, 100, 100, 25, 200
Henry Gibson, 50, 200, 200, 300, 100
Jeremiah Bashears, 75, 100, 100, 50, 200
Nathan Hammons, 100, 200, 100, 50, 150
Hezekiah Hammons, 10, 100, 75, 50, 100
M.B. Ryan, 15, 200, 50, 25, 200
_. R. Patterson, 15, 100, 75, 200, 250
_. F. Patterson, 10, 120, 100, 25, 200
Drewry Carrel, 20, 115, 250, 30, 100
Thomas York, 15, 100, 300, 25, 200
Phillip Low, 20, 200, 300, 30, 100
Josiah Terry, 10, 100, 200, 15, 75
James Slarun, 8, 60, 100, 10, 60
Bartholomew Eltel, 15, 75, 100,25, 100
Allen McDonald, 100, 21000, 3000, 250, 100
Michael Low Jr., 15, 50, 200, 15, 50
H. Thompson Jr., 20, 25, 100, 10, 50
James Newport, 30, 20, 100, 20, 100
Joseph Low, 10, 100, 200, 30, 200
John Tacket, 20, 200, 300, 20, 100
Samuel Anderson, 10, 300, 200, 30, 200
Phillip Anderson, 25, 20, 300, 30, 100
Wm. Carrol, 10, 100, 200, 20, 200
Shadden Allen , 15, 50, 100, 20, 100
M. Massengille, 30, 26, 200, 50, 200
H. Massengille, 10, 50, 100, 50, 100
M. Massengille, 5, 45, 50, 25, 200
Wm. Dicson, 20, 100, 25, 50, 100
H. Chitwood, 15, 75, 20, 50, 200
Samuel McDonald, 10, 90, 15, 20, 100
James McDonald, 200, 80, 100, 50, 50
Thomas Phillips, 20, 100, 150, 50, 100
Martin Terry, 10, 50, 100, 25, 100
Wm. Roisden, 30, 70, 150, 20, 100
John Carson Sr., 10, 90, 100, 10, 100
Jeremiah Wilson, 15, 200, 300, 25, 100
Daniel Wilson, 20, 100, 200, 25, 100
Judy Jeffers, 20, 40, 100, 30, 200
Jackson King, 10, 200, 150, 40, 150
Redin Smith, 10, 100, 150, 50, 200
John Hunnycutt, 15, 200, 100, 40, 100
Cornelious Litton, 20, 75, 200, 60, 80
Silvester Litton, 10, 80, 100, 50, 100
Nancy Roisden, 4, 100, 150, 60, 50
John Marcum, 15, 150, 200, 80, 75
Isaac Roisden, 10, 100, 300, 50, 100
Edward Baker, 15, 150, 200, 80, 200
Wm. Smithers, 16, 200, 150, 75, 50
Anderson Smith, 10, 200, 200, 80, 100
Wm. Smith Sr., 15, 100, 200, 75, 150
A.B. Slaren, 20, 100, 250, 550, 200
Wm. Smith Jr., 30, 200, 150, 100, 150
John Runnels, 20, 150, 100, 80, 100

Zachariah Young, 10, 100, 75, 50, 75
M. S. Baker, 20, 80, 200, 50, 150
Frederick Smith, 20, 0, 100, 50, 150
Joseph Bird, 20, 80, 200, 50, 150
Josiah Smith, 100, 250, 1500, 350, 250
Thomas Creekmore, 15, 100, 100, 40, 150
James Trammel, 14, 130, 100, 50, 200
Lariatt Trammel, 16, 150, 400, 25, 200
G. B. Creekmore, 100, 500, 600, 100, 350
T. M. Smith, 12, 100, 250, 15, 150

Wm. Smith, 35, 130, 400, 25, 325
A. Blankenship, 0, 0, 0, 25, 14
Jacob Lafever, 30, 200, 550, 50, 400
John Smith, 50, 115, 600, 100, 300
Wm. Smith Sr., 14, 74, 200, 25, 150
Michael Ward, 12, 88, 250, 25, 200
E. M. Dauherty, 19, 81, 200, 20, 150
James M. Gee (McGee), 14, 60, 300, 30, 300)

Sevier County TN
1850 Agricultural Census

The Agricultural Census for 1850 was filmed for the University of North Carolina from original records in the Tennessee State Library and Archives.

The following are the items represented and separated by a comma: for example, John Doe, 25, 25, 10, 5, 100. This represents:

Column 1 Owner
Column 2 Acres of Improved Land
Column 3 Acres of Unimproved Land
Column 4 Cash Value of Farm
Column 5 Value of Farm Implements and Machinery
Column 13 Value of Livestock

The (-) symbol is used to represent areas where no data was recorded.

Alman Fry, 1, 1, -, 5, 75
Wm. Yearbury, -, -, -, -, 27
John McKissick, 95, 640, 1200, 100, 525
Marvel Mcmahan, -, 640, 1200, -, -
Jacob Miller, 9, 91, 75, 10, 15
Hugh Henry, 80, 200, 150, 5, 100
Nelson Balls, 5, 15, 50, 3, 13
Wm. Henry, 5, 15,50, 3, 3
James Williams, 20, 100, 250, 50, 250
John Williams, 50, 3000, 1000, 50, 268
John Lange (Large), 65, 300, 700, 45, 88
Jacob Hartrell, 40, 150, 300, 10, 50
Anna Jeanes, 40, 10, 300, 10, 15
Martha Smallwood, 40, 140, 300, 10, 10
John Dennis, 40, 150, 200, 20, 215
Wm. Jeanes, 20, 1000, 200, 15, 110
Wm. Wilson, 18, 100, 100, 5, 45
James Wilson, -, -, -, 10, 171
Madison Heartley, -, 100, 100, 10, -
Lucy Large (Lange), 25, 100, 200, 8, 142
James Large (Lange), 50, 300, 500, 50, 281
Samuel Magha, 50, 300, 500, 3, 10
Redman McMahan, 80, 200, 600, 45, 171
Benajah Proffitt, 50, 600, 800, 30, 359
Eli Williams, 50, 600, 800, 5, 90
Wm. Baxter, 20, 50, 100, 5, 91
Salomi Williams, 100, 500, 600, 100, 240
Wm. Smith, 7, 50, 100, 3, 66
Revarge Branum, 30, 110, 180, 10, 241
Jacob Tison, 30, 2000, 500, 10, 278
John Williams, 50, 150, 400, 20, 144
Robert Mathewes, 30, 100, 500, 15, 150
Thomas Mathews, 3, 500, 50, 5, 100
Berry William, 40, 200, 20, 15, 144
Alfred Henry, 55, 65, 200, 10, 100

Wm. Williams, 55, -, -, -, 40
Joab Rolling, 100, 500, 1000, 75, 483
Alexr. Stenett, 60, 65, 325, 15, 160
Elizabeth Stenett, 20, 30, 100, 5,100
James Proffitt, -, -, -, 5, 80
Jackson Proffitt, 25, 75, 200, 20, 330
Samuel Large (Lange), 80, 100, 525, 15, 227
John Large Jr., -, -, -, 5, 119
John Henry, -, -, -, 5, 68
Wm. Ogle, 28, 100, 200, 10, 100
James Ogle, -, -, -, 3, 25
James Hurst, 25, 225, 200, 10, 75
Anderson Williams, -, -, -, -, 15
Henry Howard, 75, 150, 400, 100, 350
James Mcmahan, 75, 200, 700, 15, 200
Wm. Beck, -, -, -, -, -
John Thomas, -, -, -, -, 20
William Mcmahan, 5, 50, 100, 5,170
Archibold Mcmahan, 100, 400, 1000, 100, 500
Abijah Maples, -, 100, 25, 5, 75
Archibold Maples, -, -, -, -, 15
James Maner, -, -, -, -, 25
Samuel Mcmahan, 100, 100, 500, 44, 500
George Mcmahan, 75, 75, 1500, 60, 500
John Henry Jr., 75, -, -, -, 15
Archibald Mcmahan, 50, 225, 700, 70, 300
Archibald Mcmahan, 40, 75, 400, 25, 236
Jesse Kernel, 40, 75, -, 5, 15
Sarah Maples, 25, 100, 400, 15, 200
John mcmahan, 200, 500, 2000, 100, 1200
David Bowen, 200, 500, -, -, 40
John Breeden, Sr., 55, 120, 150, 20, 200

John Breeden Jr., 3, 47, 50, 3, 15
Elizabeth Webb, 3, -, -, -, 10
Bryant Breeden, 100, 300, 1200, 150, 500
John Burst(Hurst), -, 75, 40, 3, 35
Westley Ganner, -, -, -, -, 12
Israel Wallace, 100, -, -, 3, 50
Marell (Marvel), Breeden, 12, 75, 50, 8,
75
Henry Hurst, 10, 100, 250, 4, 75
Martha Hurst, 22, 29, 200, 5, 100
Wm. Jarman, 22, -, -, 5, 80
Wm. Breeden, 50, 200, 500, 10, 170
Josiah Breeden, 10, 150, 200, 5, 75
David Hurt, 25, 125, 300, 6, 150
Redman Smith, -, -, -, -, 120
John Jeanes, 25, 125, 300, 6, 125
Isaac Breeden, 20, 130, 100,5, 100
George Hurst, 30, 150, 200, 6, 75
Landon Breeden, 5, 25, 75, 10, 75
Noah Hurst, 30, 150, 150, 10, 150
George Lavday, 2, 48, 50, 5, 75
George Hurst St. 30, 50, 100, 15, 167
Emanuel Hurst, 7, 50, 50, 50, 5, 67
Byrun Hurst, 21, 280, 150, 6, 75
Sevier Hurst, 21, 280, 150, 6, 75
Rebecca Hurst, 21, 280, 150, 6, 10
David Conatser, 18, 200, 100, 10, 130
Joseph Webb, 20, 150, 100, 10, 75
Robt. Martin, 30, 300, 200, 20, 217
William Hurst, 12, 300, 25, 10, 150
Archibald Trotter, 75, 150, 500, 25, 407
John Breeden, 5, 100, 75, 5, 60
John Michel, -, -, -, 65, 337
Carol Martin, 11, 64, 200, 6, 115
Adam Houk, 150, 1700, 3000, 125, 696
Mary Benson, -, -, -, -, 25
Joseph Keeler, 60,215, 1500, 100, 930
William Martin, -, -, -, 15, 150
John Keeler, 55, 100, 668, 20, 368
Robt. Duggan, -, -, -,50, 334
Catharine Thomas, 50, 30, 300, 15, 560
Margaret Macom, -, -, -, -, 32
James M. Duggan, -, -, -, 50, 334
George Keeler, -, -, -, 15, 385
Jane Baxter, -, -, -, 5, 80
Daniel Duggan, 80, 300, 800, 20, 300
Archibald Duggn, 12, 160, 200, 10, 100
William Naugher, -, -, -, 5, 200
Andrew Bird, 80, 200, 1200, 100, 400
John Howard, 130, 300, 1800, 100, 500
Lemuel Bogart, 80, 122, 700, 25, 250
William Etherton Sr., 15, 10, 100, 5, 35
James Etherton, 40, 100, 500, 5, 46
William Jenkins, 40, 100, 500, 5, 45
William Etherton Jr., 10, 25, 40, 5, 75
Jacob Blazer, 40, 100, 200, 20, 200

A. L. Low, 30, 20, 100, 15, 100
Thomas Low, 30, 20, -, 40, 100
Edward Lovday, 25, 75, 200, -, 100
Cornelius Fox, 50, 300, 1500, 25, 400
John Parrot, 50, 100, 250, 10, 150
John Lovday, -, -, -, -, 75
Spencer Benson, 50, 250, 225, 10, 200
Rachel Bohannon, -, -, -, -, 15
Vance Newman, -, -, -, 10, 200
Job Lovday, 40, 100, 300, 5, 150
Elizabeth Layfollet, 50, 100, 200, -, 75
Henry Newman, -, -, -, 1, 100
Deliah Conatser, 45, 105, 200, 5, 100
Absalum Allen, 50, 225, 600, 100, 200
John Layman, 25, 75, 200, 13, 100
Elizabeth Layman, 40, 200, 300, 15, 150
Mary Patterson, 40, 240, 200, 6, 75
Hetty Jenkins, 15, -, 50, -, 50
Cornelious Patterson, 100, 150, 1000, 15,
225
Robt. M. Clewer, -, -, -, 150, 400
Mark Fox, 150, 183, 1000, 75, 250
John Fox, -, -, -, 5, 150
William Fox Sr., 100, 200, 2000, 150,
500
Asa Derrick, 200, 300, 3000, 100, 800
Joseph Shrader, 75, 300, 1500, 125, 500
William Fox Jr., 60, 140, 750, 15, 200
Lewis Bird, 100, 400, 1000, 100, 700
Joseph Sutton, 35, 300, 300, 25, 300
Christopher Shrader, 50, 125, 300, 10,
100
Washington Shrader, -, -, -, -, 150
James Stenett, 50, -, -, -, 20
Henry Shrader, 50, -, -, -, 88
Henry Bird, -, -, -, 50, 200
Simon Bird, -, -, -, -, 150
George Bird, -, -, -, -, 70
John Ivy, 18, 5, 75, -, 15
John Bird, 125, 2000,3 000, 100, 500
Adam Bird, 60, 100, 400, 150, 400
George W. Baker, 50, -, 100, 300, 100
Gilbert Baker, 150, 500, 2000, 300, 200
Samuel Baker, 60, 150, 500, 10, 350
Conord Rinehart, 60, 150, 500, -, 20
Bagus (Baqus) Francis, 15, 70, 200, 8,
175
Alexr. Vance, -, -, -, -, 75
Finly Patterson, 50, 50, 500, 15, 200
Adjus Jobe, -, -, -, -, 50
Mark Bird, 100, 125, 1200, 10, 200
John Lewis, - -, -, -, 85
George Fox Jr., 40, 150, 500, 10, 300
Mary Fox Jr., 30, 50, 100, 10, 200
George Reneau, 30, 50, 100, 10, 15
Reuben Reneau, 40, 150, 400, 10, 200

JohnWeishopt, 75, 360, 500, 50, 40
Adam Keeler, 75, 360, -, 5, 150
Emanuel Fox, 175, 200, 2000, 50, 800
Martin Baker, 85, 370, 600, 100, 500
James Baker, 85, 370, 12, 300
Lames Layman, 125, 200, 1200, 250, 60
Jane Breeden, 6, 75, 100, -, 20
Cron__Breeden, 6, 75, -, 10, 75
John Allen, 6, 75, 100, 8, 100
Even Dobkiny, 6, 75, 100, 5, 100
Hyram Miller, 6, 75, 100, 5, 105
John P. Smallwood, 9, 215, 100, 10, 75
Adempsy Maples, 35, 265, 300, 8, 75
William Allan, -, -, -, 10, 100
Alexandria Zollinger, 100, 250, 1000, 70, 300
Alexandria Sharp, -, -, -, -, 75
Preston Maples, 55, 100, 300, 12, 100
Maples Blalock, 55, 100, 300, 12, 30
Wilson Duggan, 120, 261, 2000, 78, 1100
Barbary Howard, -, -, -, -, 30
Lewis Howard, 40, 112, 350, 10, 362
John Thomas, -, -, -, -, 40
Samuel Bird, -, -, -, 5, 50
George Eslinger, 45, 195, 400, 10, 100
Vennesee Pate, 45, 195, 400, 50, 20
Ruben Watts, -, 150, 50, 50, 20
John Lindsey, 45, 150, 50, 50, 27
Wm. Lindsey, 14, 2000, 150, 3, 100
Philip Shults (Shutts), 100, 8000, 1200, 150, 800
Jesse Lindsey, 55, 950, 500, 10, 200
Perry Shults (Shutts), -, 900, 100, 3, 95
Pleasant Shults (Shutts), 25, 140, 500, 43, 135
Jackson Shults (Shutts), 30, 300, 600, 15, 132
John Ownsby, 30, 300, 600, 5, 150
Daniel Emert, 240, 1480, 3000, 50, 916
John Shults (Shutts), 30, 200, 500, 10,250
Isaac Huskey, -, 200, 500, 3, 75
John B. Parton, 3, 22, 100, 3,8
Wm. Whaley, 30, 150, 300, 3, 67
George Evans, 20, 30, 100, 5, 200
Sam Whaley Jr., 35, 2000, 1800, 10, 250
John Owndy(Ownby), 35, 2000, 1800, 5, 75
E. W. Parton, 35, 2000, 1800, 2, 15
James Mortain, 7, 140, 200, 2, 175
John Owndy (Ownby), 35, 300, 200, 4,80
John Owndy(Ownby), 35, 300, 200, 4, 50
John Huskey, 30, 50, 250, 6, 200
Richard Evans, 55, 100, 600, 25, 475
F. S. Emert, 60, 3000, 800, 25, 475
Jeremiah McCarter, 60, 3000, 800, 25, 135

Perry Whaley, 60, 3000, 800, 25, 23
Aaron Ownbey, 25, 700, 250, 8, 200
Stephen Huskey, 70, 1000, 800, 30, 250
Aaron Whatley, 15, 85, 150, 3, 81
James McCarter, 15, 75, 50, 5, 60
James Huskey, 15, 75, 50, 5, 50
Harklus Ogle, 15, 75, 50, 5, 80
Wm. Ogle, 60, 600, 300, 10, 350
Joseph McCarter, 20, 150, 200, 5, 80
George McCarter, -, -, -, -, 25
David Ownby, 6, 50, 50, 5, 25
Harklus Ogle, 30, 100, 350, 10, 165
Thos McCarter, 25, 200, 150, 8, 146
Nathaniel King, 20, 15, 100, 50, 100
Elisha Ogle, -, -, -, 3, 75
Isaac Ogle, 25, 100, 400, 100, 278
Thomas Ogle, 70, 250, 250, 48, 200
Daniel Ragan, 60, 1500, 1000, 100, 200
John Whaley, 30, 150, 300, 10, 100
Wm. Ogle, 20, 100, 250, 5, 150
Easter Trantham, 40, 300, 600, 6, 75
Richard Evans, 25, 65, 85, 10, 140
Wm. Bohannon, 16, 50, 75, 5, 75
Jacob W. Catron, 20, 280, 100, 75, 165
Jacob Houser, -, -, -, 5, 50
Joel Kerr, 45, 400, 200, 45, 100
Robt. Coner, 18, 55, 200, 5, 75
Nancy Coner, 18, 55, 200, 5, 75
Wm. Huskey, 40, 800, 400, 28, 200
David Ragan, 10, 800, 75, 5, 30
Elijah Ogle, 25, 15, 150, 5, 120
Richard Ragan, 25, 15, 150, 5, 50
Wm. B. King, 22, 15, 125, 5, 140
Henry Ogle Sr., 13, 15, 75, 3, 55
Wm. Ogle Sr., 50, 300, 350, 5, 155
Nicholas Ownby, 20, 75, 150, 5, 87
James Ogle, 20, 100, 300, 10, 125
Wm. King, 20, 100, 300, 10, 10
Isaac Ogle, 20, 500, 25, 8, 100
Preston Ogle, 6, 300, 75, 5, 100
Thomas Ogle, 30, 300, 350, 15, 87
Levi Ogle, 30, 30, 350, 15, 60
Nathaniel King, 10, 395, 100, 3, 22
Isaac Ogle, 55, 80, 400, 10, 220
Martin Cleavbough, 55, 80, 400, 10, 74
Henry Franklin, 12, 485, 125, 3, 60
George Flenar, 60, 400, 300, 75, 214
Stephen Whithead, 60, 400, 300, 78, 60
Wm. Maple, -, 50, 50, 5, 80
Jacob Kerr, -, -, -, 4, 50
Barbray Roberts, 25, 125, 100, 5, 130
David Mcmahan, 200, 6000, 3000, 150, 2000
Mcnutly Mcmahan, 200, 6000, 3000, 100, 300
Thomas Webb, -, -, -, -, 55

Thomas Weeks, -, -, -, -, 10

Sarah Brack, 20, 6000, 3000, 3, 50

Franklin Bryant, 30, 437, 300, 5, 128

Aaron Roberts, 8, 328, 67, 5, 90

Richard Crowson, 250, 700, 2300, 125, 600

Elijah Hatcher, -, -, -, 5, 120

Mary Richeson, 75, 100, 1000, -, 125

James McFalls, -, -, -, 10, 130

Nicholas Smith, -, -, -, 4, 81

John Roberts, -, -, -, -, 50

Daniel Roberts, 30, 100, 300, 5, 100

John Hatcher, -, -, -, 7, 71

Stephen Whitson, -, -, -, -, 1

George Rimel, 160, 400, 1200, 45, 476

James Hendly, 10, 240, 150, 9, 170

Ezekiel M. Broiles, -, -, -, 5, 150

Caleb Emert, -, -, -, 3, 100

Valentine Mattox, 40, 55,450, 10, 329

Reuben Hatcher, 125, 500, 900, 100, 570

Achilles Compton, 40, 230, 300, 3, 124

John Huskey Sr., 150, 500, 1000, 150, 400

Hamah McKinzy, -, -, -, -, 8

E. G. Jones, 100, 150, 1000, 78, 265

Margaret McGill, -, -, -, -, 12

Henry Harden, -, -, -, 8, 75

James Mattox, 140, 200, 1700, 200, 600

James Ridings, 12, 288, 100, 25, 100

James Cameron, 45, 75, 300, 100, 300

Aaron Cook, -, -, -, 5, 100

Margaret Cunningham, 60, 45, 800, 80, 274

Alfred Cunningham, -, -, -, 15, 100

John Lilford, 60, 45, 800, 15, 20

Joseph Miller, 60, 45, 800, 15, 30

Jonson Franshire, 50, 66, 200, 35, 300

James Cotter, -, -, -, 175, 600

George King, -, -, -, 10, 175

James Hedrick, 45, 150, 500, 15, 200

Alexr. Salty, 20, 100, 100, 5, 70

Petr Hedrick, 45, 150, 500, 35, 400

Wm. Ridings, -, -, -, -, 10

Gasaway Blanton, -, -, -, 3, 75

Charles W. King, 45, 150, 500, 5, 75

Eli Blair, -, -, -, 5, 125

Wm. Cotter Jr., 45, 150, -, 10, 300

Wm. Cotter Sr., 250, 400, 2000, 50, 400

Brice Mcfal, 25, 95, 200, 10, 60

Isaac Robbison, 9, 80, 50, 2, 95

David Cotter, -, -, -, 15, 400

John Nations, 30, 30, 200, 5, 50

Alexr. McCinsey, 4, 60, 45, -, 50

Wiley King, 2, 100, 100, -, 100

James Lawson, -, -, -, 5, 175

James Cotter, -, 50, 150, 5, 80

William Mattox Jr., -, -, -, 15, 228

Wm. Mattox Sr., 70, 153, 650, 120, 422

Alexr. James, 5, 153, 650, 5, 100

Arthur Mcfals, 60, 140, 250, 10, 114

Mary Lindsey, -, -, -, -, 14

Joel Mcfals, -, -, -, 10, 150

Jonson Adams, 75, 300, 600, 100, 400

Wm. Mcbrint, -, -, -, 5, 75

John Husky Jr., -, -, -, 5, 100

Joseph Starkey, 18, 80, 150, 5, 165

Hugh Baker, -, -, -, 5, 100

Elizabeth Murphy, 12, 25, 200, 5, 30

C. L. Cunningham, -, -, -, 5, 100

Amos Trotter, 75, 375, 1000, 200, 600

William Mcglaugher, 25, 99, 125, 30, 150

Samuel Murphy, 65, 210, 575, 20, 75

Joshua Patty, 57, 4344, 300, 40, 91

John H. Murphy, 35, 375, 125, 35, 200

Charles C. Walker, 30, 65, 100, 20, 175

John Starkey, -, -, -, 5, 50

Nancy Patty, -, -, -, -, 30

John Wear, 40, 350, 600, 75, 100

Joshua Nichols, 60, 130, 525, 75, 275

Moses Cunningham, 75, 300, 1000, 10, 230

Webb Compton, 10, 100, 100, 10, 175

John Nichols, 80, 200, 800, 100, 540

Syrus Compton, -, -, -, 5, 60

Absalem Smith, -, -, -, 70, 50

Daniel F. Murphy, 20, 157, 200, 5, 75

John Anders, 125, 650, 1200, 250, 583

James Cunnings, 23, 120, 400, 5, 150

Amos Lov_ady, 20, 55, 86, 10, 100

David _. Mullendore, 100, 700, 1500, 58, 222

Wm. Porter, -, -, -, 5, -

Alexr. Nichols, 40, 74, 300, 10, 231

James A. Burnett, -, -, -, 8,175

Aaron Dockery, -, -, -, 3, 140

Wm. Clabeaugh, -, -, -, 5, 35

John Jinkins, -, -, -, 8, 52

Robert Shields, 20, 40, 300, 10, 150

James Eldridge, -, -, -, 10, 250

John Webb, 75, 325, 600, 50, 293

Amos. Clark, 30, 170, 225, 5, 73

Andrew Henderson, 75, 66, 1200, 25, 350

Nathaniel Gipson, -, -, -, 5, 8

John Mitchel, -, -, -, -, 80

Meady Shield, 100, 300, 800, 50, 483

John White, -, -, -, 8, 143

Alphy White, 100, 165, 800, 10, 127

John Butler, -, -, -, 10, 105

Thomas Ogle, -, -, -, -, 15

George W. Seaton, 40, 90, 400, 15, 123

Henry Bohannon, -, -, -, 15, 132

James Clabber, -, -, -, 5, 30

Richard Clabber, -, -, -, 8, 86
Margaret Nichols, 12, -, 175, -, 70
Taney (Laney) Maples, -, -, -, -, 65
Elijah Maples, -, -, -, -, 13
Thomas Maples, -, -, -, -, -
Thomas Maples, -, -, -, -, 25
Campbell Maples, -, -, -, 3, 100
Madison Cate, -, -, -, 15, 267
James Clark, 100, 1500, 1200, 40, 300
James Drining (Driving), -, -, -, 5, 144
Cove (Cave, Com), James, -, -, -, 5, 100
Martha James, 65, 75, 800, 5, 105
F. S. Emert, 40, 100, 800, 20, 138
R. S. Clark, -, 100, 800, 20, 138
John B. Clark, 40, 100, 800, 5, 98
John Feazel, 100, 50, 300, 4, 180
Anna Maples, -, 50, 300, -, 15
Joseph Snapp, 200, 205, 1500, 400, 3700
Charles Innman, -, -, -, 100, 150
Clesa Robbison, 200, 150, 1600, 30, 425
Jacob Maloy, 90, 255, 1000, 2 0, 232
Fielding Justices, -, -, -, 7, 15
James Ferguson, 90, 100, 800, 100, 418
John Kerr, -, -, -, 8, 63
Phillip Roberts, 70, 400, 800, 100, 358
Phillip Emert, 100, 60, 300, 15, 115
Elisha Sezmore, 100, 60, 300, 5, 160
G. R. Maples, 200, 400, 1500, 40, 700
G. M. Maples, 80, 220, 400, 7, 150
Carrol Thomas, 100, 60, 400, 20, 175
Sanford Allen, 100, 200, 800, 40, 250
Wm. Romines, -, -, 800, 2, 10
Anace Canatser, -, 200, 800, 1, 15
Isaac Romines, 100, 200, 800, 1, 12
Ezekiel Romines, 100, 200, 800, 4, 20
Harrald Smith, 100, -, 800, 10, 100
Perry Breeden, 50, 600, 300, 15, 80
Andrew Carnalzer, 150, 240, 500, 150, 258
Henry Thomas, 150, 240, 500, 10, 100
Benjamin Maning, 150, -, 500, 8, 53
Joel Grant (Gantt), -, 240, 500, 10, 88
Martha Thomas, 150, 240, -, -, 12
Abecal Richardson, -, 240, -, -, 15
Tunis (Lunis) Scott, 80, 2 60, 1800, 30, 229
John Ellison, -, -, -, 10, 45
Nelson Mitchel, 80, 260, 1800, 10, 67
David Mitchel, 80, 260, 1800, 3, 114
Joseph Terry, 80, -, 1800, -, 30
John Fox, 100, 350, 1500, 75, 276
Westley, Fox, -, -, -, 5, 200
Wm. Snapp, -, -, -, 5, 92
John Thomas, -, -, -, -, 12
George Henderson, 160, 500, 2350, 150, 451

John Newman, -, -, -, -, 14
Cornelius Thomas, -, -, -, -, 10
John Poindexter, 100, 167, 800, 60, 382
A. J. Bradley, 2, 30, 40, 3, 20
Levi H. Eton, -, -, -, 20, 183
Jacob Hoober, 50, 150, 490, 30, 118
_. K. L. Anders, -, -, -, 90, 237
William Snapp, 50, 175, 300, 25, 115
Anderson Seaton, 50, 200, 300, 25, 250
Joby Perryman, -, -, -, -, 22
Marcy Clark, 50, 450, 300, 5, 132
Moses Seaton, 85, 75, 600, 20, 297
Alexr. Dixon, -, -, -, 10, 66
Rachel Robbison, -, -, -, -, 25
Eli Roberts, 40, 135, 200, 18, 140
Margaret Burnett, -, -, -, -, 10
Henry Trotter, -, -, -, 8, 80
John Trotter, 70, 75, 600, 150, 209
James Trotter, -, -, -, 8, 100
Mary Butler, 300, 800, 1500, 150, 450
Henry Patterson, 50, 50,1 60, 6, 238
John Raines, -, -, -, 5, -
Phillip Cope, -, -, -, 8, 45
Henry Butler Jr., -, -, -, 10, 230
Andrew Lawson, 60, 53, 266, 30, 265
Samuel Crance, -, -, -, 35, 150
John Patterson, -, -, -, 5, 10
Peter Reneau, -, -, -, 20, 94
John Kerr, 30, 116, 200, 20, 200
James A. Smith, 31, 31, 300, 30, 155
Aaron Runyons, 100, 30, 600, 100, 570
Francis Rambo, 70, 80, 600, 15, 181
M. W. Porter, 60, 75, 550, 100, 164
Archibald Scruggs, 70, 70, 500, 25, 244
Angeline Flemings, -, -, -, -, 10
Isaac Bartler(Bastler), -, -, -, 100, 120
William Mcmahan, -, -, -, 3, 60
Joseph Anderson, -, -, -, 10, 147
W. H. Trotter, 94, 473, 700, 72, 408
Isaac Trotter, -, 12, 25, 75, 200
John F. Fowler, 300, 1329, 5000, 300, 600
Andrew Lawson, -, 40, 20, 12, 146
Samuel Mcmahan, 135, 400, 3500, 108, 700
Jan McKineon, -, -, -, 5, 148
Joel Barnes, -, -, -, 15, 141
Wm. Catlett, 325, 383, 5000, 145, 4885
James P. Catlett, 100, 150, 500, -, 1893
Dennis Thomas, -, -, -, 4, 1000
H. M. Thomas, 125, 200, 2500, 100, 225
Anderson Woods, 1, -, 550, -, 82
Lewis King, -, -, -, 5, 30
John Helton, -, -, -, 5, 45
Aaron Roberts, 75, 200, 700, 20, 314
George Roberts, 75, -, -, 10, 259

Philip Gobble, 25, 50, 125, 5, 155
Amos Gobble, 25, 50, 125, 50, 217
Daniel Ernest, 25, -, -, 8, 200
James McKindley, 25, 50, 125, 4, 15
Benjamin Carry, 25, 50, 125, 4, 80
Westley Ernest, 100, 450, 1000, 40, 591
Druery Spurgen, -, -, -, 50, 30
John L. Trotter, 300, 6000, 5500, 150, 1490
Wm. J. Trotter, -, -, -, 10, 170
John Spurgen, -, -, -, 10, 60
Jacob Fanning, -, -, -, -, 22
Joseph Huff, 50, 450, 500, 5, 137
C. Miller, 125, 150, 2000, 225, 367
A. Wynne, 100, 200, 1200, 100, 292
Richard Shields, 100, 200, 1200, 20, 85
William Patera, -, -, -, 12, 184
Richard Floyd, 100, 200, 1200, 5, 75
Basdil Scragg, 40, 200, 400, 100, 121
Randel Henderson, 85, 106, 1000, 125, 412
William Henderson, -, -, -, 40, 301
Elijah Henderson, -, -, -, 20, 250
Joseph Compton, -, -, -, 20, 250
James W. Chambers, 65, 610, 1000, 150, 372
Archibald Rose, -, -, -, 4, 12
W. M. Walker, 175, 700, 1500, 155, 594
Thomas Edmondson, -, -, -, 5, 65
Phillip Seaton, 75, 165, 850, 125, 492
Catharine Lawson, 70, 600, 1200, 175, 394
Wm. Cleaubaugh, -, -, -, 8, 45
West G. Trotter, -, -, -, 75, 151
Anderson Kear, -, -, -, -, 25
Charles Cleaubaugh, -, -, -, 5, 95
Elizabeth Claugbaugh, 30, 79, 300, 75, 118
Elizabeth Hardin, 1, 69, 20, -, 10
George Archer, 50, 150, 200, 40, 84
Martha Archer, -, -, -, -, 113
John Thurman, 40, 150, 200, 27, 107
William Felton, 40, 300, 550, 70, 274
Henry Layman, 35, 75, 300, 8, 73
Rebecca Jones, 50, 140, 800, 10, 152
Eli Fox, 85, 700, 1200, 80, 483
Thomas Romines, -, -, -, -, 12
Elizabeth Stover, 50, 100, 450, 75, 370
William Anderson, -, -, -, 8, 46
Jesse Stafford, 125, 1000, 1400, 75, 200
Nelson Newman, -, -, -, 2, 20
Mathew Lawson, -, 9, 15, 3, 25
James Newman, 20, 40, 300, 100, 44
Robert Richards, -, -, -, 15, 114
Charles Petty, -, -, -, 10, 25

Samuel (Lemuel) Catlett, 40, 110, 250, 10, 150
John Romines, 8, 92, 25, 15, 53
Vinyard Thomas, 5, 45, 25, 5, 13
William Thomas, -, -, -, 10, 15
James Petty, -, -, -, 5, 66
Wilburn Bowden, -, 70, 60, 5, 18
Lofty H. Catlett, -, 500, 100, 5, 100
Mary Pate, -, -, -, -, 20
Benjamin Atchley, 80, 200, 1600, 75, 571
Uriah Lanning, -, -, -, 10, 70
Thomas Langston, -, -, -, 10, 30
Wm. S. G. Ford, 1, 200, 900, 100, 500
Martha Ford, -, -, -, -, 100
Amillia Atchly, 50, 250, 900, 40, 241
Benjamin Atchley, -, -, -, 5, 50
Benjamin Thomas, -, -, -, 3, 40
Daniel Atchley, 75, 75, 1000, 50, 279
_. T. Trotter, 100, 200, 1500, 100, 291
Samuel Pate, 300, 500, 2500, 400, 600
Daniel Kerr, 100, 330, 1000, 40, 140
Masiles Long, 40, 120, 500, 50, 202
Terrissa C. Lance, 40, 120, 500, 50, 202
George Romines, 40, 120, 500, 15, 50
Andrew Ward, 40, 120, 500, 7, 15
John Reese, 40, 120, 500, 15, 123
James Lindsey, 40, 120, 500, 5, 96
James Stevens, 40,, 120, 120, 6, 4
John Romines, 40, 120, 120, 3, 14
Juda Shahan, 40, 120, 120, 2, 33
Alfred James, 40, 120, 120, 5, 53
John Stoffle, 40, 120, 120, 3, 53
Jesse Hille, 150, 200, 2000, 40, 214
Lewis Lowery, -, 22, 112, 45, 65
Lewis Lowery, -, 22, 112, 45, 65
Rebcca Atchley, 60, 20, 400, 65, 242
Charles Cobb, 6, 45, 40, 15, 150
James _. Looney, 100, 160, 1500, 40, 774
Joshua Atchley, 50, 130, 700, 100, 202
Noah Atchley, 40, 130, 700, 3,175
Jacob Hufft, 20, 40, 75, 4, 134
Benjamin Atchly, 35, 40, 250, 5, 132
Isaac Atchly, 90, 300, 2000, 100,3 02
John Lindsey, 90, 300, 2000, 8, 88
Wm. Atchly, 55, 60, 500, 40, 180
Washington Atchly, 55, 60, 600, 10, 53
Joseph Gant, 190, 180, 2500, 150, 867
James Ray, 70, 43, 500, 40, 302
John Nelson, 70, 43, 500, 40, 302
Robert Atchley, 8, 17, 75, 50, 89
John Lewallen, 35, 37, 200, 10, 70
James Sarrett, 30, 120, 220, 12, 113
James Haggard, 30, 120, 220, 77, 80
Atchley Haggard, 55, 75, 400, 100, 293
Thos. Atchley, 45, 56, 300, 100, 42
Elizabeth Jones, 75, 124, 800, 10, 222

John F. Robbison, 75, 124, 800, 40, 107
Elizabeth Richards, 75, 124, 800, 40, 10
Len Cowder, 75, 124, 800, 18, 78
Robert Henry, 75, 124, 800, 10, 101
Able Romines, 75, 124, 800, 10, 41
David Abbot, 30, 120, 50, 10, 45
Elizabeth Romines, 25, 24, 130, 2, 40
Isaac Richards, 30, 95, 100, 8, 130
Riley James, 30, 95, 100, 60, 75
Amillia James, 30, 95, 100, 60, 20
John Stoffle, 15, 175, 100, 10, 12
Sarah Vance, 15, 175, 100, 10, 20
Martha Jenkins, 15, 175, 100, 10, 25
Clem Jarnagin, 15, 175, 100, 5, 10
John Mcmahan, 100, 300, 1600, 100, 421
John Ferguson, 75, 135, 550, 20, 253
N. M. Maker, 50, 150, 450, 18, 100
Levi Wells, 50, 150, 450, 15, 100
Asa Layman, 75, 90, 300, 10, 266
Preston Layman, 100, 200, 1000, 15, 199
Madison Howard, 50, 400, 400, 80, 222
Henry Harris, 50, 400, 400, 80, 100
John Walker, 190, 102, 2000, 300, 630
O.P. Jenkins, 190, 102, 2000, 90, 20
Henry Houk, 190, 102, 2000, 20, 238
George Fox, 250, 800, 2000, 200, 815
Wm. Mitchel, 250, 800, 2000, 200, 60
Soloman, Anders, 90, 173, 1400, 200, 690
Benjamin Anders, 90, 173,1400, 200, 100
Robert Mcmahan, 100, 400, 1800, 150, 579
John Canon, 200, 300, 6000, 200, 1000
Wm. Canon, 200, 500, 6000, 205, 1262
John Catlett, 40, 180, 1100, 400, 296
Hugh Blairs, 180, 450, 1800, 200, 821
Harrison Blair, 180, 450, 1800, 200, 30
David McCroskey, 45, 100, 3000, 75, 682
R. J. Davis, 300, 700, 3500, 200, 735
Andrew Blair, 300, 700, 3500, 8, 200
C. M. Hardin, 80, 300, 750, 100, 332
Nathan Reed, 80, 300, 750, 15, 20
Morgan Davis, 40, 460, 400, 20, 233
Wm. Maples, 10, 15, 50, 5, 20
Samuel Sarrett, 10, 15, 50, 15, 90
Daniel McMott, 10, 15, 50, 15, 12
Nathaniel Crow, 10, 15, 50, 15, 58
Wm. Paliner, 10, 15, 50, 15, 58
Cole Warren, -, -, -, 20,75
B. M. Chandler, 250, 500, 5500, 300, 950
Abraham Mcmahan, 125, 275, 1400, 175, 550
Austin Hall, 125, 275, 1400, 175, 15
George W. Catlett, 12, 48, 100, 125, 200
Hannah Porter, 90, 38, 1500, 50, 441
Charley Reed, 55, 250, 500, 100, 263

Mitchel Reed, 12, 40, 75, 5, 100
James Maples, 12, 18, 40, 15, 224
Hugh Goforth, -, -, -, 5, 100
Alexr. Ellison, -, 212, 100, 3, 25
James McCarter, -, 212, 100, 3, -
Hugh Goforth Sr., 120, 19, 1800, 62, 426
George Findley, -, 19, 1800, 20, 51
Eli White, -, 19, 1800, - 25
John Carroll, 120, 19, 1800, -, 15
H. G. Hodgets, 120, 19, 1800, 50, 297
A. J. Reed, -, -, -, -, 12
Sampson Phillips, -, -, -, 15, 100
L. W. Barnes, 100, 86, 1500, 325, 443
Joshua Atchley, 30, 170, 300, 500, 182
John Mullendoe, 140, 160, 1500, 150, 570
Martha Henderson, -, -, -, -, 15
Wm. Ellis, 200, 225, 7000, 250, 449
Wm. M. Burnett, -, -, -, 5, 85
John Toomy, -, -, -, 10, 256
Josiah Tarnel, -, -, -, 5, 25
Henry Maples, -, -, -, -, 75
Harper Henderson, -, -, -, 5, -
Joseph H. Hodsden, 200, 225, 7000, 100, 900
George McCown, 250, 1000, 4000, 100, 485
Floyd Nichols, 2, -, 50, 60, 228
John S. Mcnutt, 175, 225, 3000, 175, 580
Wellington Mcmahan, 80, 75, 2000, 40, 373
S. O. Dickey, 400, 400, 5000, 200, 930
Samuel Hammer, 3, 32, 600, 75, 125
Wm. C. Pickens, 90, 100, 1200, 400, 500
Wm. J. Hodges, -, -, -, 20, 200
John Smelser, -, -, -, 50, -
John Trundle, 110, 160, 2000, 175, 567
Elender Trundle, 135, 235, 3000, 150, 500
Andrew Newcom, -, -, -, -, 10
Ahag Ellis, 75, 40, 1800, 30, 200
Martin Houk, -, -, -, 20, 15
Samuel Keller, -, -, -, 5, 40
Margaret Clark, -, -, -, -, 25
Ann B. Patten, 100, 250, 850, 75, 100
George Wade, 250, 200, 2000, 300, 463
J. Householder, -, -, -, -, 15
Phelix Whittle, -, -, -, 10, 50
John Whittle, 75, 105, 1200, 100, 400
James McCroskey, 90, 340, 1900, 40, 225
Wm. Wayland, 150, 350, 2100, 100, 600
E. Hodges, 100, 230, 2000, 90, 856
John S McCroskey, 100, 230, 2000, 112, 240
Reese Findley, 100, -, -, 2, 75
Samuel W. Randles, 75, 200, 700, 15, 115

Sarah M. Hodges, 100, 50, 1300, 95, 386
Wm. Hodges, 90, 30, 1200, 45, 218
Mary A. McCroskey, 200, 200, 3000, 100, 661
Ruben Webb, -, 250, 200, 40, 75
John Houk, -, -, -, 75, 310
C. Lawson, -, -, -, 20, 175
James Malone, 80, 120, 500, 50, 250
Glasgo Snoddy, 100, 450, 1500, 30, 270
William Roberts, -, -, -, -, 100
Matilda Roberts, -, -, -, -, 100
Benjamin Clark, 30, 95, 100, 10, 100
Jane Cunningham, -, -, -, 10, 150
Elisha Rose, 60, 90, 250, 30, 60
Langston Cunningham, 20, 79, 200, -, 150
John Cunningham, 50, 15, 250, 5, 100
John Rose, 40, 250, 500, 10, 100
R. M. Creswell, -, -, -, 15, 125
Linsey Rose, 40, 250, 500, 5, 50
James Perry, 15, 78, 130, -, 45
George Huffaker, 45, 200, 800, 10, 164
Samuel Creswell, 45, 200, 200, 10, 289
Michael Rackard, -, -, -, 10, 16
Margaret Thomas, 45, 200, 200, 10, 100
Catharine Parmer, 45, 200, 200, 10, 20
Prior L. Whittle, 45, 200, 200, 10, 55
Samuel Widner, 50, 100, 500, 15, 175
Martin Frazier, 50, 100, 500, 30, 200
Joseph Abbot, 50, 100, 500, 10, 50
Caswell Hicks, 50, 100, 500, -, 15
Moten Williams, 103, 137, 1000, 100, 380
McCinsey Rose, 103, 137, 1000, 15, 125
Richard Randler, 103, 137, 1000, 15, 15
Jacob Widner, 103, 137, 1000, 150, 225
John G. Hodsden, 50, 100, 400, 100, 598
William Thomas, 80, 170, 850, 100, 425
Ryal Waters, 80, 170, 850, 60, 125
William Randles Sr., 80, 170, 852, 10, 125
John Randles Sr., 50, 80, 700, 60, 270
Stephen Underdown, 100, 39, 1600, 25, 232
Pleasant Underdown, 100, 39, 1600, 5, 15
Wm. Merritt, 100, 39, 1600, 10, 17
Wm. W. Randles, -, 25, 100, 10, 145
James Randles, 125, 200, 2100, 10, 100
Thomas Brabson, 241, 600, 6000, 150, 703
Elizabeth Brabson, 200, 500, 8000, 200, 838
Daniel Covington, 200, 500, 8000, 200, 18
Wm. Smith, 200, 500, 8000, 3, 15
Hugh Cowen, 160, 160, 2500, 150, 300

Andrew Berryer, 160, 160, 2500, -, 42
Adonigah Thomas, 160, 160, 2500, 10, 75
Jonson Gosett, 160, 160, 2500, 5, 46
Aarom Shamlin, 160, 2000, 100, 50, 125
John Chandler, 700, 3000, 7000, 745, 1920
P. C. Rawllings, -, 3000, 7000, 745, 30
Wm. Chandler, 250, 300, 3000, 200, 700
Archibold More, 250, 300, 3000, 200, 15
James White, 250, 300, 3000, 10, 150
James More, -, 300, 3000, 10, 700
James Shahan, -, 300, 3000, 100, 200
Berthel Allen, -, -, -, -, 22
John McCrosky, 50, 160, 500, 25, 121
Felix G. Wayland, -, -, -, 15, 100
Harvy Miller, -, -, -, 10, 60
Jorden Houk, 50, 110, 400, 30, 505
Harvy Rambo, 70, 350, 800, 50, 340
Jacob Carroll, -, -, -, -, 75
Calvin Chandler, 150, 166, 1400, 100, 500
Lewis Wayland Jr., 150, 400, 1000, 50, 339
Lewis Wayland Sr., 120, 150, 1000, 50, 360
Linsey Bales, 120, -, -, 3, 10
Alexr. McCallie, 200, 200, 2000, 150, 700
Jesse Starkey, -, -, -, 3, 16
James M. Sharp, 500, 1000, 8000, 800, 1200
Daniel L. Trundle, 130, 150, 2000, 80, 500
Abraham Fox, -, -, -, 50, 40
John Fagala, 125, 125, 1200, 150, 350
Michael Fagala, 200, 700, 3000, 285, 1080
Prudy Norten, 60, 225, 500, 100, 360
James Ellis, 200, 200, 3500, 300, 708
Richard Gilbert, -, -, -, 15, 100
Peter Snapp, -, -, -, 15
James Murphy, 100, 16, 900, 20, 400
Simeon Duggane, -, -, -, 8, 100
Robert H. Hodsden, 350, 1600, 4000, 230, 1490
John C. Yett, 250, 300, 3000, 200, 729
B. H. Toomy, 60, 64, 1800, 20, 435
Wm. Randles, -, -, -, 100, 300
James Mcnelly, 10, 150, 1000, 100, 120
Hubbard Carnes, -, -, -, 25, 158
M. A. Rawllings, ½, -, 500, 25, 40
Elijah Cate, 150, 500, 1200, 100, 382
M. W. McCowen, 1, -, 50, -, 10
Susannah Serrett, -, -, -, -, 75
J. M. Hammer, ½, -, 100, -, 80
Pleasant Carver, 8, 52, 50, 3, 30

Thomas Taylor, -, -, -, -, 50
John Harther, -, -, -, 30, 4
Phillip Esslinger, -, -, -, 6, 156
Agatha Rawllings, 25, 35, 150, -, 30
Alexr. Rawllings, 25, 35, 150, -, 100
Clabourn Baker, 15, 10, 50, 8, 75
William Baker, 20, 15, 100, 5, 65
William Gossett, 20, 15, 100, 5, 100
James M. Evans, 65, 1200, 700, 50, 400
Daniel Mcpherson, 65, 1200, 700, 50, 25
Sincler Ragan, 40, 110, 150, 20, 100
Gilbert Galyean, 40, 110, 150, 10, 75
Anlysass Thomas, 40, 110, 150, 10, 150
Zachaus Thomas, 40, 130, 200, 12, 130
Henry Thomas, 40, 130, 200, 13, 6
James Clark, 100, 400, 800, 75, 286
Lemuel Nichols, 100, 400, 800, 2, 58
Wiley Wilcoxs, 20, 5, 150, 6, 80
James Cowder, 50, 223, 400, 50, 100
Wm. Cagle, 50, 223, 400, 5, 25
Allen Cagle,-, 223, -, -, 15
Sarah Cagle, 25, 25, 50, 5, 18
George Welles, 15, 86, 30, 25, 75
John Wells, -, 86, 30, 25, 10
Phanber Cagle, 15, 86, -, -, 100
Richard Ragan, 30, 122, 50, 50, 143
George Cagle, 50, 65, 105, 65, 167
William Lathens, 50, 65, 105, 5, 100
Jacob Tipton, 50, 65, 105, 8, 12
Reuben Ragan, 50, 65, 105, 8, 20
John Sing, 30, 45,200, 10, 195
Benjamin Tipton, 75, 300, 600, 100, 300
James Lane, -, -, -, -, 3
Cramer Delozier, 30,600, 1000, 50, 300
Asa Delozier, 30, 100, 50, 30, 300
Andrew Delozier, 30, 600, 1000, 30, 175
Samuel Pickens, 200, 2000, 2000, 500, 722
Lizy Garner, 200, -, -, -, 10
Bartley Landford, 200, -, 2000, -, 15
Jonathan Wysong, 200, 2000, 2000, 60, 60
John Langford, 45, 10, 100, 60, 250
Joseph Tipton, 75, 125, 200, 20, 250
William Bowers, 75, -, -, 5, 60
Elijah Shelly, 12, 100, 75, 5, 60
Thomas Rogers, 30, 55, 100, 8, 209
William Reed, 40, 250, 250, 20, 200
Abijah Simmons, -, 250, 10, 125
John Cusick, 1, 50, 50, 15, 125
John G. Tipton, 40, 50, 130, 10, 120
John Murphy, 40, 50, 130, 10, 35
Benjamin Tipton, 50, 400, 600, 30, 375
Joseph Tipton Sr., 50, 400, 600, 30, 96
James Chandler, 70, 70, 240, 50, 345
John chandler, 70, 70, 240, 10, 124

James McCroskey, 70, 70, -, 35, 100
Jane Rinkle, 70, 70, 240, 14, 100
John Nichols, 70, 70, 240,2, 16
Samuel Cusick, 40, 300, 400, 15, 342
Joseph Delozier, 40, 200, 400, 10, 200
Malden Delozier, 50, 250, 600, 6, 200
Daniel Marris, 50, 250, 600, 6, 106
Joseph Marris, 25, 86, 106, 6, 150
John Haly, 25, 86, 106, 10, 90
William Cagle, 25, 86, 106, 10, 90
John Robbison, 60, 500, 300, 10, 150
Benjamin Thomas, 30, 44, 200, 20, 145
Ezekiel Waters, 50, 197, 220, 15, 295
John More, 50, 197, 220, 5, 10
Franklin Galyean, 50, 197, 220, 5, 100
Mary Galyean, 50, 197, 220, 5, 200
Thomas Shahan, 150, 195, 220,, 100, 150
Eli Cook, -, -, -, 5, 107
Robert Palmer, 150, 197, 220, 5, 45
John Owen, 150, 197, 220, 10, 100
Josephus Gosett, 150, 197, 220, -, 30
Pleasant Pierce, 100, 300, 1000, 80, 474
Laben Jenkins, 30, 93, 200, 5, 150
William Lewallen, 30, 93, 200, 3, 74
Caleb Jenkins, 40, 74, 200, 7, 180
Nancy Gipson, 45, 225, 245, 8, 183
Martin Ellison, 45, 225, 245, 8, 25
Henry Baker, 30, 50, 80, 5, 100
Alexr. Lewallen, 50, 20, 500, 30, 376
Anderson Bower, -, 50, 25, 25, 75
Jonathan Brown, 20, 216, 75, 50, 120
Bobbold Mcmurry, -, -, -, 25, 120
Quiller Gosett, 20, 216, 75, 25, 20
Sarah Nichols, 20, 216, 75, 25, 30
Rufus Davis, 20, 216, 75, 30, 150
George Wells, 20, 216, 75, 30, 13
James Carver, 20, 216, 75, 6, 18
Frederick Scruggs, 45, 65, 1000, 40, 294
James Monda, -, -, -, 4, 200
Joshua Cate, 500, 800, 3720, 112, 576
Perry Cate, 500, 800, 3720, 100, 400
James Pollard, 500, 800, 3720, 5, 129
Houston Cate, 500, 800, 3720, 65, 80
Levi Lewis, 500, 800, 3720, 10, 85
Levi Lewis, 500, 800, 3720, 10, 85
Fuqua Pollard, 500, 800, 3720, 8, 80
Hubbard Hickman, 500, 800, 3720, 5, 35
Humphrey Hickman, 500, 800, 3720, 10, 90
Thomas Hickman Jr., 500, 800, 3720, 10, 92
Thomas Hickman Sr., 70, 430, 500, 70, 148
John Coldwell, 100, 130, 800, 100, 890
Coleman Hickman, 100, 130, 800, 7, 35
Sarah Right, 100, 130, 800, 7, 100

John Housley, 200, 300, 2000, 100, 6348
Alexr. Stogner, 200, 300, 2000, 5, 60
Thomas Wilson, 200, 300, 2000, 5, 50
Moses Clonington, 200, 300, 2000, 5, 15
Moses Russell, 75, 150, 625, 20, 131
Jesse Ballard, 75, 150, 625, 4, 30
William Milles, 125, 200, 750, 40, 200
Alexr. Douglass, 100, 500, 1500, 80, 297
Abraham Smith, 100, 500, 1500, 10, 100
Daniel F. Jeanway, 100, 500, 1500, 7, 50
Nancy Hamilton, 60, 170, 250, 10, 84
Jesse Pollard, 200, 300, 900, 5, 250
William Hickman, 200, 300, 900, 15, 250
Guilford Brady, 200, 300, 900, 25, 130
William Right, 200, 300, 900, 25,4 8
James Miles, -, -, -, 5, 47
Radford Gatlin, 40, 200, 500, 68, 200
Edward Walles, 20, 40, 120, 5, 62
John Hickman, 20, 40, 120, 5, 68
Mary Dikes, 20, 40, 120, 4, 80
Jackson Cowen, 40, 200, 250, 10, 140
James K. Franklin, -, -, -, 10, 60
Moses Long, 40, 17, 100, 15, 100
Laterl Herington, 40, 17, 100, 15, 25
Isaac Teag, 40, 17, 100, 15, 50
Thomas Franklin, 55, 320, 400, 10, 182
Hyram Underwood, 28, 85, 56, 5, 100
George Huffaker, 28, 85, 56, 10, 39
Robt. Bales, 65, 140, 1000, 140, 496
W. B. Palmer, 65, 240, -, -, 20
Westly Huffaker, 230, 400, 6000, 150, 915
Samuel Reed, -, -, -, 2, 20
Jefferson Rose, -, 200, 100, 25, 200
Hosey Rose, 230, -, -, -, 35
Henry Randles, 75, 125, 800, 12, 241
David Keener, 20, 40, 120, 15, 300
Jesse Cunningham, 72, 40, 200, 75, 500
Payne Mcclearry, 150, 650, 3200, 200, 400
Jackson Hickman, 150, 650, 3200, -, 20
Henry Smith, -, -, -, -, 40
George Underwood, 184, 300, 1450, 150, 560
Ira Cate, 184, 300, 1450, 10, 150
James Cate, 30, 20, 100, 5, 107
AAlfred Coons, 30, 20, 100, 4, 30
Enyard Cate, 30, 20, 100, 5, 50
A. W. Bryan, -, 5, 150, 10, 173
Peter H. Bryan, -, 5, 150, 10, 173
Thomas Bryan, 200, 500, 1500, 156, 560
George Keener, 50, 50, 400, 10, 183
Rachel Shannon, -, -, 400, 10, 15
Elisha Cate, 50, 50, 400, 25, 150
John Douglass, 60, 160, 800, 15, 400

Samuel Douglas, 150, 650, 1500, 150, 611
James Perry, 150, 650, 1500, -, 100
Thomas Cate, 90, 125, 1200, 150, 645
Lea Cate, 30, 15, 275, 5, 455
Wm. Polard, 30, 15, -, 50, 40
Abraham Scarlet, 30, 15, 275, 50, 15
Marrion Patty, 30, 15, 275, 50, 25
Asher Sellers, 30, 15, 275, 50, 25
Samuel Young, 30, 15, -, -, 15
Frederick Hickman, 30, 15, 275, -, 12
Joseph McClay (McClary), -, -, -, 30, 100
William E. Bryan, -, -, -, 35, 400
Hugh Thomas, -, -, -, -, 30
Anderson Kerr, 20, 24, 200, 5, 75
Henry A. Whaley, 100, 100, 1000, 50, 100
L. D. Hicks, -, -, -, 3, 60
Robert R. Nelson, -, -, -, -,15
William Burns, -, -, -, 50, 300
William Kemp, -, -, -, -, 21
John Ellis, 150, 100, 2500, 250, 750
Ranson Mooneyham, 150, -, -, -, 12
George Russel, -, -, -, 12, 100
William Pate, -, -, -, 12, 150
Elisha Roberts, -, -, -, 100, 350
Levi Roberts, -, -, -, 5, 150
Rachel Ballard, -, -, -, -, 20
Thomas Douglas, -, -, -, 25, 300
Samuel Henry -, -, -, -, 444
Benjamin Keener, -, -, -, -, 80
Thomas Atchley, 160, 120, 1000, 25, 100
Sarah Wright, 160, -, -, -, 25
Benjamin Henry, 130, 339, 1200, 150, 323
John Atchley, 15, 95, 200, 12, 150
Rutha Moore, 15, 95, -, -, 11
Spencer Acuff, 100, 89, 400, 50, 75
David A. Bryan, -, -, -, 2, 22
William Brown, -, -, -, 3, 100
Jane Creswell, 100, -, -, -, 24
Owen Hester, 40, 45, 200, 8, 140
Eli Brown, -, -, -, -, 140
Serena Brown, 40, -, -, 5, 20
Isarah Kyle, 40, -, -, -, 15
Lewis Hancock, -, -, -, -, 25
Nancy Robertson, 30, 70, 100, 3, 100
Elizabeth Brown, -, -, -, 30
Anna Merrit, 30, -, -, -, 50
John Underwood, 80, 143, 450, 100, 170
Allen Cate, 100, 96, 600, 50, 200
Samuel Mount, 50, 300, 500, 15, 478
Amanda Reese, -, -, -, -, 15
Nathan Tolbert, -, -, -, -, 55
Richard Lanning, 1, -, 600, 80, 120

Enoch Underwood, 175, 600, 1200, 100, 475
John Underwood, -, -, -, 10, 163
Samuel H. Ellis, 40, 40, 350, 40, 125
Ephram Johnson, 100, 200, 600, 30, 166
Nancy Givinn, -, -, -, 5, 40
Elizabeth Keener, -, -, -, 15, 255
Thomas Tolbert, 150, 150, 1000, 50, 383
George Baker, -, -, -, 20, 75
Lee Henry, 30, 160, 1400, 20, 150
Thomas Henry, 80, 184, 500, 130, 400
John Runyans, -, 80, 40, -, 40
Soloman Mills, -, -, -, -, 25
John Underwood, 300, 2800, 2000, 75, 300
James Underwood, 20, 80, 300, 50, 300
Henry Underwood, -, -, -, 2, 125
Calvim M. Hodges, -, -, -, 5, 300
Sameul Huffaker, 80, 120, 800, 75, 203
Anderson Bales, -, -, -, 25, 250
Rebecca Hudson, 100, 200, 400, 15, 200
Joel Hudson, 100, 200, 400, 200, 150
William E. Hodges, -, -, -, 70, 200

William Kelley, -, 150, 150, 8, 200
Fatha Petty, 150, 300, 1300, 150, 390
Daniel Kelly, 15, 124, 150, 10, 175
Elizabeth Bryan, 250, 750, 10000, 150, 1120
James Smith, -, -, -, 5, 35
Jesse Palmer, -, -, -, -, 20
William M. Bryan, 250, 400, 2000, 150, 1803
Preston Clifton, -, -, -, -, 15
Horatio Petty, -, -, -, 5, 200
Susan Clifton, -, -, -, -, 10
William Pigg, -, -, -, 3, 50
Angelina Gist, 30, 270, 1500, 150, 460
William R. Underwood, -, -, -, 30, 300
Jane L. Haggard, 50, 50, 100, 25, 300
John T Harris, -, -, -, 100, 115
R. K. Graham, -, -, -, -, 50
John H. Sinclair, 1, -, 500, 65, 60
L. H. DeLashenet, -, -, -, -, 100
John Tedford, 36, 118, 1000, 100, 100

Shelby County TN
1850 Agricultural Census

The Agricultural Census for 1850 was filmed for the University of North Carolina from original records in the Tennessee State Library and Archives.

The following are the items represented and separated by a comma: for example, John Doe, 25, 25, 10, 5, 100. This represents:

Column 1 Owner
Column 2 Acres of Improved Land
Column 3 Acres of Unimproved Land
Column 4 Cash Value of Farm
Column 5 Value of Farm Implements and Machinery
Column 13 Value of Livestock

The following symbol is used to maintain spacing where there are no numbers: (-) In addition, the left margin has been bound too close to the edge causing some first names or initials to not be completely visible. With some names appears the entry "Entered Previously." However, I have not found the previous entries. In some cases the term "Entered Previously as No. 11" for example. I have extracted the information from line number 11 of that same page. However, there is no apparent relationship between the two people as the last names are not the same. Also, sometimes "Entered Previously" is X d out in the first block, but not second, third or 4th blocks, and a new number in the fifth block. This county's information was at times very confusing.

Silas Bryant, 25, 175, 1200, 40, 175
Joseph Kelley, 150, 350, 3500, 20, 580
Johnathan Hargus, 15, 85, 450, 55, 120
Johnathan Faulk, 55, 100, 600, 75, 400
Nicholas Boswell, 35, 65, 500, 50, 180
Wm. Truesdale, 110, 90, 1200, 100, 600
Allan Neely, 35, 45, 300, 40, 100
Newton Johnson, 25, 75, 500, 75, 150
Pat H. Brickley, 45, 63, 500, 40, 220
Ed Kelley, 25, 75, 400, 50, 240
Wm. Ballard, 20, -, , 5, 150
Samuel Kennedy, 90, 52, 972, 75, 580
Jas. C. White, 150, 280, 3440, 525, 850
Wm. B. Batte, 137, 561, 3500, 100, 612
Jef Gray, 40, 25, 600, 100, 46
John K. Branch, 23, 77, 1000, 35, 400
Geo. Douglass, 50, 300, 2000, 65, 425
D. S. Crenshaw, 80, 91, 1710, 100, 674
J. S. Dickerson, 50, 210, 2000, 150, 640
James Gillham, 50, 60, 1100, 75, 340
R. J. Byram, 40, 40, 800, 420, 500
Wm. A. Polk, 75,m 45, 1500, 70, 780
Alex. Phillips, 41, 26, 680, 25, 110
John A. Reed, 20, -, 200, 20, 225
Wm. C. Gragg, 50, 77, 1000, 50, 280
Chas. W. Timmins, 60, 70, 1300, 10, 225
Hugh Stephenson, 25, 40, 650, 50, 150

W. D. Gaither, 80, 80, 1600, 130, 375
Jas. D. Stewart, 25, 49, 700, 10, 280
Jas. C. Willie, 40, 35, 600, 40, 260
Jas. Griffith, 40, 90, 1300, 50, 250
R. L. Starks, 85, 147, 2320, 100, 725
Zelpha Ward, 40, 15, 260, 5, 230
Joel Herron, 100, 200, 3000, 500, 1150
M. R. Snead, 25, 75, 600, 20, 245
John Holt, 62, 87, 2000, 560, 340
Lucy W. Cauler (Carler,Canler), 25, -, 200, 10, 50
Saml. Dougherty, 22, -, 180, 10, 80
H. H. Glisson, 100, 190, 2500, 110, 338
D. M. Sanderlin, 300, 291, 500, 550, 1250
H. Seaward, 30, 291, 500, 10, 180
John A. Michelbery, 90, 19, 2500, 800, 880
Richd. Epperson, 12, 76, 500, 10, 133
Wm. B. Hills, 108, 265, 2500, 400, 800
John Fleming, 30, 48, 450, 40, 115
M. K. Herring, 20, 129, 1200, 40, 230
John W. Bledsoe, 230, 340, 5000, 380, 1890
Joseph Ferguson, 33, 67, 800, 50, 250
Joseph Byram, 20, 30, 300, 5, 100

Wade H. Bolton, 400, 600, 7500, 550, 1285

_. G. Bond, 45, 215, 2600, 75, 600

Jas. M. Olifant, 50, 51 1010, 65, 300

Thos. J. Ross, 120, 156, 3300, 200, 890

B. B. Goodwin, 120, 156, 3300, 10, 165

Wm. H. Patrick, 33, 47, 650, 10, 175

Jas. T. Stewart, 65, 85, 2550, 90, 390

Wm. P. Stewart, 25, 35, 1000, 98, 380

Bryant Ward, 35, 293, 2000, 10, 218

Polly Ann Shoulders, 60, 140, 2000, 5, 140

Joel S. Herring, 30, 70, 1000, 75, 220

Talbot Atherston, 40, 50, 900, 90, 315

Stephen P. King, 6, 44, 500, 30, 200

Jas. Scott, 30, 70, 1000, 45, 250

Joseph Bond, 25, 75, 1000, 80, 273

Alex Snead, 100, 161, 2615, 78, 315

Sarah Hays, 20, 50, 500, 20, 360

John M. Bond, 125, 80, 2050, 60, 450

Saml. Rankin, 22, 211, 1000, 50, 130

John Sloan, 35, 90, 350, 5, 387

H. J. Reese, 20, 108, 1000, 25, 215

John H. Jones, 60, -, 400, 5, 100

John Dement, 12, 10, 100, 8, 90

_. H. Johnson, 27, -, 270, 10, 185

Geo. S. Carr, 18, 348, 1000, 5, 85

Wm. Mustin, 20, -, 200, 14, 60

Joshua Crane, 20, 30, 500, 15, 105

Whitfield Crane, 20, 80, 400, 18, 100

Argus F. Shelby, 25, 50, 500, 18, 290

Moses S. Alexander, 20, 30, 250, 6, 70

Henry Stewart, 50, -, 400, 50, 370

Lewis Hill, 5, 200, 900, 20, 130

Richd. Hazelwood, 25, 100, 1000, 40, 228

James Sloan, 30, 100, 1000, 78, 430

Wm. S. Garner, 400 100, 4000, 900, 2600

Wm. M. Wilson, 30, 70, 600, 75, 150

James Garvin, 22, 78, 250, 60, 140

James Berryhill, 15, 85, 500, 20, 85

Robt. Robertson, 30, -, 150, 50, 400

Wm. J. Whithead, 0, 70, 500, 15, 350

Ebenezer Harrel, 30, 20, 400, 125, 230

John Owen, 19, 36, 205, 88, 290

Mary Thompson, 95, 292, 3000, 50, 250

Henry Thompson, 15, 92, 800, 15, 225

M. L. Roy, 35, 125, 1200, 20, 400

Newton Corbet, 28, 2, 300, 5, 155

Nancy Corbet, 185, 185, 370, 600, 425

A. B. C. Dubose, 300, 306, 4000, 75, 75

Wm. D. Dunn, 300, 550, 5600, 900, 2640

Danl. Corbet, 30, -, 250, 40, 580

Henry Wenders, 23, 29, 1400, 60, 225

Chamberlin Jones Jr., 300, 540, 5040, 600, 1265

Cambertagn Jones Sr., 825, 1291, 12696, 2100, 3900

Berthien Jones Est., 150, 342, 2840, 150, 880

Joel Sawyers, 15, 108, 981, 5, 30

L. B. Starks, 120, 120, 1800, 200, 640

Wm. A. Olas, 75, 185, 2000, 500, 395

Isaac _. Bolton, 550, 550, 8000, 8500, 3136

Thos. Dickens, 300, 800, 8000, 400, 1830

Francis Smith, 18, 622, 1000, 40, 400

Redick Moon (Moore), 35, 1105, 4000, 60, 517

John Carter, 33, 964, 3500, 40, 175

Mary Scott, 100, 400, 4000, 100, 900

Sarah Ward, 300, 300, 4000, 800, 900

Norman Reynolds, 70, 30, 500, 100, 480

John Geers, 170, 90, 2080, 20, 450

Wm. Reynolds, 25, -, 125, 85, 460

Robt. Reynolds, 100, 58, 1000, 720, 460

Willie G. Hardin, 30, 290, 2000, 60, 125

Peter B. Wynne, 30, 689, 6000, 425, 1125

Saml. Acock, 150, 375, 5000, 125, 1600

Stephen Harrison, 20, -, 30, 65, 250

Jas. T. Person, 85, 411, 3000, 80, 710

John Person, 750, 1101, 13000, 750, 1662

Benj. Duncan, 350, 550, 11000, 350, 1435

E. B. Harrell, 35, -, 350, 150, 515

Wm. Goodman, 23, 200, 1561, 50, 1310

J. R. Taylor, 12, 98, 4000, 60, 620

W. J. A. Bell, 120, 80, 2000, 635, 900

Allen Gladden, 12, -, 120, 5, 115

Wm. Ross, 160, 340, 6000, 500, 670

Thos Wyblood, 70, 530, 3000, 75, 320

Amos Person, 60, 190, 2500, 150, 350

Turner Person, 450, 1213, 17000, 1000, 1700

Ann Moore, 100, 150, 2500, 15, 558

John Howze, 78, 185, 2600, 150, 558

Geo. W. Halloway, 60, 260, 2560, 150, 558

Allen Reaves, 60, 260, 2560, 150, 175

Elizabeth Crenshaw, 130, 470, 4500, 100, 200

David Crenshaw, 35, 137, 850, 125, 245

Susan Gray, 20, 35, 550, 10, 70

John Marcum, 110, 250, 3600, 75, 560

Haywood Branch, 23, 1, 450, 90, 450

John Ralston, 160, 1537, 11879, 700, 1090

Allen S. Wynne, 150, 27, 1000, 50, 528

C. C. Coleman, 6, -, 60, 50, 165

John Adkins, 6, -, -, 5, 25

John Jones, 30, 66, 500, 75, 390

Danl. Harrison, 25, 49, -, 14, 400

Joseph Harrison, 22, 49, -, 5, 125
I.G. Grooms, 9, 49, -, 6, 105
T. T. Goldsby, 500, 2400, 16000, 750, 2750
A. T. Bledsoe, 230, 200, 4800, 500, 1190
John Harding, 100, 205, 3600, 150, 910
T. T. Goldsby, 60, 40, 700, 75, 320
Chas. Creshaw. 40, 400, 2500, 75, 500
Ezekiel Robinet, 35, -, -, 15, 230
Rufus Etherby, 20, 138, 1500, 75, 910
Miles W. Goldsby, 240, 190, 4000, 250, 1250
A. B. C. Dubose, 475, 500, 9000, 800, 3050
Wm. Douglas, 100, 60, 1500, 40, 702
Andrew Hallum, 20, 30, 600, 15, 100
S. S. Rembert, 450, 1250, 17000, 1200, 3000
John W. Ward, 400, 1100, 6700, 430, 550
Henry Ward, -, -, -, 31, 40
D. Crenshaw, 45, 55, 1000, 450, 365
J. B. Davis, 10, -, 100, 12, 190
John Evett, 30, 44, 740, 10, 275
Abner Clift, 15, 185, 400, 10, 85
Sumner Jenkins, 40, 600, 6000, 100, 240
Michael C. Peel, 15, 104, 6000, 100, 800
Eugene DeChallenge, 20, 1280, 8000, 100, 370
B. O'Bannion, 20, 140, 600, 10, 55
Wm. Fletcher, 200, 400, 4000, 75, 735
Edward Willis, 30, 370, 2000, 15, 210
Wm. McKnight, 12, 307, 1000, 40, 200
__hiel Jones, 16, 84, 400, 80, 825
Wm. Garrett, 20, 180, 1000, 10, 235
Saml. Barton, 30, 30, 2500, 100, 245
James (Barton), 50, 50, 500, 50, 400
Hardin Bateman, 70, 330, 2000, 125, 1175
Abraham Adams, 65, 135, 1000, 50, 475
Hosea Beatman, 40, 1600, 500, 30 385
Wm. Bland, 27, 72, 100, 5, 230
Wm. Hallum, 18, 22, 150, 48, 378
Joseph Ruffin, 25, 35, 180, 10, 40
Benj. Gregory, 12, 68, 240, 18, 100
Wm. Lubles, 20, 200, 300, 5, 75
James Carroll, 35, 165, 1000, 125, 355
Levin Wimberry, 30, 70, 500, 25, 135
James Corbet, 12, -, 60, 10, 75
Wm. React, 14, 86, 450, 10, 130
M. Plummer, 15, 35, 175, 10, 175
Robt. McBride, 37, 63, 400, 60, 330
Moses Alexander, 53, 52, 750, 100, 540
Wm. E. Roberts, 24, 50, 400, 50, 200
Lereud(Leonard) Whitworth, 14, 110, 500, 25, 120
Johnathan Reactt, 25, 150, 1700, 100, 340

Fulaeny Juter (Jeetter), 50, 40, 500, 128, 965
Boyd Williams, 18, 21, 150, 45, 140
H. M. Cough, 17, 73, 900, 65, 380
B. J. Sigler, 35, 115, 1500, 50, 370
Lemuel D. Harrell, 65, 152, 1700, 550, 1453
Robert Ware, 100, 163, 1800, 100, 715
Wm. A. Shelby, 60, 80, 1400, 100, 450
Alfred Ware, 14, 96, 600, 5, 95
L. S. Taylor, 64, 36, 1000, 10, 115
John C. Bolton, 40, 60, 800, 50, 320
Lem. Crane, 40, 60, 500, 65, 310
Chas. W. Fitzgerald, 350, 350, 5000, 350, 630
Allen Smith, 10, 90, 500, 15, 70
James W. Jackson, 23, 977, 1500, 10, 100
Blany Harper, 30, 67, 150, 25, 255
Richd. Oglesby, 30, 211, 1165, 65, 230
Saml. Watt, 49, 150, 800, 50, 578
Jeremiah Massey, 15, 140, 1200, 100, 950
S. M. Ross, 15, -, 300, 15, 230
Ezekiel Bennet, 15, 99, 575, 75, 170
A. R. Herron, 80, 68, 5000, 200, 700
R. B. Trotter, 8, 160, 210, 60, 165
Harriett Stanton (Slanton), 17,-, 8000, 100, 300
John W. Barnett, 10, -, 1000, 40, 160
Levi Prescott, 14, 6, 2500, 150, 250
Rodolph Schnetz (Schneley), 10, -, 1000, 20, 120
Willie B. Smith, 20, -, 1800, 75, 95
Joseph Dennis, 5, 20, 1250, 50, 175
John Anderson, 50, 250, 5000, 100, 300
Nancy Rice, 12, 12, 1400, 50, 125
B. R. Thomas, 200, 300, 10000, 500, 2000
Wm. Wilkins, 10, -, 750, 100, 70
Saml. Harper, 40, 30, 3500, 78, 358
Wm. Morehead, 12, 15, 1000, 100, 120
Jas. A. Morehead, 20, 20, 1600, 100, 150
John W. Morehead, 10, 16, 1000, 25, 50
Malissa Rudisell, 14, 6, 1200, 90, 100
_. H. Hawley, 30, 33, 1890, 50, 500
_. H. Coe, 100, 800, 9000, 25, 500
__ml. Lemmon, 21, 179, 4000, 41, 50
Sanford Petters, 40, 60, 2000, 30, 250
Wm. Strong, 70, 41, 3300, 400, 800
Wm. Wommack, 70, -, 1400, 20, 195
Elas Morris, 65, -, 1300, 100, 120
_. M. Gill, 50, 72, 4000, 300, 1200
_ennet Bagby, 20, 32, 20000, 50, 500
_. M. Gates, 9, 5, 4000, 78, 175
John Hooston, 10, -, 1000, 25, 900
Custis Stohl, 3, -, 400, 25, 5
Rich. Hooper, 7, -, 600, 20, 25

Sarah F. Peyton, 15, -, 2500, 5, 140
Jas. T. Leath, 70, 30, 1500, 100, 750
Seth Wheatley, 10, -, 800, 15, 250
_. S. Caldwell, 3, -, 3000, 200, 300
John Colby, 24, -, 2500, 50, 350
Jesse Isler, 40, 20, 8000, 72, 320
Wm. Wray, 18, -, 4000, 250, 275
Jas. Thompson, 6, -, 2500, 60, 130, 275
_. D. McLean, 80, 30, 7500, 200, 830
Mary Armour (Asmour), 100, 40, 5000, 100, 415
Tillman Bettis, 150, 30, 1440, 800, 1055
Chas. F. King, 40, -, 4000, 100, 385
Wm. Willie, 7, -, 2500, 100, 75
C. T. Rose, 15, 15, 3000, 78, 200
Henry Baker, 4, 1, 600, 10, 25
M. B. Winchester, 20, 180, 10000, 50, 230
B. G. Beadle, 12, 6, 900, 20, 144
W. F. Allen, 175, 225, 6600, 1500, 900
_. Goodwin, 175, 25, 2500, 500, 1103
_. D. Blue, 100, 50, 2250, 150, 1025
Wm. Braswell, 75, 130, 3280, 400, 500
Jesee Alsop, 17, 193, 1800, 50, 110
Ellis Whitworth, -, -, -, -, -
James Neel, 50, 225, 2600, 70, 525
_. R. Potts, 75, 115, 2000, 100, 455
Wm. Reaves, 120, 80, 4500, 200, 930
Wm. A. Kerr, 120, 680, 8000, 50, 390
James Huffman, 30, 46, 760, 50, 360
John C. Jones, 22, 73, 800, 15, 100
_. Brown, 33, 92, 1250, 50, 428
_. W. Floyd, 21, 61, 500, 25, 140
Thos. Etheredge, 70, 85, 1555, 50, 448
Burton R. Berry, 50, 50, 500, 15, 155
Wm. S. Wells, 65, 120, 2000, 150, 374
John N. Fuller, 100, 120, 2500, 100, 500
Benj. Duncan, 50, 51, 1000, 5, 272
John Hathaway, 227, 500, 4000, 500, 380
Wm. M. Manus (Maners, Manas), 14, 59, 300, 20, 80
Wm. G. Wickham, 79, 121, 2400, 30, 340
John B. Hodges, 60, 200, 1600, 30, 286
Sam. Smith, 60, 190, 1500, 78 385
Emanuel Baker, 10, 26, 900, 50, 235
Saml. Carr, 50,90, 1400, 100, 280
_. Carlisle, 60, 40, 500, 200, 355
Thos. J. Rawlings, 120, 623, 3500, 250, 730
Jas. W. King, 15, 10, 500, 15, 112
_. Shivers, 46, 54, 1000, 100, 425
_. C. Sanderlin, 150, 172, 4000, 75, 465
Lewis Griffith, 20, -, 200, 25, 57
Thos. Humphreys, 18, 44, 500, 5, 60
Joseph Locke, 40, -, 400, 150, 450
Wm. Magee, 30, -, 600, 60, 400

_. B. Hawkins, 80, 73, 900, 75, 285
G. D. Blair, 100, 217, 3800, 350, 690
Eli Bell, 40, 170, 1200, 20, 200
Alex. Allen, 30, 61, 550, 100, 435
_. W. Alexander, 40, 110, 1500, 60, 158
Elam Thomas, 75, 100, 1200, 100, 485
Nancy Phan (Pharr), 50, 70, 00, 10, 100
Geo. W. Jamison, 25, 195, 2500, 90, 160
Jas. Jamison, 120, 350, 5640, 500, 624
Lucy Hawkins, -, -, -, 200, -
John J. Edwards, 25, 25, 400, 5, 220
Henry B. Willerford, 120, 150, 2400, 400, 550
John Watson, 45, 43, 650, 110, 255
J. H. Alsabrooks, 60, 111, 2000, 20, 228
Narcisson Garrett, 15, -, 150, 10, 45
Alex Bradley, 38, 32, 700, 50, 190
Geo. Bentley, 60, 57, 100, 30, 135
M. McCollum, 400, 240, 3200, 350, 1570
Ira Moore, 70, 98, 1100, 10, 100
Thos. Dickens, 250, 175, 4000, 125, 600
Jas. Rodgers, 15, 45, 500, 50, 180
Thos. Carter, 20, 40, 200, 6, 30
B. Bryant, 100, 112, 2000, 60, 275
Lewis Hocott, 60, 65, 1500, 75, 260
Benj. Phillips, 16, -, 200, 15, 185
B. W. Prior, 40, 60, 900, 20, 245
Winnaford Anderson, 220, 620, 6720, 325, 1900
Jas. A. Oakley, 27, -, 270, 150, 140
Sarah Scott, 40, 160, 200, 40, 100
Isaac Brooks, 80, 20, 1000, 75, 500
David N. Meadows, 100, 560, 3200, 50, 700
Benj. Y. Winston, 50, 80, 550, 38, 180
Nancy Rodgers, 30, 70, 500, 15, 328
Elisha Cowgill, 38, 80, 500, 10, 120
Thos. Wilson, 15, 23, 220, 5, 135
Jas. W. Cowgill, 15, 15, 150, 5, 138
Allen Walton , 60, 112, 1650, 70, 195
Robt. Wallace, 30, 314, 2500, 200, 320
Jas. Oldham, 8, 400, 1200, 8 75
J. C. Hardaway, 50, 270, 2000, 30, 165
Jane Alexander, 60, 580, 6400, 105, 420
M. S. Mathewes, 35, 65, 1200, 65, 480
James Purser, 25, 58, 664, 50, 350
James Marlchain, 100, 240, 5000, 100, 430
John Diviney, 32, 98, 400, 35, 200
Ed Lewis, 20, 200, 1100, 50, 160
Fred Smith, 40, 22, 1000, 100, 360
Oswell Harris, 23, 77, 600, 10, 165
Benj. L. Branch 60, 90, 1100, 575, 663
John M. Branch, 18, 346, 1200 20, 275
Fletcher Taylor, 300, 840, 7000, 700, 1390

Willie Carlisle, 45, 55, 500, 10, 70
James Carlisle, 45, 55, -, 10, 71
G. W. Oldham, 65, 335, 1000, 60, 250
Sally Daniel, 82, 200, 2820, 120, 605
Elem Hutchens, 30, 70, 500, 15, 200
Marcus Braswell, 39, 157, 800, 21, 110
David McKnight, 40, 200, 2000, 50, 300
Albert Kimbro, 140, 45, 3700, 625, 245
John Pope, 600, 300, 18000, 650, 2550
Overall Sanderson, 40, 60, 1500, 50, 415
G. L. Holmes, 700, 200, 15000, 550, 1750
Salover(Sabra) White, 700, 436, 22720, 520, 1550
L. T. Westbrooks, -, -, -, 250, 590
Wm. H. Snead, 100, 134, 3510, 00, 445
Susannah Henry, 30, 70, 1500, 65, 225
Geo. Graham, 400, 212, 7200, 500, 1400
Stephen Coleman, 30, 64, 1300, 60, 270
James Dollar, 16, 75, 361, 20, 120
Jim Sikes, 60, 140, 1300, 80, 210
Saml. Blair, 40, 160, 400, 40, 450
Gabl. Anderson, 60, 88, 1400, 15, 300
Wm. Marsh, 300, 432, 11000, 850, 2000
Leonidas McKnight, 40, 200, 2000, 10, 300
Pat. Duffy, 40, 175, 4000, 75, 430
Epurn (Exsum, Epirn, Epurn) Dunning, 14, 26, 240, 10, 75
Bethay Maxwell, 73, 190, 1850, 55, 350
R. T. G. Hart, 150, 170, 3500, 750, 1320
B. C. Sanderlin, 100, 250, 7000, 100, 350
Elizabeth Doty, 25, 15, 500, 70, 230
C. H. Hart, 40, 32, 725, 115, 210
Kenneth Garret, 900, 580, 33600, 1000, 5730
John S. Clayton, 180, 68, 3500, 550, 1275
John W. Ward, 400, 247, 3882, 600, 990
Thos. McGowen, 180, 332, 5000, 70, 630
John M. Sanders, 17, 120, 1350, 80, 125
R. J. P. Shivers, 125, 25, 1000, 350, 900
Mathew Rayner, 125, 875, 6000, 75, 500
M. Whitehead, 25, 65, 90, 50, 175
Chas. G. Polk, 80, 420, 500, 100, 440
H. Baily, 15, 54, 700, 100, 170
M. Shivers, 180, 10, 1000, 30, 220
Robt. Staples, 25, 25, 600, 10, 305
Nancy Sparkman, 39, 61, 1000, 50, 375
David Bentley, 70, 80, 750, 60, 180
Lem. Stokes, 125, 875, 6000, -, 120
W. A. Andrews, 100, 132 1170, 100, 460
M. Edwards, -, -, -, 6, 150
Lewis Edwards, 175, 400, 2700, 125, 525
Josiah Daniel 230, 170, 4000, 455, 760
Thos. C. Crenshaw, 700, 550, 15000, 2100, 3017

Stark React (Reait), 200, 117, 3800, 200, 975
Harper MacGowen, 150, 133, 2830, 85, 390
Mathan W. McGhee, unknown, unknown, unknown, 10, 75
Fred Brick (Buck), 50, 54, 1000, 25, 175
Clement Cannon, 60, 40, 1000, 120, 445
Aron Jackson, 85, 275, 2500, 580, 740
W. Bane, -, -, -, 20, 120
Allen Davis, 28, 68, 600, 50, 60
Wm. _. Robins, 90, 90, 2000, 50, 450
Mary E. Jones, 140, 200, 4000, 60, 450
John T. Simpson, 130, 262, 2000, 50, 500
L. D. Mullins, 250, 210, 4500, 500, 725
Thos. Cole, 25, 70, 1000, 30, 125
Lucretia Willett, 100, 250, 3500, 60, 400
Wm. Hill, 220, 155, 2250, 78, 830
B. W. Hill, 25, -, 240, 8, 30
John Hill, 70, 157, 2770, 50, 950
Winfield Cole, 230, 170, 6000, 575, 1140
John Galloway, 200, 260, 4600, 400, 1115
Richd. Crouch, 150, 250, 2500, 500, 800
O. M Alsop, 140, 241, 1900, 150, 330
Charlotte Jones, 35, 67, 1000, 8, 110
John S. Abernathy, 100, 100, 2000, 500, 600
Bryan Halloway, 100, 100, 2000, 50, 65
Cintha Williamson, 300, 259, 5031, 85, 540
Saml Roach, 80,70, 2200, 120, 335
Wm. C. Anderson, 107, 100, 2500, 550, 545
N. L. Macke, 50, 75, 1000, 75, 345
Henry T. Jones, 150, 137, 2000, 175, 675
Reuben Massey, 300, 390, 6900, 525, 1130
Elijah Pulliam, 450, 325, 7750, 500, 1250
James A. Massey, 100, 100, 2000, 10, 170
Richd. Wallace, 60, 140, 1500, 10, 150
James L. Dickey, 60, 140, 1800, 120, 495
John Branch, 50, -, 500, 25, 125
D. Ferrell, 40, -, 400, 10, 200
Richd. Towns, 20, -, 200, 10, 75
Jno. W. Waddle, 75, 55, 1000, 20, 162
Micajah Woods, 35, 65, 800, 60, 210
Wm. Floray, 30, 20, 300, 75, 150
C. L. Brookes, 24, 80, 700, 75, 150
Jonathan Waddle, 300, 259, 5031, 5, 80
Jno. M. Shelby, 50, 285, 5000, 100, 500
S. Parks, 50, 50, 800, 50, 220
D. H. Walker, 100, 186, 3000, 100, 500
Robt. Parks, 40, 40, 600, 65, 440
Cyrus Parks, 40, 40, 600, 10, 190

H. L. Buckley, 60, 240, 3000, 75, 330
James Preeden, 275, 200, 5000, 80, 650
Thos. Anderson, 200, 125, 5000, 175, 900
Joseph Wesson, 30, 56, 1290, 70, 400
Joseph Willie, 120, 82, 800, 118, 210
Sam Bond, 838, 662, 22500, 1700, 3665
Washington Bond, 350, 210, 8400, 1300, 1640
Scott Bane, 200, 50, 3750, 150, 500
Richd Woolsey, 80, 120, 1050, 85, 650
Benj. Baker, 40, 47, 750, 90, 366
S. F. Willerford, 220, 235, 5000, 100, 1420
Joshua Kelly, 100, 500, 2500, 400, 480
John W. Ward, 400, 300, 5700, 500, 1100
John Bond, 260, 318, 8670, 1250, 1365
Hilared Mand (Maud), 80, 120, 2000, 75, 305
Thos. Harwell, 400, 180, 8700, 700, 1100
Wm. Maloney, 35, 965, 5000, 100, 340
Saml. Parker, 13, 965, 85, 5, 80
Chas. Hill, 30, 962, 5150, 75, 360
Larkin Branson, 8, 962, 5150, 5,80
Richmond Winklee, 53, 202, 1503, 150, 530
Neill McNair, 30, -, 300, 25, 260
James N. Massey, 53, 47, 800, 100, 530
Geo. Smith, 42, 242, 2000, 110, 472
Arch Fleming, 30, 50, 880, 100, 365
Robt. Dallis, 15, -, 150, 8, 40
E__ L. Goss, 18, 287, 3500, 80, 240
Soloman McBride, 20, -, -, 20, 200
Jas. R. Manaser, 30, 890, 5000, 50, 225
John B. Hale, 60, -, -, 100, 405
Robt. Smith, 15, 45, 725, 135, 185
Elisha Bass, 25, -, 250, 50, 415
Geo. W. Manaser, 17, -, 170, 8, 170
John McNair, 28, 972, 4000, 10, 205
Wm. Bennet, 60, -, 200, 5, 60
Hugh Rodgers, 30, -, 150, 15, 130
Alfred Smith, 30, 75, 700, 20, 190
Johnathan Keatherly, 14, 150, 800, 75, 247
Jas. M. Flanikin, 25, 45, 400, 15, 225
David P. Coffee, 20, 45, 500, 100, 370
David Appleberry, 20, -, 200, 15, 175
Terry Massey, 42, 80,800, 25, 210
Wm. Bolt, 35, 65, 500, 40, 105
Pryor Barrell, 40, 80, 700, 30, 180
J. B. Boyd, 50, 120, 900, 60, 390
R. J. Williams 70, 110, 1000, 50, 185
Joseph Miller, 110, 244, 2800, 525, 815
John J. Griffith, 30, 20, 350, 25, 565
John G. Sanderford, 30, 110, 980, 20, 130
Barnet Pattison, 100, 863, 2000, 100, 445
Geo. W. Sessons, 40, 221, 1600, 90, 370

J. M. Worthington, 50, 52, 800, 75, 295
J. H. Sink, 80, 208, 2880, 500, 440
Stephen English, 75, 100, 1500, 250, 370
Robt. N. Bond, 46, 106, 1100, 40, 413
Chas. Harrell, 30, 30, 300, 15, 145
Geo. W. Condor, 24, 56, 640, 50, 235
John Kirkpatrick, 24, 6, 300, 50, 230
Joseph S. Bosley, 60, 740, 6000, 50, 290
R. B. Jones, 35, 65, 400, 10, 290
Joseph Faulk, 80, 112, 1800, 40, 260
Saml. Harrell, 40, 20, 300, 60, 325
Benj. Sanderford, 50, 25, 400, 5, 345
Saml. G. Jones, 27, 60, 500, 125, 300
John W. Gragg, 35, 165, 2000, 50, 260
Flip Lane, 20, -, 160, 85, 250
Saml. Hill, 30, 130, 1000, 65, 360
Ridgon Grady, 100, 71, 1710, 150, 500
John Douglass, 150, 134, 2000, 150, 780
Robt. Motley, 70, 30, 700, 15, 155
B___ Harrell, 50, 50, 700, 75, 390
J. L. Orr, 38, 12, 500, 100, 270
James McDaniel, 35, 15, 500, 100, 270
Mary Milliken, 25, -, 200, 10, 100
Jas. W. Slater, 18, -, 100, 10, 60
Jas. N. Douglass, 30, 20, 400, 100, 245
Joseph Massey, 40, 260, 700, 50, 265
Wm. Battle, 550, 1200, 10000, 678, 1560
John Isom, 12, -, 100, 25, 120
Phillip Hargus, 48, 13, 800, 68, 370
James Pool, 18, -, 50, 7, 70
Edward Freeman, 30, 66, 300, 30, 170
Gabl. Oquinn, 18, 80, 300, 18, 140
John Elliott, 40, -, 150, 10, 190
Canada Howel, 42, 60, 400, 40, 300
Elizabeth Nelson, 15, 59, 300, 50, 220
Elizabeth Howell, 50, 40, 210, 10, 90
Richd. Appleberry Sr., 125, 200, 1200, 85, 530
Richd. Appleberry Jr., 125, 200, -, 5, 113
Martha Henley, 27, -, 100, 12, 100
Geo. W. Pool, 20, 40, 480, 30, 485
Jessee Phillips, 120, 580, -, 75, 475
Clayton _. Kelley, 40, 10, 400, 60, 500
Benj. Bennet, 46, 10, 500, 10, 125
Zach Ellison, 30, 42, 400, 80, 120
_. Kelly S. Van, 50, 50, 700, 10, 255
James M. Kelly, 50, 150, 1200, 650, 692
Absalom Appleberry, 40, 160, 500, 20, 300
N. W. Dill, 40, 160, 500, 78, 350
B. H. Eddins, 75, 75, 1500, 65, 328
Thulina Canada, 40, 80, 1200, 25, 135
G. M. Bartlett, 200, 273, 5000, 700, 1115
Theophilus Bland, 100, 230, 3000, 100, 650

John Blackwell, 500, 700, 12000, 900, 1922
Joseph Ward, 500, 500, 12000, 1300, 1482
Hugh McAden (McAdire), 60, 50, 300, 20, 265
Nicholas Hall, 40, 160, 2000, 50, 560
David Branch, 100, 100, 1500, 90, 450
Franklin Farley, 300, 350, 3250, 78, 710
Stark Fleetwood, 50, 150, 1500, 50, 170
Jackson Scruggs, 50, -, 150, 7, 75
Ed. D. Hale, 50, 180, 100, 15, 225
_. W. Gillespie, 25, 174, 1200, 80, 235
Paschal Ruckley (Buckley), 50, 142, 1200, 600, 400
Francis Steward, 35, 130, 450, 10, 125
Gold A. Griffin, 120, 315, 3500, 730, 550
_. L. Buckley, 50, 62, 500, 20, 370
John Scott, 40, 160, 500, 10, 140
John Revees, 40, 448, 3000, 50, 378
John B. Horne, 53, 70, 600, 60, 570
Jno. W. Steele, 54, 76, 400, 6, 65
Lewis Herring, 144, 560, 5000, 550, 550
Marshall Herring, 60, 50, 300, 10, 175
W. Chitwood, 25, 175, 1000, 45, 225
_. J. Haye (Hays), 1600, 3900, 38500, 1550, 4200
Jas. Rooks, 88, 115, 1400, 120, 545
Turner S. Hines, 200, 50, 1200, 50, 400
_. Horne, 100, 160, 2600, 550, 850
Thos. Worthan, 80, 120, 1800, 80, 225
Rich. _. Worthan, -, -, -, 10, 90
Wm. Griffin, 500, 300, 4000, 678, 1765
Lucy Ellis, 100, 301, 1500, 5, 65
Moses Button, 80, 120, 1600, 25, 130
S. B. Berryhill, 35, 80, 1200, 25, 320
Joseph Thompson, 65, 37, 1000, 150, 340
C. J. Berry, 100, 35, 1000, 75, 455
Margaret Williams, 60, 70, 500, 20, 275
Wm. Black, 50, 66, 700, 38, 235
J. S. Whitley, 30, 18, 500, 5, 105
Hiram Sturgis, -, -, -, 10, 240
Wm. Bond, 250, 270, 3000, 610, 900
Richd. Jones, -, -, -, 10, 130
Henry Williams, 90, 40, 1600, 200, 450
Jno. H. Becton, 600, 550, 1500, 700, 1215
Jno. L. Woodson, 40, 110, 750, 40, 555
Joshua Harding, 30, 80, 800, 50, 110
Wm. Griffin Jr., -, -, -, 30, 140
Jas. Ferguson, 60, 40, 300, 60, 278
Sarah Gunter, 50, 200, 1500, 50, 240
Alex. H. Williams, 60, 40, 400, 25, 105
Joel W. Royster, 150, 250, 5000, 600, 1040
Robt. W. Ricks, 30, 70, 800, 110, 535

Jno. D. Hines, 60, 80, 600, 5, 225
Phillip Sowards, 40, 135, 700, 5, 90
Henry Powell, 100, 100, 500, 25, 300
Thos. Anderson, 50, 150, 600, 40, 160
Stephen Jones, 35, 183, 800, 15, 250
Richd. Jones, 65, 125, 1000, 55, 480
James Gillespie, 100, 340, 2640, 450, 350
Alex. Donaldson, 300, 657, 5742, 640, 1435
Sam Donaldson, 350, 650, 4000, 700, 1725
John Donelson, 250, 582, 6000, 50, 795
Elijah King, 100, 100, 1400, 575, 420
Geo. Cherry, 100, 150, 1750, 75, 628
Joek Ooek, 48, 52, 500, 5, 700
Smith Beloate, 40, 240, 1450, 60, 365
Geo. Beloate, 40, 45, 300, 20, 350
Robt. Goodloe, 30, 54, 400, 40, 78
Davis Harding, 60, 150, 1680, 100, 305
D. F. Blackwell, 250, 140, 2145, 550, 1060
Wm. Redd, 60, 100, 1600, 50, 275
Alfred Neal, 100, 92, 1200, 25, 400
A. Calhoun, -, -, -, 25, 214
Mary Anderson, 45, 137, 1000, 125, 300
Geo. Hallison, 5, 45, 300, 50, 270
John Taurinan, 150, 74, 872, 95, 800
Stephen Herring, 50, 96, 1000, 100, 200
James Sloan, 35, 115, 1000, 25, 185
_. W. Mitchell, 38, 107, 700, 15, 140
_. T. Land, 40, 55, 800, 75, 460
Thos. _. Wherry, 40, 160, 1000, 50, 240
Silas Wherry, 50, 74, 1000, 70, 360
Edwin Herring, 100, 313, 1800, 175, 335
Jessee Willie, 48, 155, 1500, 75, 160
Jessee Lynn, 50, 150, 1600, 50, 340
Frances Gillespie, 64, 170, 1892, 90, 350
F. P. Thomas, 50, 100, 900, 35, 280
Minerva Owen, 20, 50, 500, 8, 150
Lewis Willie, 30, 82, 500, 8, 110
Jno. M. Thompson, 25, 200, 1600, 50, 320
Mary Ferguson, 60, 140, 1600, 10, 175
Chas. Hallum, 50, 36, 1000, 40, 160
Thos. P. Willie, 50, 10, 300, 10, 130
Thos. Wherry, 90, 130, 1100, 700 520
John Wherry, 60, 140, 1000, 100, 428
Chas. H. Starr, 260, 480, 8880, 780, 1417
Sam Leaks, 350, 650, 10000, 1000, 1310
Peter Anmen, 70, 130, 3000, 178, 435
Ann C. Thurmin, 160, 340, 3000, 428, 875
Jas. Harris, 35, 65, 900, 60, 187
Rich. Leak, 250, 290, 5000, 350, 187
E. D. Peoples, 152, 100, 2500, 180, 680
James Gray, 79, 400, 3000, 100, 560

Wm. Walsh, 73, 148, 3000, 20, 385
Robt. Guerrant, 15, 45, 400, 10, 105
John Nobles, 30, 70, 700, 28, 120
Berry N. Smith, 70, 30, 500, 125, 420
A. O. Edwards, 120, 68, 1500, 800, 960
Jno. S. Waddle, 45, 99, 1000, 40, 326
Thos. Garrett, 30, 170, 1200, 125, 165
P___ Jones, 80, 163, 1944, 28, 290
Lucan Button, 50, 100, 1200, 8, 220
Isaac Jenkins, 50, 62, 784, 10, 150
C. B. Soward, 200, 320, 3300, 100, 710
Winnaford Williams, 80, 50, 1040, 28, 502
L. B. Munglum, 69, 100, 1400, 128, 285
Robt. Williams, 80, 50, 1300, 100, 355
John James, 25, 110, 652, 50, 190
John Gray, 100, 105, 2000, 100, 180
Thos. B. Crenshaw, 800, 1286, 16668, 1028, 2630
Nancy S. Allen, 175, 295, 3500, 130, 505
Geo. W. Davis, 122, 100, 1500, 25, 648
Wm. Sigler, 120, 173, 2300, 80, 790
Hugh McClellan, 45, 55, 800, 130, 2200
Wm. Crenshaw, 623, 534, 11770, 1200, 2816
Tabitha Burns, 30, 78, 324, 5, 100
David Hecklers, 160, 140, 1800, 20, 178
Jesse Marks, 50, 50, 500, 40, 245
Lewis H. Pyrn, 19, 9, 200, 78, 235
Olivia Webster, 40, 60, 600, 15, 400
Jas. Edwards, 120, 170, 1750, 600, 700
James Beavers, 800, 1286, 16668, 50, 80
Jourdan Sawyers, 70, 32, 600, 40, 345
Danl. Talley, -, -, -, 8, 150
Hervey Grenade, 70, 85, 1000, 40, 240
Jeremiah Baugh, 120, 140, 3000, 40, 390
_. M. Tate, 80, 122, 1600, 100, 870
Jno. Williams, 200, 640, 11000, 650, 1000
Z. M. Tate, 40, 80, 720, 35, 210
Elizabeth Allen, 160, 240, 4000, 500, 925
Walter Allen, 100, 400, 2000, 50, 520
Robt. Ecklin, 220, 680, 5000, 650, 1490
Jo. Patrick, 25, 79, 400, 50, 185
W. Clifford, 25, 79, 400, 10, 145
Joshua Ecklin, 150, 293, 3000, 120, 685
Asbury Crenshaw, 600, 807, 8445, 1057, 2461
Osmund Field, 200, 200, 2000, 700, 780
Wm. Strong, 50, 50, 500, 10, 100
Ezekiel Sanderlin, 60, 75, 1200, 500, 540
B. F. Nelson (Meson), 45, 1858, 500, 75, 200
Henry McKinney, 30, 25, 325, 30, 30
Danl. Boytee, 60, 40, 500, 50, 278
Peter J. Randol, 30, 45, 375, 25, 140

John Houston, 80, 80, 1200, 175, 305
Wm. Perry, 18, 25, 250, 50, 95
Peyton Fletcher, 250, 250, 3000, 150, 500
Edwin Rodgers, -, -, -, 5, 60
Wm. G. Hooker, -, -, -, 10, 230
F. A. Hooker, 140, 130, 2000, 650, 785
Jethro Harrell, 140, 230, 2500, 100, 476
Jas. Webber, 40, 10, 350, 15, 150
Joseph P. Duvall, 75, 170, 250, 50, 275
Isaac Stutman, 35, 5, 500, 10, 200
H. C. Stark, 800, 240, 8000, 1050, 1830
B. W. Webber, 35, 55, 600, 25, 300
Wm. A. McDowell, 80, 170, 250, 75, 420
Joseph T. Allen, 150, 156, 2000, 75, 477
Blakely Husky, 60, 150, 1000, 35, 210
Robt. Williams, 40, 20, 500, 25, 345
Milly Williams, 50, 100, 1000, 20, 125
Saml. W. Rice, 75, 125, 1600, 60, 240
Chas. E. Williams, 250, 150, 3200, 650, 600
Wm. Little, 300, 179, 3000, 100, 1100
Wm. Priddy, 125, 85, 1800, 50, 275
Wm. R. Warthens, 150, 270, 3200, 80, 510
Geo. A. Little, 60, 40, 760, 20, 217
Wm. W. Little, 60, 40, 800, 75, 258
Mathew Weber, 400, 500, 9000, 835, 1630
John Ashley, 85, 115, 2000, 78, 370
John Webber, 106, 200, 2400, 110, 635
McNeill Powell, 25, 15, 30, 5, 125
Alex. Davis, 45, 105, 1000, 75, 360
Pleasant Houston, 50, 133, 1800, 640, 420
Eliza Riley, 70, 9, 1000, 50, 300
Wm. Yarbrough, 30, 20, 500, 10, 230
Elizabeth Compton, 300, 155, 4440, 25, 860
John Kirk, 79, 300, 2653, 125, 555
Jeptha Wiles, 42, 38, 700, 120, 290
Saml. McNeely, 30, 50, 500, 10, 150
Jas. Houston, 35, 45, 800, 160, 385
Wm. Marter (Martin), 50, 50, 1000, 60, 240
Benj. Strong, 60, 90, 800, 100, 278
John Howel, 42, 60, 700, 10, 135
A. M. Bryan, 40, 28, 408, 15, 250
Sherrod Jones, 50, 390, 1500, 25, 140
Wm.Rutledge, 25, 156, 1000, 85, 290
Jane Spears, 35, 15, 150, 20, 150
Wm. Hamner, 150, 280, 2500, 120, 587
Wm. Nolly, 72, 149, 600, 15, 100
Wm. B. Houston, 30, 57, 500, 20, 480
Chas. Rutledge, 40, 60, 600, 75, 195
Wm. Baxter, 20, 30, 450, 60, 130
Wilson Loyd, 60, 46, 500, 95, 66

Geo. W. Randol, 20, 54, 50, 10, 130
N. A. West, 35, 215, 1250, 15, 175
Wm. Howard, 30, 160, 1000, 5, 70
W. C. Moore, 40, 60, 600, 60, 230
Theophilus Rodgers, 60, 150, 600, 60, 280
McGilvery Rodgers, 150, 300, 4000, 480, 310
Wesley Cole, 130, 267, 3500, 800, 740
Cullen Rodgers, 60, 140, 2500, 10, 345
John Gant, 60, 70, 1300, 105, 370
Wm. Owen, 67, 290, 2000, 55, 365
Wm. R. Wallace, 30, 70, 700, 10, 278
Wm. Ellis, -, -, -, 12, 60
Wm. Conn, 20, 30, 350, 5, 85
Hiram Wiles, 40, 40, 600, 56, 230
Saml. Goodman, -, -, -, 5, 80
Wm. Stovall, -, -, -, 130, 400
Robt. Allen, 140, 160, 3300, 200, 820
Benj. Gates, 48, 60, 500, 5, 50
Andrew Cox, 14, 76, 400, 5, 130
Thos. Yeats, 40, 60, 1000, 35, 190
P. C. Gilmore, 50, 55, 500, 60, 235
Geo. C. Patrick, 35, 125, 1280, 60, 277
Hugh Wilson, 80, 18, 500, 70, 260
Pulaski Arnola, 18, 32, 200, 10, 140
Howard Owen, 50, 135, 1000, 40, 300
Thos. Lowry (Livory), 22, 28, 250, 8, 190
Baxter Carter, 70, 76, 1500, 60, 170
Robt. Shother, 100, 250, 2500, 50, 265
Ezriah Denny, -, 250, 40, 215
Rob. M. Galloway, 230, 70, 3900, 128, 1085
John Wilson, 100, 230, 2500, 200, 600
Mathew Brown, 75, 75, 2000, 150, 315
Wm. P. Vaden, 312, 400, 5700, 500, 800
James Rafter, 385, 420, 8000, 900, 1790
Wm. T. Bettis, 116, 100, 1700, 240, 225
Vincent Bangus, 53, 200, 2500, 65, 200
Thos. Dismukes, 120, 800, 2400, 110, 345
Virginia Dismukes, Entered Previously, Entered Previously, Entered Previously, 4, 150
Middleton Black, -, -, -, 20, 255
Jno. A. Hays, 95, 105, 1800, 100, 300
W. H. Mitchel, 40, 60, 500, 5, 110
Uriah Keller, 30, 86, 250, 40, 355
Robt. Littlefield, 35, 165, 800, 5, 80
Wm. Thompson, 46, 26, 600, 110, 195
D. Faucett, 60, 240, 3500, 65, 100
Hardy Owen, 120, 459, 5790, 500, 690
Ed. W. Kenny, 450, 497, 12000, 1000, 2380
Benj. Carroll, -, -, -, 10, 40
A. J. Sanders, 20, 51, 500, 100, 285

J. W. Yeats, 275, 262, 6000, 200, 1200
Sam Yeats, 25, 65, 800, 25, 365
Paulina Sanders, 300, 170, 2000, 75, 340
Jonathan Albright, 42, 58, 1000, 50, 210
James Gwin, 125, 175, 3000, 70, 400
John Briley, 100, 185, 2000, 35, 400
Hardeman Abingdon, 500, 592, 10920, 700, 1585
Green Dees, -, -, -, 60, 250
_. J. McDonald, 40, 60, 800, 25, 300
Wm. A. Lowry, 60, 288, 3000, 500, 665
David Biggs, 200, 360, 5600, 500, 940
Jos. Edmundson, 100, 100, 1000, 150, 350
Ann H. Montgomery, 60, 70, 1250, 80, 405
A. C. Edmundson, 40, 160, 700, 60, 290
John Kelly, 76, 127, 1250, 25, 140
Lewis Revel, 30, 170, 800, 60, 300
Thos. Hunter, 50, 43, 1100, 550, 180
Jos. B. Lane, 26, -, 250, 60, 155
Wm. Bass, 30, 90, 1500, 20, 250
Redin Corbett, 30, 70, 800, 115, 550
J. W. Koen, 90, 26, 3460, 100, 675
Wm. Woodworth, 45, 55, 1000, 60, 300
Olsy B. Armor, 12, 88, 1000, 5, 100
Turner Woodle, Entered Previously, Entered Previously, Entered Previously, 8, 80
Joel E. Rhodes, 60, 100, 800, 90, 265
Thos. Mackey, 100, 60, 1600, 80, 540
James Walker, 40, 15, 500, 75, 65
S. H. Winford, 33, 41, 750, 20, 335
P. C. Halley, 50, 50, 1000, 80, 300
Wilford Sullivan, 80, 20, 1000, 65, 245
F. H. Berry, 25, 47, 720, 50, 155
James Hart, 52, 50, 1000, 70, 120
Jno. F. Boyet, 50, 110, 1920, 78, 170
W. T. Farley, 254, 466, 9000, 675, 920
J. E. Hendrick, 170, 150, 4000, 500, 750
T. B. Ellis, 110, 50, 1600, 100, 550
Jno. M. Fleming, 130, 70, 2000, 700, 1200
W. F. Farley, 320, 320, 6000, 600, -
C. Sullivan, 85, 35, 1200, 60, 305
J. C. P. Hammand, 400, 240, 6400, 555, 850
Nelson Ferrell, 110, 76, 1800, 150, 300
Wm. M. Warner, 140, 60, 2000, 100, 545
Evenezer Best, 130, 30, 1800, 400, 230
John Jarmon, 450, 450, 10000, 750, 1695
Sam Gilleland, 135, 345, 6000, 165, 1027
B. O. Watson, 200, 110, 5000, 870, 1175
Jesse Applewhite, 400, 240, 8000, 925, 915
Peter Baker, 25, 32, 600, 12, 135

Collin Person, 60, 37, 1000, 75, 475
W. H. Parker, 70, 41, 1000, 115, 270
Jesse T. Brown, 75, 70, 1200, 105, 443
Thos. Moore, 200, 75, 2437, 405, 960
Green Williams, 110, 157, 2670, 125, 765
Jno. W. Moreland, 275, 135, 5000, 700, 1285
W. W. Talley, 60, 100, 2250, 175, 390
Wm. Phillips, 45, 55, 1250, 75, 300
R. W. Smith, 300, 353, 10712, 578, 1060
John Applewhite, 215, 312, 6587, 625, 810
H. R. McSwine, 200, 320, 5200, 690, 1045
And. Tayloe, 850, 806, 20000, 1130, 1975
Chas. Davis, 70, 90, 2000, 200, 500
Alex G. Neal, 60, 100, 1250, 50, 195
John B. Beasley, 25, 55, 600, 6, 105
E. P. Strickland, 125, 195, 2200, 850, 815
Wm. Coopwood (Coopmoon), 500, 300, 8000, 680, 1600
Wm. Cannedy, 50, 110, 850, 60, 360
Alex F. McKenney, 500, 1300, 18000, 700, 1345
Benj. Jones, -, -, -, 40, 150
Wm. P.Kyle, -, -, -, 60, 625
Robt. S. Spencer, 150, 50, 2500, 610, 730
Danl. T. Edains, 125, 115, 3000, 110, 805
R. S. Flinn, 60, 100, 1000, 80, 375
Wm. Polk, 130, 510, 8000, 80, 900
Mos. Slough, 80, 20, 500, 90, 220
Edmond Harrison, 89, 200, 1500, 60, 420
Schuyler H. Roberts, 300, 336, 6000, 280, 1060
Thos. J. Trueheart, 400, 270, 6700, 110, 1275
Danl. Smith, 115, 85, 2500, 683, 595
Mathew Nevil, 120, 80, 4000, 750, 590
Jane Smith, 200, 100, 4000, 75, 560
Clotila_ Jay, 75, 25, 1000, 50, 190
John W. Vaughan, 70, 90, 2000, 125, 460
William Vaughan, -, -, -, 20, 225
Landon Harvey, 122, 100, 2400, 75, 580
Mary B. Trueheart, 300, 235, 6000, 600, 828
Benj. Baker(2 names written over with third), 250, 120, 5000, 705, 700
R. G. Miller, 74, 25, 1000, 20, 400
John W. Harrison, 150, 234, 3840, 100, 602
Thos. C. Blakely, 30, 17, 1000, 10, 300
Isaac Mitchell, 40, 10, 700, 25, 200
Joel H. Hall, 180, 150, 3300, 330, 690
Rolfe Eldridge, 200, 110, 3100, 330, 700
Randolph Webb, 103, 70, 2800, 100, 555

R. F. McClure, 25, 47, 500, 70, 50
R. McIver, 400, 400, 8000, 500, 125
Isaac Mendenhall, 40, 85, 900, 75, 460
Wesley Moore, 70, 260, 1400, 50, 350
Thos. Simpson, 50, 250, 1000, 60, 450
Britain Carr, 30, 170, 1200, 40, 120
Joseph Eckles, 50, 66, 1160, 50, 250
Henry Lee, 80, 81, 1612, 420, 200
Henry C. Massey, 160, 215, 4687, 450, 650
Elijah Brook, 220, 94, 3600, 800, 845
Margaret Suggs, 80, 67, 1470, 175, 580
Benj. Thompson, 810, 81, 1612, 25, 590
R. C. Ledbetter, 300, 300, 6000, 60, 2000
Jas. C. Anderson, 165, 168, 3000, 1000, 730
James Barber(Barker), Entered Previously, Entered Previously, Entered Previously, 30, 300
George Small, 100, 60, 1600, 125, 695
Wm. B. Burk, 115, 31, 1606, 125, 790
David Wilson, 130, 190, 3200, 75, 575
A. C. Stephenson, 300, 265, 5600, 540, 980
Stephen W. Rutland, 300, 180, 6000, 400, 1100
Wm. _. Dillard, 120, 30, 1800, 50, 340
Penny Harrison, 400, 360, 6020, 750, 1320
Willie M. Rutland, 65, 255, 3200, 30, 280
James D. Blackborn, 150, 170, 3000, 15, 175
Willis G. Eddins, 110, 50, 1920, 120, 580
John Gray, 86, 74, 500, 95, 430
Benj. Reid, 120, 40, 1600, 125, 755
Moses Neely, 250, 440, 6900, 715, 1055
T. W. Goodrich, 440, 200, 7000, 750, 1160
Richd. W. Tubberville, -, -, -, 18, 150
Addison Kelly, 65, 235, 1600, 85, 205
James Brooks, 120, 105, 2250, 100, 365
James Brooks, 60, 75, 1350, 5, 90
Arthor Matson(Masson), 60, 75, 1350, 40, 295
Wm. F. Hamlin, 460, 200, 6600, 700, 1300
Newton Ford, 400, 280, 6500, 650, 1050
J. J. Todd, 190, 84, 3400, 150, 1155
Thos. H. Todd, 140, 50, 400, 500, 790
Henry Jackson, 225, 151, 400, 225, 780
Britton Duke, 338, 375, 7110, 620, 1275
Frances Wright, 160, 1840, 20000, 150, 625
Sarah Walker, 240, 280, 4160, 420, 715
Nathanl Thompson, 100, 83, 2250, 155, 500

Benj. Mosby, -, -, -, 150, 680
James Hodges, 30, 36, 600, 10, 90
Wm. N. Morgan, 12, 10, 1750, 75, 215
Lovet (Loret) Fellow, 60, 100, 1120, 75, 450
John Wilson, 100, 100, 1000, 70, 495
John W. Stout, 125, 115, 3000, 78, 795
Job A. Lewis, 52, 51, 1545, 120, 375
James Kimbrough, 500, 724, 15000, 680, 1707
John Jackson, 125, 105, 2500, 50, 550
Elijah Webb, 65, 575, 6400, 120, 320
John B. Bettis, -, -, -, 60, 55
Wm. Carter, 350, 290, 6000, 750, 1425
W. W. Joice, 150, 231, 3800, 200, 300
Geo. W. Trueheart, 40, 10, 500, 50, 200
J. M. M. Cornelius, 130, 70, 2400, 80, 630
A. H. Lucken, 30, 15, 1000, 20, 178
John S. Dennis, 75, 43, 2000, 145, 450
Richd. Eldridge, 110, 90, 2000, 75, 300
Wm. C. Harrison, 300, 157, 5484, 725, 750
Joseph Brooks, 150, 470, 8000, 650, 285
John Harding, 125, 75, 2500, 500, 540
Thos. Rutherford, 60, 30, 1000, 40, 250
Wm. D. Vaper, 25, 192, 5, 110
Mary Melton, 21, 86, 400, 10, 75
Thos. Walsten, -, -, -, 5, 50
Geo. Vaper, 35, 65, 500, 45, 240
Robt. M. Allen, 75, 135, 2000, 150, 410
John Kesterson, 100, 220, 1500, 50, 365
Thos. J. Coybill, 200, 440, 640, 600, 990
Duncan McFadgen, 40, 20, 800, 15, 100
Arthur Callis, 91, 66, 1200, 15, 300
John P. Winford, 45, 55, 1000, 40, 300
Wm. Winford, -, -, -, 5, 100
Wm. Harrison, 80, 33, 800, 30, 130
Wm. Barnet, -, -, -, 5, 210
Thos. M. Moore, 120, 180, 2000, 100, 425
Allen Rutland, 320, 420, 7400, 690, 995
Benj. R. Ellis, 210, 110, 3000, 700, 1040
Arch A. Reid, 200, 120, 3200, 55, 460
Phillip McNeill, 300, 140, 4400, 65, 795
Henry Harrison, 160, 60, 2200, 580, 620
Wm. S. Williams, 400, 280, 8000, 260, 1340
Robt. G. Fellows, 55, 36, 1000, 148, 450
Wm. A. W. Maner (Mann), 300, 340, 4000, 700, 1120
Thos. J. Rodgers, 55, 10, 400, 30, 145
Wm. Darby, 560, 627, 12000, 485, 1858
Chars. F. Dandridge, 135, 185, 2800, 55, 550

J. C. Dougherty, 420, 220, 6500, 800, 1080
G. W. Cole, 250, 750, 10000, 200, 800
Saml. Roseboro, 180, 240, 5000, 200, 2100
F. A. Owen, 330, 357, 12000, 500, 1570
John K. Nelson, 200, 400, 4000, 120, 570
Lewis Featherson, 125, 55, 2160, 200, 450
Thos. Brownlee, 250, 70, 4000, 150, 525
Johna Lundy (could be John A. Lundy), 50, 50, 3000, 150, 400
Thos. Warren, 25, 55, 640, 40, 140
W. Howard, 450, 75, 8000, 600, 1245
N. Trezevant, 450, 224, 10000, 850, 1100
Joseph Mason, 40, 10, 5000, 50, 310
Jas. Titus, 75, 58, 2000, 100, 525
Newert Drew, -, -, -, 60, 175
Pauline Dunn & son, 575, 185, 9600, 335, 1387
John B. Todd, 130, 80, 4500, 150, 925
Saml. Gibbons, 300, 340, 12000, 810, 1570
Eppy White, 300, 200, 15000, 540, 1455
Wm. N. Kimball, 100, 420, 5000, 75, 620
Jas. R. Williams, 220, 260, 7680, 775, 1080
Eliz Epps, 40, 126, 1500, 55, 200
Wm. N. Gregory, 50, 148, 1000, 10, 325
Geo. Mccarty, 14, 36, 200, 5, 110
Wm. Davis, 70, 85, 3000, 175, 490
Benj. A. Hildebran, 300, 660, 10000, 230, 578
Jas. Epps, 230, 34, 4000, 820, 1350
Wm. Hutchins, 80, 80, 2000, 18, 150
N. Kennedy, -, -, -, 12, 210
Jas. T. Wilcox, 100, 170, 3375, 80, 450
Jas. O. Thweatt, 350, 278, 10000, 625, 935
John W. Elam, 400, 354, 15000, 700, 1130
B. S. Davis, 30, 50, 800, 100, 633
N. S. Palmer, 50, 150, 2000, 25, 130
Saml. H. Rodgers, 60, 100, 2400, 35, 450
Henry Holman, 60, 210, 2700, 115, 850
A. H. Herran, 400, 157, 5370, 800, 1715
Wm. P. Bradley, 200, 200, 4000, 100, 485
Jane Walker, 200, 444, 6440, 500, 915
Thos. Holman, 120, 480, 8000, 400, 595
Jas. S. Lemaster, 450, 415, 10810, 740, 1320
M. W. & J. Deadrik, 600, 460, 25000, 950, 2465
Geraldus Brintin, 775, 569, 25000, 750, 2050

Wm. Echols, 200, 212, 6180, 510, 1040
Math. Ragland, 350, 134, 7260, 450, 1120
D. S. Greer, 250, 488, 9222, 1350, 1117
Edward S. Elam, 135, 317, 4520, 100, 735
John F. Hamlin, 480, 360, 10000, 600, 1985
Daryl Pierson, 150, 206, 3560, 40, 475
W. & J. Norbert, 375, 265, 5400, 375
Ila Douglass, 150, 220, 3700, 550, 515
E. S. Simms, 60, 100, 1000, 75, 400
E. W. Mathews, 160, 160, 3200, 70, 420
John Lucket, 10, 80, 700, 30, 230
Hugh N. Steward, 60, 30, 900, 30, 235
Neaty C. Gallagher, 90, 70, 1500, 35, 295
E. A. Watson, 90, 70, 1500, 60, 300
Jery Williams, 70, 90, 1000, 236, 250
Thos. Alsabrook, 75, 85, 1200, 150, 535
J. Branaugh, 60, 100, 1200, 100, 258
N. W. Welbonner, 320, 160, 4800, 90, 1170
J. S. Welbonner, 100, 120, 1600, 140, 955
Isaac Welbonner, 80, 177, 2570, 80, 445
A. C. Welbonner, 274, 300, 6000, 528, 800
Wm. N. Allen, 190, 5, 1750, 30, 270
Felix Allen, 120, 100, 2500, 100, 600
Wm. Imes, same, same, same, 8, 80
Moses Grooms, 64, 86, 1500, 50, 265
Cath. Vance, 100, 60, 800, 50, 250
Robt. Holmes, 170, 150, 4000, 705, 780
J. H. Vanhook, 70, 250, 2500, 100, 380
T. Davis Est., 400, 240, 6400, 650, 1660
Licurgus Davis, -, -, -, -, 335
Nath. Hazlewood, 20, 60, 500, 5, 75
Josiah Cook, 25, 55, 500, 10, 135
N. Douglass, 90, 230, 3200, 78, 345
M. Waddell, -, -, -, 10, 225
Wm. Edmonson, 325, 175, 7500, 1280, 1210
John Watts, -, -, -, 8, 70
R. C. Edmonson, 70, 247, 4750, 135, 475
J. E. Felts, 80, 80, 2000, 500, 525
Geo. Vincint, Entered, Entered, -, 15, 160
Chas. Harris, Entered, Entered, -, 50, 310
Wm. B. Guing, 40, -, 500, 5, 100
Wm. Pittman, 350, 226, 15000, 500, 1200
H. D. Small, 20, -, 2500, 78, 200
Thos. Casner, 25, -, 3000, 100, 100
Arron Botts, 100, 100, 5000, 100, 430
S. D. Key, 250, 250, 1000, 200, 1200
E. P. Stewart, 6, -, 2500, 50, 225
H. N. Moon, 13, 6, 16000, 65, 260
Jas. L. Delaway, 50, 150, 8000, 150, 650
W. B.(R) Morris, 20, -, 1000, 100, 405

W. B. Miller, 12, 18, 3000, 30, 250
S. J. Lester, 4, 2, 600, 10, 140
Mich McName, 3, -, 2500, 150, 430
Joshua Watson, 5, 2, 500, 75, 220
Clayton Frazer, 19, -, 3000, 75, 240
Paulina Dunn, 130, 100, 1500, 50, 625
Wm. Neely, 7, -, 1500, 15, 70
E. D. Bray, 16, 10, 3000, 70, 169
Henry Pitt, 32, -, 800, 50, 250
M. B. Ragan, 25, 25, 3000, 100, 530
S. Rozell, 200, 285, 12000, 100, 880
Thos. N. Giles, 10, 30, 3000, 15, 400
T. Whitfield, 15, 5, 3000, 50, 400
Ed Bradshaw, 90, 122, 6360, 78, 530
Richd. Strickland, 9, -, 500, 10, 50
A. A. McKey, 13, -, 1500, 100, 350
Jas. C. Lewis, 4, -, -, 100, 175
Thos. P. Danerson, 12, -, 1500, 50, 166
Joseph White, 7, -, 4000, 78, 170
Jas. Robinson, 12, 8, 4000, 50, 400
E. W. M. King, 8, -, 4000, 30, 300
P. W. Porter, 12, -, 3000, 15, 85
Joseph Lenon, 16, -, 4000, 200, 450
M. S. Simms, 19, 10, 5000, 50, 140
Wm. Tanner, 4, -, 1000, 30, 15
John A. Wilson, 8, 4, 5000, 30, 400
L. W. Wren, 8, 3, 3000, 28, 100
J. T. Mitchell, 9, -, 900, 75, 125
J. M. Walker, 75, 77, 10000, 100, 350
S. R. Brown, 6, -, 6000, 75, 150
L. M. Williams, 18, -, 6000, 150, 250
Egbert Wo__rige, 4, -, 2500, 75, 840
Wm Gilbert, 62, 0-, 12000, 200, 546
Jas. H. Murray, 2, -, 2500, 50, 850
Silas Buck, 25, -, 5000, 50, 250
John Morrison, 30, 720, 7500, 100, 620
Mrs. Carr, 150, 376, 20000, 75, 500
John Trigg, 100, 280, 25000, 100, 1450
Chas. Lofland, 100, 250, 20000, 200, 600
John D. Plunkett, 130, 170, 4500, 1150, 870
Albert Madden, -, -, -, 150, 350
Lemuel Farrar, 300, 180, 8000, 700, 1810
Geo. W. Smith, 300, 180, 6000, 380, 1065
Chas. Isbell, 40, 105, 1000, 50, 255
John B. Holmes, 250, 343, 6000, 550, 850
Meredith Johnson, 100, 150, 3000, 85, 350
Abner C. Wilbourn, 100, 100, 2000, -, -
Wm. F. Baker, 400, 408, 12000, 275, 1325
A. N. Plunkett, 35, 189, 3000, 80, 210
Wm. M. Dunn, 460, 400, 17200, 950, 2120

Edward Mallory, 120, 100, 4000, 100, 605

Albert G. Blakemore, 50, 30, 2500, 80, 275

Wesley Bateman, 30, 130, 5000, 88, 1300

Micajah Mason, 88, 76, 2000, 120, 500

Morgan Vance, 250, 1650, 38000, 450, 2000

S. D. Irwin, 75, 85, 1250, 200, 600

Danl. Lake, 250, 123, 4000, 400, 1032

Levi Lourance, 105, 300, 2000, 128, 2085

Levi W. Lorance, 45, 755, 3200, 50, 650

Thos. G. Davis, 30, 70, 500, 100, 800

James Rodgers, 200, 400, 7200, 400, 1380

James Tweedle, 10, 55, 325, 75, 250

Daria Williams, 27, 173, 4000, 15, 920

Wm. Persons, 405, 1395, 15000, 500, 1500

Wm. Mitchell, 300, 980, 30000, 250, 1455

Jas. F. Batte, 80, 80, 1600, 50, 350

Jacob Glenn, -, -, -, 30, 100

John Arnola, 52, 72, 2480, 100, 325

Wm. Person, 400, 600, 5000, 128, 1200

D___ Johnson, 220, 180, 3000, 400, 1500

Wm. L. Lundy, 300, 282, 8000, 375, 2000

Alfred Eldridge, 400, 204, 7200, 240, 1279

A. A. Weatherall, 65, 148, 2500, 600, 600

Wm. P. Mathews, 58, 45, 900, 30, 210

John M. Hunt, 70, 95, 1650, 100, 300

Henry Thompson, 12, 148, 1000, 8, 60

Seth Wheatley, 480, 2110, 25600, 1400, 1500

Sneed Harris, 30, 130, 1500, 75, 250

Wm. R. Peoples, 165, 102, 2670, 300, 650

G. Brinlyod, 700, 260, 9600, 600, 2300

James Johnson, 80, 240, 4000, 78, 562

Joel Mays, 85, 75, 800, 50, 300

John W. Nelson, 300, 340, 1500, 1000, 1425

Mrs. Richd Person, 145, 575, 10000, 300, 1150

Frances M. White, 270, 370, 12000, 375, 1715

Thos. Newsom, 70, 110, 1000, 200, 300

Smith County TN
1850 Agricultural Census

The Agricultural Census for 1850 was filmed for the University of North Carolina from original records in the Tennessee State Library and Archives.

The following items represent categories below and separated by a comma: for example, John Doe, 25, 25, 10, 5, 100.

Column 1 Owner
Column 2 Acres of Improved Land
Column 3 Acres of Unimproved Land
Column 4 Cash Value of Farm
Column 5 Value of Farm Implements and Machinery
Column 13 Value of Livestock

The following symbol is used to maintain spacing where there are no numbers: (-) In addition, the left margin has been bound too close to the edge causing some first names or initials to not be completely visible.

Jefferson Jones, 40, 25, 300, 20, 485
Wm. W. Averett, -, -, -, -, 100
John W. Marriss, 14, 43, 100, 25, 136
John Fiviash, 12, 23, 350, 41, 91
Wm. Chandler, 45, 55, 300, 20, 250
Miles H. Biles, 50, 50, 200, 20, 398
William Grospine, 35, 65, 250, 8, 320
Thos. Clariday, -, -, -, 5, 67
Davis Marriss, -, -, -, 7, 131
Tiney Suet, 10, -, 150, 10, 202
Wm. M. Bells, -, -, -, -, 140
_____ Hawkins, -, -, -, -, 225
Silas Baram, -, -, -, 8, 104
Jas. M. Spain, 7, 77, 150, 400, 208
Elizabeth Bridges, 60, 54, 300, 20, 178
Matthew Mooningham, -, -, -, 2, -
Martha Tunstall, 30, 10, 150, 10, 44
Joel L. Flancers, -, -, -, 12, 370
Drusilla McAlister, 100, 250, 1200, 200, 684
Wm. F. McAlister, 60, 160, 720, 100, 485
Daniel H. Binford, -, -, -, 20, 128
Mary A. Massey, 30, 20, 50, 10, 197
Wm. W. Chambers, -, -, -, 25, 195
Hickerson Barksdale, 300, 612, 5000, 100, 990
Demsey Marris, -, -, -, 60, 109
Martin Fisher, -, -, -, 5, 65
Wm. Kelley, 40, 80, 100, 10, 75
Mathias Dice, -, -, -, -, -
Mary Fiviash, 25, 25, 75, 15, 260
John Hicks, 30, 100, 60, 15, 137

Robert Barton, 50, 77, 75, 50, 224
Benj. Burford, 1, -, 50, 10, 52
John W. Hughes, -, -, -, 10, 127
Agnes Penn, 70, 15, 75, 15, 235
Saml. Evetts, -, -, -, 5, 90
Moses Evetts, -, -, -, 5, 53
George Evetts, -, -, -, 20, 122
Jas. Filston, 25, 47, 30, 6, 99
John Dice, 18, 43, 50, 10, 156
Salaman Dice, 100, 200, 200, 499, 750
Elizabeth Dice, 80, 150, 100, 125, 435
Lucy Kelley, -, 65, 6, 5, 132
Samuel Burdine, 150, 330, 2000, 100, 950
Benjamin Javansaw, -, -, -, -, 16
James F. Seal, -, -, -, 1, 20
Henry Ward, 200, 100, 1600, 100, 1055
Nancy Spain, 50, 68, 500, 20, 370
Saml. Spring, -, -, -, 15, 187
James Devenport, -, -, -, 2, -
John Page, 100, 300, 1100, 100, 521
Elmore D. Page, -, -, -, 188, 420
Margaret Owens, 20, 173, 200, 300, 69
James Hawkins, -, -, -, 8, 117
Archibald Read, -, -, -, 200, 10
Green Bowens, -, -, -, 8, 147
B. E. Warren, 30, 20, 350, 30, 300
Sarah Marris, -, -, -, 2, 5
Wm. J. Rose, 18, 14, 150, 3, 119
George W. Rose, 30, 50, 150, 3, 119
Abraham Carmicle, 25, 75, 100, 50, 228
Anderson Woods, 20, 44, 200, 20, 139

James Clariday, -, -, -, 5, 42
Alfred Sary, -, -, -, 6, 67
John Rauls, 75, 175, 1500, 100, 540
Ed. M. North, 25, 40, 375, 10, 332
Wm. W. Reeves, -, -, -, 12, 26
T. M. Violett, -, -, -, 2, 9
Leed S. Halley, 40, 55, 350, 20, 151
George H. Day, -, -, -, 5, 50
Joseph Bishop, 40, 122, 400, 30, 300
Elizabeth Carmicle, -, -, -, 20, 12
Zachariah Hawkins, -, -, -, 10, 70
Charlotte Hawkins, -, -, -, 10, 100
Luke Ford, -, -, -, 15, 136
Martha Woods, -, -, -, 5, 12
John P. Norris, 50, 55, 500, 40, 410
Jane Norris, 35, 43, 250, 10, 252
Jefferson Link, 100, 100, 800, 100, 323
Drury Clariday, 60, 132, 800, 110, 618
Saloman Reed, -, -, -, 5, 81
Thos. W. Page, 120, 94, 1500, 78, 704
Miggett Cuterell, -, -, -, 15, 167
Harrell T. Rucks, 75, 107, 1460, 125, 590
Elizabeth Bradley, 75, 120, 750, 20, 336
Leroy Bradley, 90, 165, 1200, 50, 1600
Clinton Hooks, 10, 5, 100, 5, 88
Elizabeth Rucks, 300, 550, 1500, 50, 675
John H. Bates, -, -, -, 10, 170
Lewis Bickers, 30, 13, 200, 100, 263
O. S. Ewing, 35, 43, 400, 60, 63
J. M. Jones, -, -, -, 3, 363
Ellis Beasley, 11, 1, 550, 400, 1150
Berryman Turner, 80, 33, 600, 100, 474
Grandison Jumper, 3, 3, 25, 58, 157
Henry Page, 2, 4, 20, 75, 345
James Shelton, 300, 370, 3600, 200, 970
Tabitha Moore, 400, 200, 2500, 125, 1590
George Gaddy, 45, 62, 500, 10, 136
John R. Etheby, 150, 85, 2500, 85, 915
William Harris, 75, 12, 800, 95, 433
Benj. Cooksey, 50, 70, 500, 15, 272
Joseph Cooksey, 50, 140, 350, 6, 205
E. P. Haley, -, -, -, 7, 80
David McCall, 200, 60, 2500, 200, 860
Dorotha Owen, 5, 13, 40, 5, 10
James Gill, 150, 150, 1200, 75, 475
John Campsey, -, -, -, 10, 485
John Barbee, 140, 160, 2000, 250, 495
Wm. Federick, -, -, -, 1, 5
John Bankins, -, -, -, 5, 73
Ben. B. Smith, -, -, -, 15, 166
Nancy Armstrong, 50, 550, 1500, 10, 363
Mary E. McCall, 150, 750, 2445, 150, 676
John Mccall, 100, 383, 1000, 100, 1036
John D. Bass, 55, 70, 1100, 55, 294

Nancy Norris, 50, 90, 800, 20, 368
Richard Parker, -, -, -, 1, 60
Ed. Harrison, 90, 100, 1000, 60, 477
John M. Jones, -, -, -, 10, 120
James Thomason, -, -, -, -, 40
John J. Worthy, -, -, -, 3, 650
Mariah Wilson, 30, 10, 300, 5, 185
Saml. Bickers, 15, 30, 300, 150, 446
James C. Crutcher, -, -, -, 4, 310
John Hauk, -, -, -, 1, 6
Geo. Satterfield, 1, -, 200, 1, -
John Roe, 50, 110, 100, 50, 455
Wm. M. Price, 40, 60, 400, 35, 261
Thos. A. Flippin, 75, 155, 900, 150, 464
Frances Flippin, -, -, -, 10, 174
Thos. Bridges, 100, 100, 600, 150, 800
Elizabeth Douglass, -, -, -, 1, -
John D. Hazzard, 50, 500, 400, 50, 300
Ira B. Purnell, 45, 55, 700, 30, 242
John Kittle, -, -, -, 5, 21
Thos Kirmey (Kinney), 45, 60, 300, 50, 401
Anna Carpenter, 45, 60, 300, 50, 401
Sander Halley, 100, 130, 1000, 75, 555
Joseph Bridges, 36, 70, 400, 50, 213
Pleasant Douglas, -, -, -, 5, 36
Robt. Kinny, 70, 275, 1000, 100, 390
Francis Hale, -, -, -, 2, 10
Wm. Kittle, -, 8, -, 7, 130
Wm. Reaves, 50, 148, 900, 25, 293
Calvin Arrington, -, -, -, 7, 116
James Read, -, -, -, 7, 94
Albert Arrington, 30, 50, 300, 8, 138
Thos. Arrington, -, -, -, 5, 77
Joshua Wilson, 30, 34, 350, 100, 298
Mary Owens, 40, 180, 400, 15, 143
Saml. Owens, -, -, -, 7, 150
Thos. G. Litchford, -, -, -, 75, 207
John W. Redman, -, -, -, 18, 217
Benj. Redman, -, -, -, 2, 21
Eunice Payne, 200, 400, 3000, 40, 632
Joseph Payne, 125, 102, 1700, 125, 882
Henry Carpenter, -, -, -, 10, 155
W. C. Roe, 100, 600, 1500, 150, 645
James Rawland, 115, 75, 1000, 125, 645
Eliza J. Payne, 60, 140, 700, 75, 538
Lavell Carter, 40, 600, 150, 8, 178
Wm. Hickman, -, -, -, 5, 31
Pleasant Roberts, -, -, -, 6, 107
Newton Payne, 50, 80, 400, 50, 533
John T. Violett, -, -, -, 5, 68
Mille Muckluoy, -, -, -, 2, 9
Thos. Wooton, 200, 110, 2500, 200, 1350
Thos. A. Frohawk, -, -, -, 10, 150
Thos. Hale, 60, 30, 300, 65, 301
John P. Carter, 100, 125, 1000, 500, 573

John Stewart, 75, 120, 1200, 60, 856
Milton Whitsett, -, -, -, 10, 215
John Thomas, -, -, -, 5, 25
Harris Alliner, 150, 116, 1000, 75, 695
Henry Sadler, 30, 20, 200, 30, 210
Benjamin Wooton, 30, 50, 400, 70, 428
Orville Greene, 100, 150, 1200, 300, 643
Wm. B. Denton, 63, 137, 800, 10, 420
Chapman Violett, 30, 50, 300, 30, 255
Willis Wilson, 45, 41, 350, 78, 312
Eunice Pope, 40, 42, 300, 10, 224
Robt. W. Denton, 60, 30, 500, 175, 540
Elizabeth A.(H) Denton, 40, 50, 200, 80, 386
David A. Tyree, 30, 35, 20, 45, 216
Kiziah Pope, 20, 33, 50, 5, 130
Matthew Carley, 20, 36, 250, 30, 317
Lucinda Selfs, 30, 20, 150, 1, 67
Calvin Pope, 35, 65, 300, 10, 175
Wm. P. Douglass, 60, 105, 1000, 1200, 205
David Palmer, 75, 75, 900, 50, 516
Geo. W. Catran, -, -, -, 1500, 150
Soloman McGee, 60, 164, 400, 18, 287
Bryant Ward, 350, 625, 3000, 200, 1800
Lydia Hughes, 80, 40, 1600, 85, 631
Edwin Thompson, -, -, -, 20, 200
Johnson Undersood, 11, -, 300, 6, 456
C. W. Ferguson, -, -, -, 3, 180
Thos. S. Violett, -, -, -, 8, 96
Martha Hare, -, -, -, 8, 119
John Gan, 100, 50, 1500, 290, 1159
Nelson Cissism, -, -, -, 3, 26
Stewart Montgomery, 70, 60, 50, 105, 518
Saml. P. Williams, 40, 35, 450, 300, 200
John Williams, 25, 63, 250, 10, 100
Milton Montgomery, -, -, -, 1, 75
Wm. Gann, 50, 150, 300, 15, 361
Tilman B.Flippin, 100, 100, 1000, 140, 650
Right Rigsby, -, -, -, 15, 85
Enoch Gann, 65, 90, 900, 175, 495
Harvy D. Wilson, 35, 65, 300, 10, 316
E. I. Williams, 60, 65, 900, 30, 416
Edard Hicks, -, -, -, 5, 82
Jesse W. Hicks, -, -, -, 5, 78
Ezekiel Hicks, -, -, -, 7, 95
James Craig, 25, 75, 200, 30, 249
John Enochs, 40, 70, 400, 22, 300
Elizabeth Hires, 50, 50, 350, 10, 230
Henry Hires, 30, 70, 400, 10, 230
Wm. Everett, 25, 25, 112, 10, 170
Thos. Morefield, -, -, -, 5, 38
Wm. Woods, -, -, -, 3, 30
Sarah Cunningham, 30, 50, 300, 10, 100

John Litchford, -, -, -, 3, 96
John Hasten, -, -, -, 12, 240
Joseph W. Hare, -, -, -, 5, 59
Robert Hasten, -, -, -, 5, 80
Jas. Morefield, -, -, -, 5, 375
Frances Litchford, 25, 60, 250, 5, 230
Moses Eastes, 59, 147, 1000, 60, 694
Thos. Tolbert, 6, 9, 60, 10, 83
Benj. Tolbert, -, -, -, 10, 80
Reese Enochs, 25, 25, 250, 40, 454
Aziah Griffin, 40, 95, 400, 20, 317
Elizabeth Bell, 50, 87, 500, 15, 310
Jas. M. Motes, -, -, -, 5, 85
John W. Motes, 75, 125, 750, 25, 465
John Smith, -, -, -, 1, 12
John Reeves, 70, 70, 700, 130, 675
Mathew Ward, 100, 300, 700, 25, 615
James Barnett, 100, 200, 800, 70, 539
John Hale, 35, 315, 700, 90, 326
Saml. H. Wilson, 35, 120, 600, 25, 550
Joel F. Preston, 25, 36, 300, 8, 247
Wm. G. Jennings, -, -, -, 10, 130
Ewing Harris, -, -, -, 12, 126
Geo. W. Williams, 80, 398, 650, 80, 490
Henry Williams, 50, 75, 500, 100, 302
Christiana Baines, 45, 120, 800, 10, 263
Alfred L. Bains, 45, 120, 800, 110, 230
Lewis (Louise) Liles, -, -, -, 5, 23
Jane Harper, 45, 180, 300, 65, 283
Wm. C. Minton, -, -, -, 4, 78
John O. Pope, 80, 60, 700, 130, 478
Thos. Williams, 35, 35, 300, 35, 180
Elbridge Mercer, -, -, -, 5, 94
Robt. Gann, 200, 150, 200, 20, 471
Jefferson Brasher, 35, 35, 250, 5, 132
Elisha Daugherty, -, -, -, 10, 26
Alexr. Rigsby, -, -, -, 5, 129
A. H. Ross, 50, 50, 500, 50, 1188
Jas. W. Grissim, 200, 150, 4500, 255, 3160
Reuben G. Hays, -, -, -, 10, 125
Washington McGee, -, -, -, 5, 73
Jas. W. Denton, 75, 325, 800, 50, 500
Mary A. Rauntree, -, -, -, 5, 46
Keren H. Haynes, 12, 13, 275, 60, 284
Eliza Carl, 20, 20, 500, 60, 445
Elizabeth Green (Greer), -, -, -, 3, 55
James Williams, 35, 60, 250, 12, 245
Margaret Wilson, 100, 125, 1000, 40, 400
John F. Farmer, -, -, -, 10, 167
James Barrett, 285, 365, 2500, 135, 920
John Denney, -, -, -, 10, 238
Mary Alliver, 55, 60, 500, 40, 471
Johnathan H. Gallick, 100, 300, 500, 200, 504
Joseph Smith, -, -, -, 1, 2

Ann Neeley, -, -, -, 1, 45

A. J. Maran, 16, 25, 150, 10, 240

Thos. J. Slaughter, 80, 130, 700, 30, 371

Richard Gray, 40, 70, 300, 18, 316

John Green (Greer), 16, 60, 200, 7, 122

Alex Bray, -, -, -, 5, 3

Anderson Paschal, 60, 60, 600, 25, 350

John Squires, -, 73, -, 5, 80

Meredith Ballinger, -, -, -, 5, 168

John D. Bradley, 50, 70, 400, 40, 303

Jesse Pope, -, -, -, 5, 91

L. B. Cheak, 25, 105, 50, 10, 219

Vincent Bradford, 70, 170, 1100, 47, 540

George Glass, 20, 34, 100, 12, 197

Wm. Baker, 65, 110, 600, 55, 318

Jas. R. Dickerson, -, -, -, -, 20

Josiah Baze, -, -, -, 10, 86

Danl. Wilkerson, 50, 60, 400, 35, 420

Stephen Barrett Sr. 12, 35, 150, 5, 127

Stephen Barrett Jr., -, -, -, 4, 47

Thos. Ballinger, -, -, -, 5, 350

Van Herrald, -, -, -, 5, 80

Martha Douglass, 50, 50, 300, 15, 300

Edmond Hasking, -, -, -, 5, 38

Martin Waggoner, 50, 56, 300, 10, 140

Thos. A. Clark, -, -, -, 5, 145

Campbell Crutchfield, 200, 250, 2000, 60, 878

Elizabeth Crutchfield, 180, 178, 1000, 50, 285

Thos. Crutchfield, -, -, -, 5, 916

Mary Baker, 4, 120, 300, 5, 160

Caswell Brown, -, -, -, 10, 96

David Brown, 20, 39, 200, 5, 58

Alex. McCowen, -, -, -, 10, 175

Wm. Taylor, -, -, -, 10, 40

Adam McCowen, -, -, -, 3,104

Edmond Carley, 30, 120, 400, 35, 292

Wm. Carley, -, -, -, 10, 104

George Waggoner, 45, 80, 500, 45, 402

James Risen(Riser), 35, 40, 150, 10, 204

Benj. P. Tyree, -, -, -, 10, 107

Hezekiah Stallings, 75, 80, 400, 35, 315

James Tyree, -, -, -, 6, 18

David Hodges, -, -, -, 6, 18

Thos. Butler, -, -, -, 5, 111

Wm. Bandy, -, -, -, -, -

John Owens, 50, 57, 600, 10, 233

Wm. Denney, 150, 150, 2500, 100, 1572

Elizabeth Neeley, 135, 250, 850, 100, 785

Aaron Ward, -, -, -, 10, 201

Tennessee Alman, 30, 20, 300, 30, 140

Christopher Balkman, 30, 20, 300, 10, 435

David M. Bradford, 45, 120, 600, 35, 575

Martin J. Everett, -, -, -, 10, 143

Anthony Heilmanteler, 25, 15, 150, 14, 90

Rebecca Nowlen, 25, 50, 350, 10, 225

Asa Nowlen, -, -, -, 5, 112

Wm. Carter, -, -, -, 1, 12

Elizabeth Grier, -, -, -, -, 11

Benj. Grier, -, -, -, 2, 17

John Tweedwell, -, -, -, 2, 10

Wm W. Heutcheson, -, -, -, 5, 10

John R. Moore, -, -, -, 150, 415

Elizabeth Moore, 175, 725, 2000, 80, 530

Thos. Gill, 60, 108, 500, 50, 480

Ammon Hause(House), 40, 50, 250, 5, 343

Enoch Rollings, 80, 25, 500, 80, 1000

John Manning, 40, 90, 250, 12, 215

Francis Hefflin, -, -, -, 1, 47

Wyley Denney, 30, 120, 300, 100, 474

John Bray, 20, 8, 100, 10, 165

Matthew Denney, 15, 30, 200, 10, 118

Wm. Mannin, -, -, -, 5, 150

Alex. Andrews, -, -, -, 1, -

Nancy Carley, 20, 80, 200, 60, 225

Rebecca Nowlin, -, -, -, 10, 175

Willis McClinahan, 50, 58, 250, 57, 275

James Rollings, 70, 30, 250, 5, 174

Sarah Mercer, -, -, -, 5, 35

Agnes Hause (House), 130, 200, 1000, 45, 245

Jesse Brumley, -, -, -, -, 20

Warner Lambreth, 124, 29, 1000, 110, 460

Eli Shy, 75, 75, 800, 60, 1160

Benj. Atwood, -, -, -, 10, 162

S. B. Hankins, 10, 10, 150, 25, 35

Rowlon W. Newby, 80, 120, 1200, 150, 1165

Jas. Cooksey, 35, 40, 400, 4, 335

Whaley Newby, 20, 30, 175, 3, 90

Nancy Newby, 150, 350, 1200, 115, 2215

John _. Jenkins, 50, 30, 300, 20, 156

Joel T. Shepherd, -, -, -, 3, -

Michael Sary, 10, 10, 100, 10, 116

Benj. Payne, -, -, -, 10, 270

Thos. F. Maran, -, -, -, 90, 317

Jeremiah Hubbard, 64, 12, 500, 12, 160

Daniel Seay, 200, 472, 3000, 150, 2186

Elizabeth Hearn, 70, 130, 1000, 78, 557

George F. Cook, 100, 100, 2000, 3065, 745

Jas. Shepherd, -, -, -, 2, 80

John Gholston, -, -, -, 60, 578

Elizabeth Federick, -, -, -, 5, 10

Ambrose Owen, -, -, -, -, 12

Timothy W. Hankins, -, -, -, 80, 214

Catharine Smith, 32, 17, 200, 15, 221

John R. Rollings, 120, 700, 240, 50, 1120
John Brumley, -, -, -, 5, 10
Wm. Phibbs, -, -, -, 2, 10
Drury Phibbs, -, -, -, 5, 79
John W. Fry, 10, 30, 150, 10, 109
Jas E. Fry, -, -, -, 10, 138
Frances P. Gill, 45, 95, 500, 85, 215
Mary Barnett, -, -, -, 5, 175
Saml. Paschal, 125, 145, 1875, 176, 555
Richard Nowlen, -, -, -, 100, 251
Geo. F. Carpenter, 200, 201, 2300, 200, 1825
Peter Hubbard, 150, 50, 300, 100, 814
Wm. Garrett, 35, 10, 200, 40, 132
John Hause, 70, 200, 1000, 45, 384
Martin Hughes, -, -, -, 11, 47
John Stephens, 140, 420, 1650, 163, 1580
Martin Fulks, 40, 140, 600, 45, 660
Champin Thomas, -, -, -, 10, 218
Edmund James, 50, 122, 500, 40, 360
Edmund James, -, -, -, 23, 119
David C. Averett, 50, 186, 300, 150, 565
Judah Clariday, -, -, -, -, 20
David Whilly, -, -, -, 5, 20
M. D. Mason, 60, 80, 600, 40, 380
James Tuggle, -, -, -, 5, 50
Elizabeth Baze, 15, 50, 250, 16, 260
Abraham Taylor, -, -, -, 5, 45
Martha Tuggle, 30, 70, 250, 5, 113
Tempey Whitley, 50, 175, 400, 30, 217
James Clariday, -, -, -, 7, 177
Jane Liggan, 8, 75, 75, 5, 43
Wm. Samson, 20, 30, 100, 5, 80
James Stallins, 30, 70, 200, 20, 235
Eliza Baze, 5, 45, 50, 5, 145
Elizabeth Paty, 16, 80, 100, 5, 20
James Paty, 15, 20, 75, 5, 75
Sarah Whitley, -, -, -, 5, 15
Wm. Hopkins, -, -, -, 5, 50
Wm. Dennis, -, -, -, 10, 140
Jesse B. Andrews, 70,38, 800, 45, 355
Thos. Liggan, 50, 90, 500, 140, 225
Joel Minton, 10, 5, 100, 5, 160
Reuben Braswell, 30, 20, 200, 40, 310
Jacob Waggoner, 40, 60, 500, 40, 325
Saml. D. Hughes, -, -, -, 5, 35
David P. Hodges, -, 10, -, 40, 411
Richard Hodges, 60, 120, 700, 30, 438
Douglass Violett, -, -, -, 5, 135
John Dowdy, -, -, -, 2, 5
Lucy Bartley, ½, -, 200, -, -
Daniel Ramack, -, -, -, 10, 150
Andrew J. Sary, -, -, -, 10, 155
James C. Sanders, 200, 400, 2000, 475, 433
Wm. Jackson, -, -, -, 15, 50

Lucinda Jones, -, -, -, 1, -
Jonathan H. Smith, 10, 45, 150, 50, 225
John R. Smith, -, -, -, 5, 60
James Galaspie, -, -, -, 5, 180
Susan Thompson, 55, 47, 550, 40, 569
John O. Paty, -, -, -, 10, 140
Margaret Gibbs, -, -, -, 10, 120
Americas Bolton (Balton, Botton), -, -, -, 78, 400
Chas. Bolton, 100, 100, 1000, 35, 627
Joseph T. Armsted, -, -, -, 5, 197
Jas. Balton, -, -, -, 4, 101
Chas. Balton, -, -, -, 5, 130
John Lyon, -, -, -, 5, 36
Chas. Thompson, 80, 100, 600, 75, 423
M. Grasity, -, -, -, 10, -
David Black, 40, 10, 400, 28, 245
Wm. Hunt, -, -, -, 5, 123
John Jones, -, -, -, 5, 115
Henry Gibbs, -, -, -, 25, 180
Vincent Thompson, 75, 125, 700, 50, 470
James Balton, 100, 190, 1000, 20, 416
Wyley McKinney, 30, 70, 200, 5, 75
Wm. Lack, -, -, -, 5, 85
Wm. Dawson, 40, 80, 400, 100, 332
Bartlett B. Hughes, 10, 20, 50, 10, 200
Wm. McKinney, 1, 1, 50, 10, 200
Wm. Hodges, -, -, -, 10, 60
Mary Butler, 25, 95, 300, 25, 188
John Jones, -, -, -, -, -
David Baze(Boze), -, -, -, -, 5, 20
Jefferson E. Baran, 35, 32, 500, 50, 231
Sabra Minton, 0, 10, 200, -, 45
John Marris (Morris), 5, 96, 100, 10, 85
Matthew W. Morris, -, -, -, -, 20
Sarah Taylor (Gaylor), -, -, -, 1, -
Wm. H. Tyree, 10, 45, 150, 10, 75
Elizabeth Carter, 10, 52, 150, 5, 65
Mahala Minton, 16, 45, 200, 5, 80
John Gibbs, -, -, -, 20, 61
Wm. Farley, 45, 155, 600, 10, 297
John Smart, 50, 130, 700, 120, 245
Richard Baze, -, -, -, 10, 60
James Skelton, 50, 70, 500, 20, 270
Andrew Williby, 20, 56, 150, 5, 25
Wm. Snarday, 40, 40, 200, 10, 193
James H. Liggan, 35, 50, 300, 25, 300
Wesley James, -, -, -, 5, 43
James M. Wilkerson, 30, 25, 250, 1, 180
Coleman C. Liggan, -, -, -, 5, 70
Joel Bates, -, -, -, 10, 50
John Bates, -, -, -, 8, 70
Stephen R. Samson, 20, 110, 100, 10, 110
Lawson Allen, 35, 98, 300, 13, 148
John Clariday, -, -, -, 3, 80
Burton Allen, -, -, -, 5, 138

Coleman Samson, 100, 100, 1000, 4, 470
John McGee, 30, 100, 70, 30, 475
Wm. B. Whitley, 125, 271, 1500, 140, 804
N. W. Farat, -, -, -, 5, 50
Geo. W McGee, 25, 25, 400, 30, 261
A. J. Baker, 25, 40, 100, 5, 78
Daniel Parham, -, -, -, 3, 108
George Barker, 50, 130, 500, 105, 430
John Wells, 20, 20, 145, 10, 105
Charles Paty, 35, 60, 250, 30, 255
Rufus P. Goss, -, -, -, -, 20
Henry J. Cockram, 50, 70, 500, 38, 278
Berry Coleman, 25, 12, 350, 10, 210
Yerby Orange, 40, 10, 400, 10, 315
Evan Raglin, -, -, -, -, 50
Diggs W. Thomas, 70, 90, 800, 131, 375
John D. Owen, 140, 130, 2500, 250, 2000
Matthew Harper, -, -, -, 10, 135
Alfred Harper, -, -, -, 10, 325
Sarah Harper, 80, 270, 1500, 50, 475
Ira W. King, -, -, -, 10, 180
Wm. Allen, 400, 950, 5000, 150, 1560
Wm. R. Betey, 150, 225, 2000, 30, 1200
James Sadler, 75, 125, 1000, 150, 775
Peter Parten, -, -, -, 10, 210
Holly Ward, 50, 130, 1000, 40, 500
John A. Farmer, -, -, -, 40, 95
Joseph Carter, -, -, -, 1, -
Pleasant Gold, 180, 200, 1500, 100, 695
James Williams, -, -, -, 5, 100
Mary Winfrey, 100, 150, 500, 20, 350
Daniel Bailey, -, -, -, -, 12
Jonathan W. Agee, 25, 50, 200, 28, 176
Jonathan Agee, 50, 84, 250, 12, 120
Danl. B. Agee, -, -, -, 5, 102
Judea Cocks, 15, 30, 75, 5, 255
Abraham Cocks, -, -, -, 5, 75
Ephraim Agee, 100, 180, 1000, 150, 660
Wm. D. Agee, -, -, -, 10, 168
Wm. Oakley, 40, 81, 250, 30, 251
Nicholas Oakley, -, -, -, 5, 95
David Davis, 60, 60, 500, 20, 380
Jethin Durham, 40, 60, 500, 125, 585
Wm. McClaine, 120, 300, 1500, 200, 1100
John Buckner, 45, 141, 300, 40, 313
John R. James, 100, 340, 1000, 75, 1195
Soloman Thomas, -, -, -, 10, 131
Jane Durham, 50, 58, 500, 40, 232
Carder Stone, 50, 87, 1000, 30, 525
R. D. Allison, 100, 200, 1000, 30,650
Hiram Patterson, 70, 70, 500, 55, 689
S. D. Early, -, -, -, 2, 135
James Manners, 40, 60, 200, 25, 275
Jackson Gilliam, -, -, -, 1, 3

Wesley Hilmentaler, -, -, -, 1, 15
Geo. Clemmans, 30, 40, 100, 30, 180
Wm. W.Washbourn, 60, 65, 600, 100, 419
Stephen Nawlin, 95, 43, 1200, 65, 270
John Madison, -, -, -, 2, 10
Martha Coffee, 50, 25, 300, 10, 138
John Lamberson, 40, 85, 600, 50, 368
Alex. Hilmentaler, -, -, -, 5, 130
W. W. Lock, -, -, -, 5, 153
Wm. Clifton, -, -, -, 5, 12
Ira B. Cowen, 100, 125, 1500, 50, 817
Carnwell Pepper, -, -, -, 1, 12
James Stewart, 30, 70, 150, 45, 145
James W. Stewart, 20, 80, 60, 5, 210
Mathew Petteris, -, -, -, 10, 140
Jas. W. Petteris, 30, 475, 300, 10, 60
Jas. Eskew, -, -, -, 5, 30
H. B. McDonald, 350, 730, 8000, 300, 2650
Saml. L. Bailiff, -, -, -, 10, 395
Thos. Bailiff, 25, 240, 400, 200, 160
Susan Harris, -, -, -, -, 10
H. C. Jones, 5, 40, 50, 5, 35
J. A. Duncan, -, -, -, 5, 25
Charlott Clements, 15, 35, 100, 5, 244
Lavel Hefflin, 65, 85, 350, 40, 437
Jas. Arendel, -, -, -, 5, 60
Wm. Hefflin, 30, 15, 100, 10, 288
Willis M. White, 28, 72, 200, 10, 255
H. H. Collier, 12, 50, 75, 25, 195
Lucretia Calia, 15, 85, 75, -, 39
John A. Paschal, -, -, -, 30, 48
Francis Manners, -, -, -, 3, 16
Hawkins Heflin, 125, 412, 1200, 35, 745
John Read, -, -, -, 8, 95
Burket Davis, -, -, -, 5, 77
Thos. Scudder, 8, 42, 75, 5, 106
John Mannin, -, -, -, 5, 25
Thos. C. Marchbanks, 200, 1200, 3000, 300, 1175
Thos. Apple, -, -, -, 5, 50
Allen Manners, -, -, -, 2, 10
Michael Manners, -, -, -, 2, 45
Wm. Heflin, -, -, -, -, 3
Major L. Sikes, -, -, -, 10, 52
Michael Manners, -, -, -, 2, 10
Thos. Howard, -, -, -, 2, 10
Alexr. Brown, -, -, -, 2, 86
Ellender Brazzell, -, -, -, -, 20
Thos. Lancaster, 527, 873, 6000, 130, 2750
Wm. Lancaster, 80, 120, 800, 85, 1000
Michael Lancaster, -, -, -, 5, 980
Wm. E. Walden, -, -, -, -, 90
Wm. Brazzell, -, -, -, 5, 177

Geo. Carter, 50, 150, 150, 40, 247
John Harrison, -, -, -, 5, 69
A. M. Bettey, 55, 200, 800, 100, 645
Martha Palmer, 30, 60, 300, 60, 355
Elizabeth Hogan, 100, 200, 1500, 100, 646
Sarah Shares (Shores), -, -, -, -, 18
Hannible McDonald, -, -, -, 10, 40
Sarah McDonald, -, -, -, 6, 30
Sarah Adams, -, -, -, 5, 50
Israel Bush, -, -, -, 5, 100
Chas. Harris, -, -, -, 5, 70
Philip Sadler, 40, 100, 600, 160, 670
Elizabeth Moss, 15, 35, 150, 50, 100
John A. Moss, 40, 50, 500, 50, 325
Uriah Walden, -, -, -, 5, 12
Jas. Alcam, -, -, -, 5, 80
Thos. Lancaster, -, -, -, 100, 3900
John G. Nollen (Nolluer), -, -, -, 15, 150
John H. Nallman, 18, 78, 150, -, 75
John Simpson, 50, 400, 600, 25, 415
John Thomas, -, -, -, 5, 90
James Denney, -, -, -, 5, 125
Peter Webster, -, -, -, 2, -
George Fisher, 20, 130, 100, 4, 300
Joshua Coffee, -, -, -, 8, 230
Thos. Fisher, 80, 320, 1000, 50, 405
R. H. Fisher, -, -, -, 5, 140
G. W. Close, 10, 20, 200, 50, 168
Sarah Lamberson, 100, 150, 1500, 40, 325
Stephen Hickman, 20, 100, 150, 5, 140
John T. Stokes, 400, 673, 3500, 200, 1700
E. W. Hale, -, 200, -, 40, 175
Jas. H. Corder, -, -, -, 5, 62
B. F. Butler, -, -, -, 5, 90
Henry Robertson, -, -, -, 10, 175
Silas Kelley, 10, 212, 150, 8, 152
Jackson Prentice, -, -, -, -, 20
Randolph Lewis, -, -, -, 10, 50
Sandy Tittis, 75, 325, 500, 75, 537
Richard Pepper, 3, 40, 15, 5, 15
Benj. Christian, -, -, -, 5, 65
John Starnes, 20, 130, 100, 10, 125
Federick Starnes, 45, 130, 400, 10, 262
John Tittis, 25, 75, 150, 5, 89
Bennet Brazzell, 50, 125, 500, 25, 445
Jesse Mcbride, -, -, -, 5, 57
Henry Starnes, 40, 160, 300, 25, 230
Jefferson Williams, -, -, -, 5, 40
Susan McGinnis, -, -, -, 5, 150
Chas. Starnes, 45, 55, 300, 10, 295
JohnWilliams, 20, 30, 150, 10, 208
Cornelius Mires, -, -, -, 5, 50
Wm. Jones, 50, 75, 500, 25, 245
Wm. Kelley, -, -, -, 5, 205

Wm. Kelley, -, -, -, 4, 215
Mary Kelley, -, -, -, 50, 495
James Bates, 80, 370, 600, 10, 175
John Coggins, -, -, -, -, 10
Thos. Clackston(Clarkston), -, -, -, -, 30
George P. Kelley, 60, 140, 300, 3, 185
Wm. P. Kelley, -, -, -, 30, 270
Isaac Bates, 250, 550, 2000, 55, 930
Saml. Brent, -, -, -, 5, 40
James Fletcher, -, -, -, 5, 2
Thos. Bailiff, 80, 60, 1000, 70, 319
A. M. C. Robertson, -, -, -, 4, 93
Martha Plunket, -, -, -, 5, 222
Joseph Baughn, -, -, -, 3, 40
Trissa Bates, -, -, -, 5, 55
Matthew Scudders, 12, 120, 150, 10, 225
Joseph Bates, 45, 60, 200, 30, 250
Saml. Mclane, -, -, -, 5, 100
Elizabeth Vake, -, -, -, 2, 20
Walter Gunter, -, -, -, 5, 80
Wm. H. Christian, 40, 60, 400, 40, 375
Ann Sullivan, 150, 400, 2000, 150, 858
John Carley, 125, 175, 1500, 20, 938
Stephen Carley, -, -, -, 5, 20
Martha Williams, -, -, -, 3, 35
Nathan Cartey(Carley), 30, 70, 200, 5, 20
John Willis, -, -, -, 5, 50
Jackson Malone, 80, 80, 500, 28, 304
J. H. Freemont, 140, 250, 1500, 50, 441
A. J. Jackson, -, -, -, 25, 265
Daniel Driver, 80, 120, 600, 50, 380
Thos. Driver, -, -, -, 10, 225
Francis Tubbs, 25, 75, 300, 10, 220
James Winfrey, 60, 70, 500, 40, 400
Hardin Hardcastle, -, -, -, 5, 130
Josiah Inge, 15, 34, 200, 5, 68
Artiminson Pullun(Puller), -, -, -, -, 13
D. H. Fanner, 10, 40, 150, 153, 110
J. C. Fisher, 45, 40, 300, 40, 217
Rebecca Fisher, -, -, -, -, 10
Jonathan Dedman, 45, 40, 400, 85, 618
Thos. Washer, 60, 190, 700, 20, 330
Thos. B. Eskew, 150, 295, 1000, 10, 270
Spencer Webster, 40, 60, 300, 10, 305
Susan Wesbter, -, -, -, 10, 135
B. H. Akins, -, -, -, 10, 255
Pharis Wilson, -, -, -, 5, 60
Saml. Simson, -, -, -, 5, 100
James Cable, -, -, -, 5, 100
Elvina Fauch, -, -, -, 3, 10
Richard Roberts, -, -, -, 3, 12
Jasper Eaton, 20, 50, 100, 5, 110
Saml. Oakly, 50, 80, 300, 10, 285
Ann Hall, 8, 12, 180, 5, 238
Cintha Armminett, 35, 25, 300, 5, 250
John Debdu_n, 60, 80, 300, 12, 410

James Pitman, -, -, -, -, 85
Wm. Oakly, 80, 20, 600, 75, 478
James Roberts, 30, 70, 300, 10, 315
Andrew Williams, 75, 155, 400, 75, 585
James Warford, -, -, -, 3, 60
James Jones, 40, 65, 300, 5, 530
John Washer, 100, 140, 800, 60, 330
Phebe McCamack, 45, 65, 400, 5, 205
Wm. Williams, -, -, -, 3, 200
Jackson Yergin, 8, 75, 100, 5, 150
Phebe Chapman, -, -, -, -, 10
Henry Malone, -, -, -, 5, 100
Isaiah White, 30, 20, 300, 15, 320
John Chatman, -, -, -, 5, 90
Elizabeth White, -, -, -, 2, 20
Braxton Malone, 28, 40, 200, 5, 230
Ge___ Allen, 4, 40, 50, 5, 100
Archibald Allen, 30, 20, 250, 3, 155
Allen Jones, 50, 30, 400, 12, 180
James Warford, -, -, -, 5, 45
John Fisher, 25, 50, 300, 10, 271
Thos. Simpson, 100, 125, 700, 60, 615
Matthew Parker, -, -, -, 65, 300
Robert Sandlin, -, -, -, -, 15
Tabitha Sims, -, -, -, -, 100
Saml. Fauch, -, -, -, 5, 165
Wm. Malone, 80, 70, 800, 40, 435
Carrall Malone, -, -, -, 5, 205
George Thomason, 40, 35, 275, 40, 110
Wm. Davis, -, -, -, -, 12
John Jones, 40, 40, 500, 110, 335
Wm. Grindstaff, 75, 80, 400, 60, 407
W. W. Bamar, 130, 170, 1200, 178, 1114
Jas. R. Bamar, 80, 100, 700, 50, 263
Lucinda M. Gann, -, -, -, 10, 122
Thos. G. Sary, -, -, -, 20, 246
Ann Bamar, 25, 70, 200, 2, 103
Levi Fauch, 40, 93, 600, 10, 523
Lucy Preston, 40, 60, 250, -, 70
Cobb Preston, -, -, -, 10, 70
Mahala Whitley, 50, 110, 300, 10, 264
Archibald Battoms, -, -, -, -, -
Valentine Floyd, -, -, -, -, 30
Barberry Floyd, -, -, -, -, 30
J. T. Hallis, 40, 70, 800, 125, 315
Jas. N. Turner, -, -, -, -, 60
Edward Turner, 100, 42, 800, 60, 800
Henry Rutland, -, -, -, 65, 395
Milbry Woodson, -, -, -, -, 20
John Simson, 30, 20, 400, 150, 400
Isaac R. Moore, 80, 100, 1000, 80, 213
Saml. Brown, -, -, -, -, 80
Wm. Turner, 35, 15, 250, 40, 158
H. C. Burks, -, -, -, 80, 225
Edward R. Willis, 60, 78, 600, 95, 415
Isaac Jones, 150, 150, 2000, 100, 878

Jas. W. Washburn, -, -, -, 5, 285
E. G. Hudson, 39, 20, 400, 13, 195
Richard Belcher, -, -, -, 5, 155
Louisa Dowell, 85, 85, 1500, 60, 910
Daniel Hunt, -, -, -, 5, 114
Abel Hunt, -, -, -, 5, 160
Jas. H. Davis, 30, 12, 200, 10, 165
Benj. Davis, 100, 50, 1500, 60, 430
A. S. Allen, -, -, -, 5, 175
Eli Davis, 70, 90, 1000, 20, 500
Reason Rawler (Rawlen, Rowlen), -, -, -, 5, 130
Presley Balia, 30, 30, 300, 5, 330
Sarah Hudson, 40, 45, 600, 10, 130
David T. Winfrey, 75, 75, 1000, 20, 304
Jane Bruce, 20, 30, 250, 60, 140
Griffin Hogg, -, -, -, -, 12
Edward Lawrence, 200, 400, 3000, 130, 1100
Joseph Haley, -, -, -, 5, 191
Elizabeth Booker, 25, 45, 300, 10, 100
Lewis Pendleton, 50, 150, 600, 50, 375
Jesse M. Boone, 50, 50, 500, 10, 352
B. M. Langford, -, -, -, 10, 111
Wyley Clark, -, -, -, 10, 41
George Cateney, 35, 65, 500, 10, 190
Henry Boone, 30, 30, 300, 10, 137
Catharine Hicks, -, -, -, -, 10
Thos. Brown, -, -, -, 10, 134
Harrison Fagan, 30, 70, 300, 10, 813
Peyton Garrison, 40, 10, 40, 5, 50
Lucinda Williford, -, -, -, 2, 15
Logan Heflin, -, -, -, 2, 15
George Whitlock, 50, 50, 500, 10, 175
Jas. Lancaster, 40, 39, 400, 10, 236
Louis Washburn, 130, 70, 1300, 80, 600
Lucinda Hill, -, -, -, -, 1
Thos. Lancaster, 45, 50, 400, 10, 228
Jesse H. Barde, -, -, -, 45 870
Lewis Hawl, 125, 25, 800, 35, 480
Elizabeth Hilmantaler, 40, 10, 200, 10, 355
Josiah Baird, 80, 100, 800, 25, 620
Abner A. Flippin, -, -, -, 5, 100
Saml. F. Patterson, 250, 150, 3500, -, 2925
Francis Dowell, 250, 250, 4500, 500, 2132
Sterlin Dowell, -, -, -, 4, 50
Jesse Langford, -, -, -, 5, 15
Elizabeth Dowell, 200, 56, 2000, 100, 645
Wm. J. Wright, -, -, -, 10, 885
David Wright, -, -, -, -, 125
Paschal Wright, 150, 100, 2000, 50, 430
Nancy Moore, 100, 100, 1000, 50, 380

Stephen H. Wright, 75, 75, 600, 10, 210
Edward Webster, -, -, -, 10, 55
Winslow Carter, -, -, -, 5, 115
Willis Dowell, 150, 100, 2000, 500, 3440
Nancy Upton, 80, 157, 1200, 75, 303
Willis C. Montgomery, 75, 27, 800, 75, 1158
Francis Allison, -, -, -, 2, 25
Saml. Allison, 60, 77, 1200, 100, 2200
Lewis Allison, 100, 110, 1500, 100, 555
Jourdan Kitzer, 60, 94, 1000, 15, 597
Sarah Hooper, 60, 30, 400, 10, 163
Wm. Hooper, -, -, -, 10, 159
Wm. Hale, 49, 50, 500, 120, 218
Joseph Bradford, 70, 90, 1100, 50, 550
Mary Rollins, 25, 15, 300, 5, 165
Elias Jenkins, 75, 25, 500, 150, 278
James Campbell, 50, 30, 700, 45, 515
Wm. A. Harris, 10, 37, 200, 20, 130
Isham Fuller, 65, 72, 600, 195, 1000
Kizziah Barnett, 80,1 40, 1200, 15, 398
Philip Bradford, -, -, -, 5, 180
Wm. Moore, 75, 71, 450, 75, 285
Gregory Moore, 200, 50, 2500, 100, 1140
Wm. Baker, 25, 75, 400, 10, 225
Saml. McClennan, 50, 69, 400, 10, 150
Bergess Swaney, -, -, -, 5, 175
Estes McClennan, -, -, -, 3, 25
Joshua Pruett, 55, 100, 600, 330, 430
Nathaniel Macan, -, -, -, 8, 75
John F. Waters, -, -, -, -, 85
Wyatt Jenkins, 60, 300, 750, 50, 409
Pleasant C. McBride, -, -, -, 7, 154
Greenville Linzey, -, -, -, -, -
Danl. McCathrine, 175, 125, 2300, 250, 3500
L. W. Fuller, -, -, -, 15, 241
Benj. W. Gill, -, -, -, 10, 260
Gilbert Butler, 45, 20, 400, 10, 222
Henry Arington, 60, 70, 400, 150, 550
Thos. Gill, 45, 168, 1000, 20, 340
Richard Butler, -, -, -, 10, 260
Harris Tuggle, 80, 130, 1500, 150, 850
Wm. W. Seay, 460, 388, 12000, 600, 6395
L. G. Squires, 50, 150, 400, 350, 340
Sarah Mercer, -, -, -, 10, 100
John H. Bedford, -, -, -, 110, 736
Jas. L. Thompson, -, -, -, -, -
H. J. Compton, 65, 90, 800, 100, 281
Edward Upton, 150, 350, 3000, -, 160
Uriah Maran, -, -, -, 10, 155
Jeremiah Maran, -, -, -, 10, 80
John Parker, -, -, -, 5, 105
Wm. Parker, -, -, -, 5, 50
James Sanderson, -, -, -, 6, 145

Isaac A. Parker, -, -, -, 7, 111
Bartlett James, 60, 100, 1000, 150, 725
Alexr. James, -, -, -, 5, 20
Sarah James, 40, 100,3 00, 30, 370
Mary Barde, 60, 270, 1000, 10, 110
John Pigg, 60, 150, 600, 150, 1300
Wm. Pigg, 10, 40, 125, 10, 15
Charles Pigg, 10, 40, 125, 10, 407
Linb__ Chandler, -, -, -, 10, 20
Benj. Paris, -, -, -, 10, 55
Wm. Johnson, 65, 65, 600, 50,5 40
James M. Paris, -, -, -, 10, 226
James G. Paris, -, -, -, 10, 80
_____ Parris, 40, 60, 500, 15, 240
John Avans, 30, 23, 250, 10, 155
Robt. L. Walker, -, -, -, 5, 125
Sarah Avans, 20, 40, 250, -, 100
Wm. Paris, 15, 45, 100, 5, 100
Geo. Tweedwell, 20, 40, 200, 5, 110
Jeremiah Barde, 40, 35, 300, 75, 400
Saml. Bridgewater, 75, 100, 1500, 400, 855
Elizabeth Crook, -, -, -, -, 30
Travis Samson, -, -, -, 2, -
Milly Coleman, 6, 9, 60, 5, 30
Fielding Ward, 20, 30, 100, 10, 100
Nathan Ward, 120, 110, 2500, 250, 745
L. B. Hughes, -, -, -, 10, 190
J. R. Smith, 132, 236, 2000, 110, 840
G. W. Easter (Eastes), -, -, -, -, 85
Steart Doss, 80, 85, 1000, 30, 572
Jas. Garrison, 75, 80, 400, 100, 305
Wilson Garrison, -, -, -, 5, 165
Harrison Burnett, 25, 75, 300, 10, 540
Jane Miggett, 38, -, -, 3, 15
Allen Harvill, 60, 100, 500, 40, 770
Henry Hilmintaler, -, -, -, 5, 87
Robt. Malone, -, -, -, 5, 170
__na Cates, 65, 125, 500, 65, 170
Wm. W. Willis, 65, 38, 500, 100, 525
Edwin Webster, -, -, -, 5, 60
Saml. Hall, 50, 30, 400, 25, 175
Bethel Dedman, 40, 70, 300, 85, 340
Jane Reasonauer, 2, -, 25, 10, 192
John Dedman, 130, 60, 600, 100, 765
James Eaton, 50, 50, 500, 50, 198
James N. Eaton, -, -, -, 10, 130
Wm. Eaton, 12, 38, 150, 10, 160
James R. Cheak, 50, 110, 500, 50, 350
Charles Denney, 200, 95, 1000, 50, 464
Jonathan Denney, -, -, -, 5, 96
Benj. Denney, -, -, -, 10, 110
Catharine Denney, 25, 40, 200, 5, 210
Margaret Oakley, -, -, -, 5, 150
Charlotte Nickson, 35, 25, 250, 20, 495
James Roberts, -, -, -, 10, 60

Robert Sikes, -, -, -, 2, -
Laban Driver, 100, 143, 600, 28, 400
Wm. Driver, -, -, -, 5, 100
Isaac Wellaby, 50, 68, 500, 15, 270
_. R. Hardcastle, -, -, -, 5, 160
Jas. Oakley, 93, 40, 500, 8, 130
Parson Gartney, 50, 133, 500, 40, 243
_. H. Cheak, -, -, -, 4, 70
W. H. Cheak, 40, 83, 500, 25, 375
Ephraum Cheak, 60, 115, 800, 60, 600
Jesse Huddleston, -, -, -, 1, 13
David Miggett, - -, -, 5, 30
John G. Roberts, 45, 100, 500, 25, 470
Wm. White, -, -, -, 5, 50
Jas. Stevins, 30, 145, 300, 25, 245
Edmond Newbell, 100, 180, 900, 100, 505
John H. Newbell, 100, 180, 900, 100, 505
Thos. Penn, -, -, -, 2, 40
Jno. W. Newbell, 30, 100, 300, 25, 215
John A. Andrews, 16, 65, 200, 15, 220
Jas. W. Moss, -, -, -, 3, 70
Joseph G. Moss, 35, 200, 350, 25, 254
W. P. Moss, -, -, -, -, 30
Wm. W. Clemmans, 15, 50, 100, 10, 175
Luch Gartney, 30, 30, 200, 10, 155
__thel Eskew, -, -, -, 8, 75
_arner W. Hopson, -, -, -, 10, 186
John Gartney, 60, 100, 600, 35, 270
Jeremiah Agee, 50, 150, 300, 15, 225
Joel J. James, 40, 40, 200, 10, 220
Benj. Sanderson, 40, 60, 250, 30, 225
L. H. Walker, 25, 65, 300, 75, 175
Wm. W. Jones, 20, 42, 250, 25, 215
John Porter, 18, 30, 200, 5, 75
Joshua Sikes, -, -, -, 5, 50
James Newbell, 56, 40, 500, 10, 755
Joseph Reasonauer, 150, 370, 1500, 600, 871
Jeremiah Reasonauer, -, -, -, 125, 400
___diah Jenkins, 15, 10, 300, 100, 96
Emily Turner, 55, 45, 600, 50, 304
Wm. F. Terry, 2, 2, 450, 5, 25
Cornelius Davis, -, -, -, 5, 85
Mary Wood, 90, 253, 5000, 300, 528
_. C. M. Buckley, 55, 45, 500, 15, 260
Felix F. Mann, 40, 50, 250, 30, 359
Darrall Denney, -, -, -, -, 1500
David Risen, -, -, -, 2, 17
Basil Foley, 45, 695, 500, 50, 450
Stephen Stone, 40, 60, 400, 50, 480
___iet Goodall, 50, 75, 1000, 30, 485
___man Booker, 15, 114, 300, 150, 240
___rmelia Allegy, -, -, -, 5, 30
John Boran, 20, 13, 175, 10, 50
Jeremiah Smith, 35, 160, 400, 30, 510

Robert Enochs, 30, 60, 600, 30, 275
__ry Hughes, -, -, -, 10, 15
Moses Reeves, 70, 330, 1200, 100, 600
_____ Jones, 20, 10, 175, 10, 150
_____ Estus, 80, 120, 800, 40, 1010
__nl Robertson, 80, 112, 800, 45, 481
Jefferson Wright, -, -, -, 10, 225
Elizabeth Wright, 100, 80, 1200, 128, 745
Richard Belcher, 70, 15, 400, 10, 280
___ H. Johnson, -, -, -, 10, 320
John Johnson, 150, 250, 1200, 155, 800
___ K. Fagon, 100, 100, 800, 178, 530
Harriet Moore, -, -, -, 10, 110
Wm. A. Lancaster, 60, 120, 400, 75, 250
Francis Bradley, 35, 30, 300, 10, 325
Wm. Craighead, 20, 73, 250, 30, 400
Saml. Givins, -, -, -, -, -
Matilda Prawell, 18, 15, 150, 10, 100
_. A. L. Gardon, -, -, -, 5, 105
John Gardon, 200, 600, 4000, 400, 1610
David Fry, 60, 80, 600, 100, 450
Edward Atwood, 50, 80, 500, 120, 450
Elizabeth Springfield, -, -, -, 2, 80
Hannah Proctor, 40, 30, 170, 40, 380
W. W. Philips, 60, 60, 700, 100, 530
John Grindstaff, 45, 55, 700, 40, 475
Rebecca Davis, 100, 20, 1000, 50, 621
B. J. Cardwell, 60, 50, 500, 50, 635
John W. Patey, 130, 82, 1200, 100, 810
Erenzar P. Paty, 45, 27, 400, 5, 217
_liver Turner, 150, 54, 1300, 75, 630
David Thomason, 50, 20, 200, 10, 120
Nicholas Eastes, 25, 80, 500, 5, 75
Robt. M. Barry, -, -, -, 5, 617
Josiah Baird, 300, 333, 2000, 125, 815
R. J. Davis, 150, 80, 1500, 15, 300
Thos. Alvis, -, -, -, 10, 130
John Hall (Hull), 80, 60, 500, 100, 620
Elisha Dowell, 40, 20, 400, 15, 230
___ Rogers, 31, -, 300, 50, 280
Cherniah (Chemiah) Nunner, -, -, -, 2, 45
Hezekiah Turner, -, -, -, 12, 138
Sterling Hale, 22, 56, 500, 100, 258
Moses Allen 70, 20, 600, 200, 710
James Barry, 100, 140, 1200, 150, 970
James Allen, -, -, -, 10, 129
May Kitchen, 40, 40, 300, -, 89
Soloman Strang, -, -, -, 10, 315
_ariah Manning, 60, 40, 250, 10, 260
Elijah Soloman, 50, 50, 500, 125, 405
Jesse Fuller, -, -, -, 18, 260
Benj. Davis, 60, 80, 500, 10, 440
_. H. Morris, 60, 54, 500, 100, 296
Obadiah Paris, 35, 55, 450, 100, 525
John Hunt, -, -, -, 10, 150
David Clark, -, -, -, 88, 100

Thos. Litchford, -, -, -, 5, 150
Benj. Enochs, 50, 135, 500, 30, 375
Jesse Fuller, 50, 160, 800, 50, 560
Sarah Wilkerson, 60, 85, 1100, 15, 550
__arken Carley, -, -, -, 100, 405
John A. Smart, 70, 125, 1200, 125, 950
James Agee, 35, 45, 450, 15, 300
Wm. Croocke, -, -, -, 15, 130
Elizabeth Waters, -, -, -, 2, 60
Nancy Barrett, 30, 15, 400, 5, 50
Samuel Barrett, 50, 20, 400, 30, 490
_aren Denney, 45, 49, 600, 20, 280
Darran B. Harris, 75, 75, 1200, 50, 425
George Walker, 30, 20, 350, 200, 860
Thos. Kitchen, 50, 90, 700, 125, 680
John L. Davis, 25, 30, 250, 10, 200
Jas. Langford, -, -, -, 5, 20
John N. Proctor, -, -, -, 10, 140
Stephen Willis, 35, 40, 600, 15, 500
Geo. Morrison, -, -, -, 10, 105
Raleigh Stott, 100, 133, 2500, 100, 950
James Brame, 25, 35, 150, 10, 125
Richd. J. Brame 50, 75, 450, 40, 450
Adam C. Parkem, 30, 30, 100, 35, 150
Wm. Gregory, 20, 9, 150, 5, 100
Dan Adcock, 12, 38, 100, 10, 270
May Numley, 70, 130, 1000, 60, 300
Rhebe C. Cary, 50, 50, 500, 30, 400
James Martin, 125, 25, 1200, 20, 160
John G. Martin, 120, 30, 1200, 100, 650
Larry H. Cage, 550, 30, 600, 150, 950
John S. Scott, 37, 3, 500, 15, 470
David Stanford, 150, 23, 1800, 100, 815
David H. Stanford, 25, 40, 500, 35, 200
James W. Warf, 15, 5, 50, 10, 200
Henry Roark, 50, 30, 500, 5, 50
Lewis McFarland, 150, 120, 2000, 125, 750
John M. Tunstall, 150, 87, 1500, 120, 800
Baxton Harris, 100, 175, 3600, 50, 325
John Culbreath, 35, 65, 534, 10, 200
Bretton Brewer, 60, 144, 4000, 30, 300
Nathl. B. Anderson, 40, 10, 650, 35, 200
Henderson Halvy, 60, 140, 1500, 40, 365
Larissa Halvy, 60, 60, 800, 10, 275
R. H. Cato, 100, 90, 3000, 50, 300
Wm. W. Anderson, 100, 200, 5000, 100, 370
Major A. Beasley, 100, 100, 1500, 60, 500
Sylvester H. Harkreade, 45, 21, 1000, 50, 415
Joseph Dereckson, 217, 83, 3000, 150, 885
Gabriel Beasley, 60, 240, 2400, 150, 865
Charles Tate 20, 120, 500, 50, 200

Elizabeth Bramford, 100, -, 1200, 60, 460
Prescilla Black, 84, 100, 1200, 78, 215
Henry Brooks, 110, 50, 2500, 400, 1000
Ed. S. Bradley, 75, 125, 2400, 150, 500
Chas. F. McKee, 40, 68, 700, 10, 225
Wm. Hart, 70, 54, 1000, 50, 250
John Carman, 70, 72, 600, 50, 750
Chas. J. Coker, 120, 422, 2762, 150, 600
Wm. Payne, 140, 202, 400, 50, 390
Moses Lay, 40, 33, 190, 10, 170
Eli Gammon, 250, 400, 3000, 250, 1000
John Stafford, 75, 75, 400, 30, 180
Stephen Stafford, 25, 50, 400, 10, 240
Saml. Satterfield, 14, 60, 200, 5, 100
B. M. Richardson, 70, 200, 1350, 40, 1015
John Stafford Jr., 40, 130, 250, 10, 90
Josiah Richardson, 100, 100, 600, 20, 400
Larkin Payne, 120, 100, 1200, 150, 800
Benj. E. Towns, 150, 133, 850, 50, 650
Arthur Bramford, 40, 120, 600, 5, 180
Jesse Smith, 40, 85, 350, 30, 30
Martin H. Bursus, 60, 70, 350, 5, 60
Thos. J. Oldham, 90, 90, 225, 15, 150
Wm. Marrey 50, 100, 400, 40, 350
John G. Anderson, 45, 215, 450, 60, 425
Wm. A. Garrett, 75, 97, 400, 50, 300
Leml. A. Hammack, 150, 286, 1200, 300, 1140
Jerh. Gamman, 150, 350, 1200, 128, 810
Wm. Gamman, 40, 60, 300, 10, 200
Wm. M. Robinson, 10, 7, 200, 5, 90
Ganery Wilbourn, 30, 70, 400, 10, 260
Green Wright, 70, 280, 800, 25, 460
Hamelton Payne, 40, 120, 250, 15, 200
Jacob M. Cleavland, 50, 100, 500, 10, 60
Benj. Welbourn, 25, 75, 200, 10, 150
Robt. Welbourn, 25, 100, 300, 10, 215
Wm. Reece, 25, 25, 200, 10, 125
Henry L. Day, 20, 15, 225, 10, 65
John D. Day, 70, 90, 800, 60, 450
James Climer, 35, 65, 400, 10, 225
Philip T. Day, 35, 40, 250, 35, 175
Solo. McMurry, 100, 80, 300, 70, 400
Martin McMurry, 100, 150, 900, 100, 1500
Henry D. Day, 40, 60, 400, 10, 175
Hosea M. Carman, 75, 45, 300, 30, 300
Thos. Carman, 100, 130, 2500,100, 650
John a. Debow, 200, 144, 3000, 150, 900
Bayel Carman, 30, 25, 250, 100, 200
Thos. McClanahan, 50, 70, 400, 5, 200
Lawrence Thompson, 300, 120, 1500, 200, 700
Wm. Kirby, 65, -, 800, 40, 600
John Madden, 150, 25, 1750, 250, 1610

Patience S Wood, 40, 22, 800, 10, 125
Margaret Rutherford, 100, 250, 1000, 50, 300
John J. Jones, 30, 40, 200, 10, 275
John Wallace, 25, 100, 625, 10, 80
Carn Stafford, 50, 250, 600, 50, 290
Richardson Roberts, 30, 10, 150, 3, 40
Thos. Stafford, 50, 50, 300, 10, 300
Jacob F. Stone, 100, 100, 500, 40, 750
A. A. Bernard, 150, 107, 3000, 200, 1265
Joseph L. Carter, 300, -, 5000, 250, 1710
John J. Gamman, 33, 46, 240, 30, 200
Joseph Johnson, 200, 157, 1785, 150, 575
Morris Woodmore, 35, 18, 300, 15, 200
Thos. Woodmore, 66, -, 600, 40, 300
James Woodmore, 70, 90, 1000, 30, 190
Josiah Marshall, 210, 66, 2800, 50, 1000
Geo. C. Gifford, 46, 60, 1000, 80, 225
Elmereth Donoho, 70, 20, 1000, 65, 1835
Saml. C. Debow, 150, 48, 1800, 100, 800
Wm. Thomas, 100, 88, 1880, 35, 450
James Kirby, 80, 40, 1000, 30, 665
Nat. M. Adams, 150, 110, 2600, 50, 950
Nelly Mangle, 60, 67, 1200, 40, 200
Marshall B. Duncan, 100, 100, 3000, 75, 700
John Lipscomb, 80, 70, 1500, 80, 400
Tandy P. D. Hall, 100, 60, 1280, 75, 380
Thos. M. P. Hall, 200, 60, 3900, 150, 1000
Malinda Hall, 27, 6, 330, 40, 125
James Parmley, 60, 43, 1000, 100, 545
Wm. W. Horsley, 60, 61, 2000, 30, 320
James Furlong, 20, 15, 300, 5, 125
Mosely Lipscomb, 150, 56, 2500, 150, 810
Alexr. Stubblefield, 100, 55, 1550, 100, 500
Edward B. Haynie, 125, 200, 2000, 50, 630
James J. Gregory, 40,73, 350, 10, 200
Brice H. Piper, 30, 52, 200, 7, 350
Wm. L. Oldham, 40, 75, 350, 35, 228
Thos. Shoulders, 30, 62, 300, 5, 250
John S. Winkler, 40, 35, 350, 30, 175
Levi C. Winkler, 50, 30, 500, 50, 500
Wm. Edens, 12, 88, 200, 10, 200
James Edens, 16, 54, 200, 8, 90
John Hiett, 50, 694, 1200, 25, 250
John Payne, 120, 280, 2000, 65, 600
Logan D. Key, 150, 96, 550, 65, 600
Mary Davis, 22, 78, 300, 5, 65
John Roberts, 13, 13, 100, 5, 125
Nathan Hall, 30, 20, 200, 8, 115
Wm. S. Hailey, 50, 120, 600, 40, 450
Thos. Hailey, 60, 98, 550, 35, 600

May Toller, 30, 60, 400, 7, 140
Ramsey Vance, 15, 21, 225, 40, 120
Joel L. Gregory, 45, 70, 350, 5, 50
Margaret Beasley, 100, 140, 1200, 50, 300
Abner Smith, 30, 30, 300, 35, 200
Madison Angel, 25, 75, 300, 5, 250
Danl. Smith, 100, 140, 1000, 40, 750
Henry L. Beasley, 20, 60, 250, 5, 50
John Shoulders, 25, 105, 300, 10, 250
Mary Nickson, 100, 100, 600, 30, 600
Thos. Gregory, 40, 90, 350, 40, 300
Pitts Gregory, 30, 40, 200, 40, 275
Betsey Gregory, 90, 80, 900, 40, 500
Hugh McKinness (McKinneys), 25, 50, 250, 15, 250
Henry Nelson, 25, 65, 400, 5, 125
Henry M. Gregory, 20, 70, 250, 15, 100
George W. Beal, 15, 55, 200, 5, 130
Bethel J. Gregory, 60, 40, 300, 35, 250
Solomon Smallen, 60, 140, 400, 25, 60
Clebourn Mathews, 20, 30, 100, 4, 100
Elizabeth Mathews, 25, 35, 150, 10, 175
Nanny (Nancy) Bishop, 30, 170,2 00, 25, 200
Wm. Nickson, 75, 85, 500, 40, 700
Henry B. Haynie, 75, 150, 1500, 100, 700
Wm. Kirby, 35, 240, 450, 40, 360
John Davis, 70, 230, 750, 40, 450
Wm. Brockett, 25, 40, 300, 7, 200
Williamson Reece, 100, 181, 2000, 40, 250
B. J. Cardwell, 90, 90, 1330, 65, 400
Wm. M. Knight, 60, 188, 1200, 15, 450
Henry M. Knight, 30, 30, 150, 10, 150
Wiley Jones, 50, 146, 700, 20, 550
Sarah Evans, 25, 88, 250, 35, 250
Aulsa Kemp, 60, 100, 700, 25, 250
C___ Pankey, 25, 75, 300, 5, 25
Edmond Sutton, 50, 280, 1000, 20, 450
James O. Wilbourne, 200, 200, 4000, 125, 1600
James Sutton, 50, 80, 600, 30, 350
Mulin Lam (Lane), 25, 26, 175, 10, 180
R. C. Cartwright, 100, 200, 1500, 40, 500
Henry Wakefield, 25, 100, 350, 10, 125
James Kirby, 35, 147, 550, 10, 150
Richd. H. Holland, 80, 162, 550, 35, 250
Matilda Holland, 60, 120, 400, 100, 450
Peyton Huddleston, 130, 450, 1500, 60, 500
L. A. Smithwick, 30, 80, 500, 10, 300
Nancy Russell, 75, 269, 600, 23, 500
James Russell, 18, 32, 235, 10, 140
Stephen Kennedy, 35, 78, 500, 40, 300
James Philips, 25, 125, 200, 8, 125

John Evans, 20, 230, 300, 10, 100
Barnet Cornwell, 40, 66, 250, 40, 330
Philip Austin 22, 63, 350, 6, 100
Levi Austin, 90, 110, 2000, 75, 405
Parthenia Winkler, 30, 90, 600, 40, 200
Reuben Good, 40, 60, 300, 10, 250
Malcom Smith, 27, 35, 200, 5, 200
Christian Austin, 20, 210, 330, 10, 400
Neil Patterson, 30, 120, 600, 10, 200
Rebecca Grin___, 25, 115, 300, 5, 125
Edwd. Sanderson, 100, 160, 2000, 100, 600
Archd. McKinson, 20, 213, 800, 50, 250
Alexdr. Patterson, 20, 80, 250, 5, 250
John O. Cosby, 220, 537, 4160, 100, 1300
Oliver F. Richardson, 50, 62, 600, 50, 310
Saml. McClellan, 50, 150, 600, 100, 400
John H. Davis, 75, 55, 600, 50, 200
Wm. Young, 200, 220, 5000, 300, 2500
Allen Holladay, 30, 20, 150, 5, 150
Joseph Yearman, 80, -, 500, 40, 150
Wm. L. McClellan, 10, 90, 300, 10, 175
Richd. Jones, 75, 45, 700, 10, 100
Rowland Wheeler, 40, 60, 500, 20, 300
Micajah Duke, 125, 515, 1500, 50, 1200
Henry Franklin, 70, 230, 1200, 40, 1280
Joseph Meadows, 40, 145, 450, 50, 300
Mary Woodcock, 35, 95, 750, 5, 175
Saml. Russell 30, 30, 500, 40, 260
Pleaman Graves, 100, 100, 1000, 75, 800
Isaac Kitrell, 60, -, 500, 40, 310
A. P. Cardwell, 35, 45, 900, 15, 40
Jo. T. Jones, 60, 38, 1200, 75, 175
Clabourn West, 50, 60, 2000, 100, 350
Thos. Martin, 40, 102, 400, 40, 640
John Robinson, 52, 100, 550, 20, 500
James West, 30, 145, 1200, 40, 285
Josiah Reece, 160, 214, 2000, 50, 415
F. B. Norwood, 60, 241, 2950, 50, 400
James Powell, 30, 45, 400, 10, 250
Geo. Powell, 35, 69, 400, 20, 185
Edmond Powell, 20, 20, 200, 20, 230
L. J. Cardwell, 180, 297, 4770, 50, 430
Isaac Webb, 75, 375, 3000, 70, 510
Wm. Low(Law), 38, 111, 400, 38, 250
Richmond Marman, 35, 345, 650, 40, 325
Ed Kitrell, 175, 150, 3000, 50, 330
D. A. Witt, 50, 70, 500, 90, 250
Cyrun Craighead, 25, 40, 300, 5, 100
E. W. Cornwell, 25, 72, 700, 60, 125
Malinda Marman, 40, 61, 444, 10, 350
Delila Davis, 25, 55, 300, 10, 150
Obediah Craighead, 25, 25, 200, 10, 100
Saml. Dyer, 10, 23, 50, 3, 40
Rebecca Mason, 50, 68, 500, 2, 25
Robt McHood(Hood), 30, 40, 300, 5, 110

Saml. Fitzpatrick, 20, 100, 400, 50, 473
Geo. Petty, 90, 51 100, 5, 75
Danl. M. Apple, 50, 40, 400, 30, 220
Philip Rhodes, 10, 70, 200, 10, 80
Zara Dillard, 26, 41, 200, 5, 75
John Ballard, 40, 90, 500, 40, 492
David Smith, 150, 250, 2500, 50, 750
Robt. Johnson, 25, 25, 200, 5, 90
James Ballard, 386, 386, 3500, 75, 720
Chas. Ballard, 50, 20, 300, 10, 100
Green B. Wood, 75, 75, 350, 5, 320
Josiah (Jonah) Bush, 30, 5, 80, 5, 190
Jefferson Wood, 60, 110, 500, 10, 150
Turner Harris, 30, 30, 300, 5, 200
Moses Ballard (Bellah), 60, 40, 400, 20, 200
Elisha Dillard, 100, 100, 1000, 5, 440
Chas. Bellah, 40, 10, 150, 10, 200
Damon Fields, 40, 64, 250, 20, 225
H. L. Traywick, 30, 90, 300, 10, 150
Jas. Stewart, 30, 90, 300, 5, 150
Clement Gillshan, 24, 36, 300, 7, 200
Wm. Dillard, 200, 680, 1500, 50, 500
Johnathan Dillard, 50, 150, 500, 60, 600
Wm. Wade, 75, 25, 200, 8, 150
Isham Clark, 50, 150, 400 40, 175
James Tromdale, 50, 130, 600, 50, 600
Isaac A. Massey, 20, 80, 400, 10, 150
W. W. Briley, 300, 218, 5000, 200, 1500
Mary Tromdale, 50, 64, 800, 20, 565
John Condett (Condill), 10, 90, 250, 5, 160
John Farmer, 40, 68, 400, 30, 200
Alinas Ferguson, 200, 200, 800, 50, 470
Benj. Jones, 40, 140, 300, 5, 400
Thos. Sexton, 30, 120, 300, 5, 120
Madison Fields, 10, 31, 82, 5, 120
Wm. Cullom, 700, 50, 10000, 300, 4500
Martin Morefield, 80, 210, 1000, 10, 85
Danl. Huddleston, 140, 345, 2300, 60, 570
Hardy Calhoun, 75, 58, 1100, 35, 150
Jas. H. Hart, 50, 133, 600, 30 300
Mathew Nichol 100, 200, 1500, 60, 1315
Archibald Taylor, 35, 80, 500, 10, 200
Mary Winfree, 50, 95, 450, 40, 400
Joseph Gass, 40, 110, 1000, 40, 250
Rebecca Cooper, 70, 80, 800 35, 185
Winneford Mitchell, 20, 10, 150, 30, 250
Richard Johnson, 8, 42, 50, 5, 100
John Bats, 40, 100, 300, 15, 315
John D. Vaden 60, 140, 600, 5, 150
Stephen Mann, 130, 140, 3300, 100, 1328
Geo. C. Mann, 25, 34, 425, 15, 230
Timothy W. Mann, 30, 45, 600, 30, 420
John Timberlake, 40, 60, 600, 25, 150

Robt. Allen, 25, 55, 400, 10, 250
Jesse Beasley, 60, 90, 750, 30, 275
Jeremiah M. Beasley, 10, 85, 500, 4, 135
Fielding Condett, 60, 80, 800, 50, 950
John H. Mann, 54, -, 700, 50, 275
Joel M. Nichol, 75, 125, 800, 100, 300
Clem McKinney, 40, 160, 600, 35, 300
C. C. Ford, 50, 50, 500, 10, 250
Catherine Brown, 60, 84, 800, 30, 415
Robt.. Warren, 60, 106, 650, 50, 490
Harrison L. Lee, 40, 60, 600, 50, 250
Geo. Daugherty, 30, 50, 200, 30, 275
Thos. J. D. Ferrell, 50, 86, 600, 30, 250
Burton G. Ferrell, 35, 90, 300, 10, 250
Wm. M. Armistead, 50, 60, 350, 50, 400
Robt. W. Mann, 10, 190, 500, 75, 240
Wm. Moreland, 30, 80, 340, 40, 200
Wm. F. Allen, 30, 75, 500, 50, 310
Wesley Carlisle, 25, 75, 500, 20, 150
Henry Pendergrass, 10, 23, 150, 5, 60
Jacob Null, 50, 325, 750, 15, 500
Jason Winchester, 35, 466, 700, 20, 400
Riley Lengin, 100, 111, 2000, 30, 690
Hezekiah Love (Lore), 125, 175, 1200, 100, 785
Rachel Hallum, 85, 150, 1600, 50, 813
A. Moore, 100, 120, 1400, 150, 1482
Daniel (David) Harrell, 27, 53, 200, 5, 160
Ab H. King. 15, -, 1100, 15, 330
George Apple, 50, 60, 500, 10, 300
Wm. T. Williams, 10, -, 200, 30, 300
Jeremiah Jamison, 273, -, 3000, 175, 1000
A. Ferguson, 80, 120, 4000, 100, 950
Ladwick Vaden, 170, 100, 1000, 100, 900
Henry Good, 40, 48, 900, 40, 300
Sam. B. Hughes, 100, 160, 1500, 50, 392
Timothy Walton Jr., 350, 310, 7000, 200, 2840
Sarah S. High, 150, 225, 16500, 75, 350
B. D. High, 6, 150, 700, 50, 250
A. W. Overton, 400, 600, 30000, 500, 2850
Wm. M. Payne, 100, 500, 500, 15, 75
Hezekiah Taylor, 60, 70, 500, 35, 300
Jamima B. Porter, 50, 40, 400, 25, 235
Francis G. Baker, 100, 142, 800, 65, 550
Claiborne Hall, 40, 7, 175, 50, 270
Wm. B. Campbell, 70, 34, 3500, 200, 1000
Jos. C. Dickens, 100, 75, 600, 150, 500
William Thomas, 10, 17, 500, 10, 120
William Robinson, 120, 126, 1500, 50, 200
Winston Perry, 100, 177, 1200, 25, 630

L. H. Cardwell, 100, 200, 2000, 50, 610
Joshua Snoddy, 8, 72, 200, 6, 100
Thomas Snoddy, 60, 40, 500, 20, 245
Hyram Lyles, 130, 100, 2300, 110, 800
Jesse Robinson, 18, 32, 1500, 12, 150
John Robinson, 60, 80, 3000, 100, 400
John Snead, 45, 69, 700, 25, 300
Sarah H. Cardwell, 40, 60, 800, 40, 455
Thomas Hinds, 53, -, 400, 20, 140
Ellis E. Knight, 170, 68, 650, 50, 403
John High, 100, 198, 3000, 100, 500
Winston High, 100, 30, 750, 60, 410
Martin S. Simons, 20, 31, 200, 10, 170
Bedford Haddock, 129, 42, 1100, 45, 352
O. J. Simmons, 12, 39, 300, 12, 115
Saml. Garret, 35, 60, 300, 50, 340
Mary Glover, 35, 35, 300, 35, 350
Nancy Glover, 35, 35, 350, 35, 205
P. F. Conwell, 50, 42, 600, 50, 310
Bedford L. Herring, 12, 24, 225, 5, 100
Wm. Pendarvis, 40, 60, 800, 25, 300
Jacob Roberts, 25, 51, 200, 8, 194
Wm. T. Hackett, 60, 40, 300, 15, 260
Peter Hackett, 50, 50, 300, 30, 361
Aelin Mathews, 45, 80, 500, 30, 179
Van H. Allen, 150, 150, 5000, 125, 1700
James High, 350, 611, 5000, 200, 1430
Wm. Overstreet, 30, 20, 200, 50, 310
Henderson Overstreet, 30, 40, 350, 10, 200
Wm. H. Hubbard, 40, 40, 350, 5, 150
John C. Hopkins, 10, 45, 150, 8, 95
Polly Hubbard, 100, 200, 1000, 15, 300
Dixon Dickens, 50, 50, 450, 30, 160
James M. Vance, 4, 70, 200, 15, 70
Jerh. Belk, 100, 100, 700, 50, 537
Robert Belk, 5, 5, 10, 25, 20
Isham Beasley, 225, 505, 5000, 350, 1620
Wm. Strother, 100, 10, 950, 40, 380
Rufus Perry, 70, 13, 700, 60, 460
Joshua Good, 70, 42, 1000, 50, 531
Jacob Hubbard, 150, 171, 2500, 150, 675
Elizabeth Strother, 150, 190, 3400, 50, 377
John B. Hughes, 150, 240, 3000, 250, 1013
Saml. Hunter, 55, 50, 800, 35, 400
Irwin Hughes, 100, 50, 1500, 50, 180
Wm Shoemake, 50, 80, 1000, 100, 442
Robt. Holladay, 50, 38, 1000, 20, 356
Blake B. Thackston, 40, 60, 1000, 40, 384
Lewis Franklin, 125, 50, 1220, 50, 920
Robt. Mosley, 150, 150, 1500, 40, 375
Wm. Massey, 50, 171, 700, 40, 409
John Maggard, 70, 160, 1000, 10, 445
Wm. Croslin, 60, 151, 400, 60, 380

Benj. Croslin, 30, 70, 300, 40, 180
Virginia Maggard, 20, 80, 100, 5, 160
Carroll Dillard, 8, 29, 125, 3, 27
Wm. Hall, 20, 71, 600, 50, 287
Sanford Gregory, 20, 17, 150, 25, 95
John Dickens, 40, 60, 400, 50, 371
Benj. Arindall, 20, 93, 350, 10, 210
Wm. A. Cook, 22, 55, 250, 10, 75
James Shoemake, 25, 75, 350, 6, 85
Joshua Dickens, 30, 70, 250, 10, 142
Martha M. Flowers, 20, 76, 250, 5, 70
Robert Beasley, 50, 200, 800, 15, 287
Darcus Anderson, 30, 100, 400, 10, 170
Lee C. Glover, 10, 30, 150, 10, 130
O. B. Anderson, 30, 70, 400, 10, 115
Chas. R. Blair, 100, 540, 1000, 75, 760
Michael Shoemake, 100, 200, 1500, 75, 468
Henry Beasley, 25, 45, 200, 15, 270
Davidson Draper, 150, 250, 700, 50, 750
George R. Dillard, 60, 30, 800, 50, 400
Robt. J. Glover, 50, 150, 700, 50, 375
Matlock Roberts, 15, 85, 400, 10, 100
Federick Wyatt, 15, 35, 150, 50, 235
Saml. Mays, 20, 30, 100, 5, 43
Elias Booker, 20, 30, 125, 10, 200
John M. Vance, 24, 76, 300, 6, 125
George W. Meacham, 35, 40, 275, 35, 225
Benj. or J. vaden, 125, 275, 1500, 100, 746
John L. Cowan, 20, 120, 300, 7, 63
Milton Haynie, 30, 170, 500, 25, 250
Jason R. Sloane, 100, 100, 1000, 50, 300
Wm. Gibbs, 20, 45, 250, 10, 180
Wm. Durall, 200, 50, 2000, 100, 250
Robt. W. Knight, 100, 175, 2000, 40, 300
Henry J. Perkins, 30, 45, 350, 40, 150
Allen Pyher (Pgher), 90, 110, 1264, 35, 200
Alexander Armistead, 64, 90, 800, 5, 250
Jerh. Coggins, 200, 440, 2000, 200, 1500
David Harris, 100, 425, 1500, 25, 200
D. K. Timberlake, 90, 131, 1200, 50, 560
John Armstead, 100, 280, 1200, 50, 700
Isaac Lynch, 100, 120, 1500, 20, 100
Jesse Hale, 40, 110, 650, 25, 85
P. W. Presley, 40, 120, 325, 10, 200
John Johnson, 80, 280, 600, 50, 590
Reuben Alexander, 50, 75, 300, 20, 100
John Merrett, 65, 135, 400, 40, 960
Thos. J. Lee, 40, 160, 400, 10, 290
Mathew W. Exum, 20, 30, 200, 5, 150
Martha Smith, 15, 60, 150, 5, 235
William Garner, 40, 185, 175, 30, 660
Valentine Presley, 20, 60, 200, 50, 250

Wm. Coggins, 30, 50, 250, 10, 250
James R. Jones, 25, 100, 700, 40, 250
Thos. Finley, 5, 67, 300, 5, 160
_____ Austin, 65, 435, 600, 23, 350
James Hall, 30, 270, 300, 7, 190
Isaac Burton, 20, 163, 200, 5, 190
_ilvay Smith, 50, 150, 400, 25, 430
Johnathan Smith, 30, 105, 250, 5, 600
Sarah Garner, 20, 30, 100, 8, 140
Anderson Winchester, 20, 65, 200, 5, 225
John Ponder, 25, 175, 500, 5, 75
Wm. McGinness, 40, 60, 700, 10, 275
_. P. Coggins, 30, 35, 400, 40, 300
John L. Powell, 5, 35, 200, 25, 200
Wm. Exum, 35, 90, 500, 15, 240
__nchen D. Exum, 20, 80, 300, 5, 310
Allen Coggins, 100, 50, 1500, 50, 710
Jefferson Rowland, 100, 100, 1800, 75, 500
Margaret Alexander, 15, 35, 400, 10, 300
Joseph Mitchell, 80, 300, 1030, 50, 475
Stephen Petty, 40, 30, 400, 20, 285
Wm. Petty, 175, 185, 3000, 100, 1500
Jesse Pickard, 30, 120, 175, 10, 270
James Haynes, 5, 125, 200, 5, 100
Robert Smith, 50, 80, 400, 10, 110
_etty Haynes, 35, 15, 200, 5, 90
Wm. D. Evans, 70, 269, 1050, 80, 350
Isaac A. Huddleston, 100, 100, 400, 40, 535
Jonathan E. Jarred, 45, 105, 350, 10, 160
_elton T. Apple, 20, 150, 400, 75, 200
Elijah S. Banks, 40, 78, 1000, 60, 375
Saml. Smith, 25, 18, 250, 5, 200
Gella Simons, 40, 160, 600, 40, 470
Susan Perry, 30, 50, 300, 10, 200
Wm. Kemp, 30, 95, 400, 5, 50
Wm. Harris, 20, 400, 3000, 150, 980
Ellis B. Kemp, 70, 168, 1400, 100, 460
Andrew Carter, 35, 165, 250, 40, 230
Nath. Terry, 60, 188, 1450, 50, 525
Isreal McClellan, 100, 171, 1500, 250, 650
Wm. B. Williams, 20, 76, 600, 15, 175
Kitty C. Bennett, 100, 500, 6000, 50, 350
Wm. R. Costello, 25, 50, 225, 5, 80
Nancy Thomas, 30, 70, 600, 35, 200
Danl. Young, 100, 200, 3000, 125, 735
John Richardson, 100, 150, 2400, 60, 1035
Sampson McClellan, 800, 700, 10000, 200, 3000
Wm. _. Dyer, 20, 12, 150, 25, 150
Miles F. West, 75, 237, 1000, 40, 405
Wm. A. Smith, 60, 100, 1000, 45, 100
Wm. Knight, 40, 60, 300, 10, 240

Jinks Kemp, 14, 73, 250, 5, 150
Beverly S. Kemp, 35, 100, 400, 28, 200
Susannah Dillehay, 85, 375, 1200, 50, 400
Robert West, 100, 150, 1500, 50, 700
Obadiah Gregory, 40, 35, 250, 10, 150
Thos. Climer, 25, 35, 300, 40, 245
Brackston Butler, 20, 30, 250, 7, 130
Wm. West, 60, 90, 700, 40, 500
Burrel Kemp, 30, 70, 280, 30, 200
Anthony Holland, 80, 125, 1500, 25, 250
Botheul Bradley, 35, 15, 250, 10, 50
Berry West, 40, 35, 600, 10, 140
Saml. King, 30, 151, 500, 30, 260
Nathan Kent, 56, -, 56, 25, 250
Benja. Payne, 75, 69, 1500, 100, 520
Isaac M. Cardwell, 30, 92, 750, 50, 250
Wm. J. Payne, 30, 36, 300, 40, 200
Abraham King, 9, 1, 30, 8, 80
James K. King, 60, 3, 300, 40, 130
Rhoda Chambers, 40, 70, 500, 5, 180
Geo. W. Anderson, 39, 50, 440, 3, 85
Ridley R. West, 100, 109, 1225, 35, 635
Wm. Draper, 50, 101, 1000, 45, 505
Danl. Clay, 40, 30, 500, 50, 250
John Parker, 75, 90, 800, 40, 370
Wm. Snead, 18, 32, 350, 7, 150
Elan Russell, 75, 118, 700, 35, 500
Hilas Russell, 25, 60, 350, 15, 150
Jesse Lam (Lane), 100, 51, 400, 25, 300
John Donoho, 70, 100, 1100, 50, 710
_. F. Young, 200, 537, 4097, 45, 400
Willis Dean, 175, 677, 2400, 200, 1310
Jefferson Dean, 55, 115, 937, 40, 250
Wm. R. Pistole, 50, 150, 1000, 40, 600
Thomas Dean, 70, 183, 700, 40, 280
Wm. Donoho, 25, 100, 450, 40, 405
Wm. Donoho Sr., 100, 113, 500, 15, 430
Thomas Cartwright, 100, 203, 500, 20, 550
Robert Green, 60, 58, 750, 45, 300
Wm. L. Kemp, 35, 83, 300, 30, 150
Stephen Good, 35, 79, 500, 10, 150
Lasiter (_asitta) Page, 150, 150, 1200, 40, 510
Henry Cornwell, 125, 105, 1800, 150, 540
Elizabeth Lam, 30, 29, 300, 5, 150
Henry Lam, 10, 10, 150, 10, 105
Leroy Carter, 80, 120, 1200, 140, 646
David Hogg, 250, 170, 3360, 200, 2000
Leonidas D. Hogg, 40, 10, 500, 10, 1615
_. P. Pate, 100, 50, 1500, 50, 415
Fielding Kittrell, 40, 75, 500, 20, 140
Philip Draper, 50, -, 330, 30, 305
John Kemp, 110, 40, 800, 30, 310

Evin McCormick, 60, 54, 800, 35, 20
_ey Kemp, 40, 66, 1250, 35, 625
John Carver, 150, 50, 800, 15, 200
John _. Turner, 100, 160, 1200, 50, 515
_. S. Russell, 40, 120, 400, 20, 125
Mathew Smith, 35, 132, 400, 40, 260
David Smith, 35, 200, 500, 10, 220
John Chambers, 60, 100, 1000, 50, 200
George Cook, 30, 30, 200, 5, 150
Robert Smith, 25, 25, 200, 5, 135
George Bartow (Baston), 100, 500, 2200, 50, 500
Danl. A. Wilkinson, 12, 13, 150, 8, 100
Miles Austin, 15, 33, 300, 10, 100
David Parkhurst, 20, 95, 300, 5, 125
Jefferson Jenkins, 25, 125, 300, 5, 200
Rawlston Jenkins, 20, 130, 300, 5, 130
James Jenkins, 20, 80, 200, 5, 150
Archibald Jenkins, 15, 10, 160, 5, 140
_beil McDuffy, 15, 10, 200, 15, 200
Rebecca Gregory, 25, 125, 500, 30, 400
Wm. J. Ballom (Ballow), 40, 60, 600, 60, 300
B. P. Lipscomb, 30, 114, 600, 45, 350
Ann Ballom (Ballow), 5, 145, 160, 10, 350
John Russell, 40, 132, 800, 25, 250
Robert A. Russell, 20, 82, 400, 10, 150
Hampton Wakefield, 15, 170, 500, 5, 200
Wm. C. Taylor, 20, 102, 150, 8, 125
Johns M. Taylor, 50, 181, 750, 75, 300
John M. Turner, 35, 165, 500, 30, 300
Wm. Dament, 28, 172, 500, 15, 250
Wm. Porter, 50, 62, 400, 50, 500
Wm. Arneth, 45, 122, 400, 50, 300
Chas. S. Long, 40, 110, 800, 10, 275
Thomas. D. Gregory, 70, 30, 300, 175, 275
John Nickson, 35, 65, 500, 10, 250
David Evetts, 18, 59, 200, 5, 200
John Halliburton, 40, 68, 200, 10, 200
Abel Gregory, 40, 85, 575, 30, 300
Johnson Dillehay, 40, 60, 300, 10, 200
Wm. L. Smith, 70, 70, 550, 15, 450
Levi G. Smith, 15, 135, 100, 3, 130
James T. Taylor, 15, 85, 200, 10, 125
Daniel Taylor, 40, 135, 450, 100, 350
John Barton, 20, 40, 300, 5, 150
James Curlee, 35, 65, 300, 60, 200
Susah C.Nash, 50, 96, 450, 50, 250
Ephraim P. Nash, 25, 110, 300, 5, 125
Richard Chambers, 50, 108, 1500, 25, 525
Joseph Evetts, 30, 50, 300, 5, 200
Othiel Johnson, 250, 100, 1700, 200, 2700

William Watson, 30, 107, 400, 10, 125
David Diar, 60, 107, 400, 15, 270
Ezekiel Parkhurst, 70, 30, 1500, 120, 400
Edward Bradley, 60, 200, 2500, 25, 450
Abraham Lee, 30, 45, 200, 50, 165
George W. Lanch, 30, 45, 500, 15, 250
Thomas Porter, 65, 135, 600, 35, 500
Chas. H. Tunstall, 60, 80, 1200, 100, 800
George W. Walker, 150, 150, 1600, 60, 900
Thomas Moss Jr., 75, 57, 500, 30, 287
Thomas Moss Sr., 50, 180, 600, 40, 350
Wyatt Parkman, 9, 25, 125, 5, 165
David Burford, 350, 450, 10000, 200, 1500
James S. Bradley, 275, 200, 3500, 200, 2755
James L. Alexander, 300, 700, 10000, 200, 1510
Francis Kirby, 144, -, 1500, 75, 805
James Bradley, 180, 87, 1000, 50, 815
Robt. A. Burford, 40, 182, 3000, 100, 400
Bias Russell, 25, 32, 500, 50, 575
James M. Murtry, 90, 175, 2500, 30, 800
James H. Vaughn, 150, 150, 3500, 300, 2000
John McMury, 75, 63, 1700, 125, 500
James McMurry, 60, 90, 1500, 200, 600
Saml. Black, 15, 35, 250, 10, 100
Hugh A. Bradley, 200, 120, 6000, 300, 1000
Thomas Tunstall, 60, 170, 1500, 125, 450
Thomas Hinton, 100, 81, 1000, 50, 550
Albert G. Donoho, 300, 65, 2500, 150, 1230
Soloman Debow, 220, 7, 3500, 150, 1400
William Stalcup Sr., 150, 207, 2000, 50, 1100
Franklin Erwin (Ervin), 100, 50, 1200, 80, 350
Wm. Stalcup Jr., 170, 56, 1600, 80, 450
Chas. McMurry, 10, 13, 100, 10, 100
Marcus Donoho, 75, 60, 1500, 50, 550
Elizabeth Blackwell, 44, 43, 700, 15, 275
James M. Blackwell, 30, 32, 300, 10, 180
Adam Stafford, 25, 29, 100, 5, 100
Herbert Saddler, 50, 94, 1000, 10, 200

_addock Beasley, 0, 88, 1600, 50, 670
__hert Porter, 75, 96, 675, 100, 700
Lee D. Ballom (Ballow), 80, 120, 1500, 100, 800
Wm. L. Bine, 13, 12, 125, 5, 150
Peer Herrod, 100, 202, 2260, 100, 725
Joseph Sloane, 100, 200, 700, 25, 300
Abel Smith, 75, 149, 600, 80, 350
Joshua W. Smith, 100, 50, 600, 50, 615
John N. Hesson, 35, 121, 500, 10, 250
John Ballard, 100, 267, 700, 20, 700
James Piper, 200, 100, 2000, 200, 800
Sally Oldham, 20, 12, 300, 10, 350
George W. Oldham, 50, 150, 800, 80, 300
James D. Gregory, 100, 75, 500, 15, 400
Henry Piper, 30, -, 300, 15, 175
Edwin T. Bomb, 75, 36, 1000, 50, 325
Lane Haynie, 35, 95, 800, 15, 325
James Chambers, 50, 110, 650, 35, 300
James W. Taylor, 75, 175, 500, 150, 350
_. W. Roysten, 120, 100, 1200, 75, 1200
Hugh K. Patterson, 50, 50, 2000, 50, 250
Henry Beasley, 250, 70, 4000, 200, 840
Saml. J. Bradley, 100, 110, 1600, 200, 700
Sam. J. Alexander, 120, 180, 3000, 200, 900
Washington Payne, 60, 190, 400, 40, 430
Wilson N. Martin, 300, 366, 5000, 150, 1600
__has. Mace, 25, 85, 1000, 10, 200
Thompson Mace, 200, 300, 2000, 50, 2745
Humphrey Smithwick, 75, 50, 800, 25, 500
Wm. B. Weatherford, 80, 24, 600, 180, 300
Mathew Anderson, 40, 48, 400, 10, 175
Elizabeth Cleavland, 40, 48, 400, 3, 80
Moses Evetts, 50, 10, 400, 30, 260
John H. Ligon, 200, 160, 2500, 150, 600
Elias Johns, 200, 50, 3000, 75, 500
John J. Burns, 20, 37, 200, 20, 285
__ine McMury, 150, 112, 1700, 100, 700
John M. Bransford, 44, 44, 400, 15, 210

INDEX

Berryer, 50
Berryhill, 55, 60
Besson, 83
Best, 62
Betey, 72
Bettey, 73
Bettis, 57, 62, 64
Bevin, 17
Bickers, 68
Bigbee, 4
Bigdon, 16
Biggs, 3, 62
Bigham, 14
Bigley, 41
Biles, 30, 67
Bine, 83
Binford, 34, 67
Binkley, 3, 9-10
Bird, 16, 40-41, 44-45
Birdsong, 15
Birdwell, 34
Birney, 5
Bishop, 24, 68
Bivens, 12
Bivins, 13-14, 21, 24
Black, 7, 19, 21, 27, 60, 62, 71, 77, 83
Blackborn, 63
Blackley, 15
Blackman, 30
Blackwell, 60, 83
Blackwood, 22
Blair, 29, 46, 49, 57-58, 81
Blairs, 49
Blake, 32
Blakely, 63
Blakemore, 66
Blalock, 45
Bland, 56, 59
Blankenship, 32, 42
Blanton, 28, 46
Blazer, 44
Bledsoe, 54, 56
Blesing, 33
Blue, 57
Bobbett, 8
Bobett, 33
Bobo, 8
Bohannon, 44-46
Boles, 12
Bolin, 17, 23
Boling, 37-40
Bolt, 59
Bolton, 55-56, 71
Bomb, 83
Bond, 55, 59-60
Bonds, 19

Bone, 28
Bonus, 26
Booker, 16, 23, 74, 76, 81
Boone, 74
Boothe, 26
Boran, 76
Boren, 1, 11
Borman, 16
Bosley, 59
Boswell, 54
Bottoms, 22
Botton, 71
Botts, 65
Bour, 19
Bourn, 8
Bowden, 48
Bowen, 15, 17, 43
Bowens, 67
Bower, 51
Bowers, 51
Bowman, 13-14, 18, 24, 27-28, 33, 35
Boyd, 23, 31-33, 59
Boyean, 15
Boyet, 62
Boyles, 6
Boytee, 61
Boze, 71
Brabson, 50
Bracey, 9
Brack, 46
Bracy, 33
Bradford, 18, 25, 70, 75
Bradley, 9-10, 20, 27, 47, 57, 64, 68, 70, 76-77, 82-83
Bradly, 23
Bradshaw, 65
Brady, 15, 34, 52
Brakefield, 2
Brame, 77
Bramford, 77
Branaugh, 65
Branch, 54-55, 57-58, 60
Brandon, 15, 18, 24
Bransford, 83
Branson, 59
Branum, 43
Brasheares, 34
Brashears, 36
Brasher, 69
Brashere, 20
Braswell, 6, 57-58, 71
Bray, 65, 70
Brazzell, 72-73
Breeden, 43-45, 47
Brent, 73
Brewer, 3, 14, 18, 26, 77

Carver, 50-51, 82
Cary, 77
Casner, 65
Cassey, 37
Casterman, 37
Castleman, 25
Cate, 47, 50-52
Cateney, 74
Cates, 15-17, 75
Catlett, 47-49
Cato, 77
Catran, 69
Catron, 45
Caudle, 4, 40
Cauler, 54
Cauthern, 14
Cavender, 21
Cayce, 28
Ceall, 38-39
Cellers, 7
Cenedy, 32
Chambers, 8, 38-40, 48, 67, 82-83
Chambless, 9
Chance, 7
Chandler, 6, 25, 49-51, 67, 75
Chapman, 2-3, 6, 74
Chatman, 74
Cheak, 70, 75-76
Cherry, 60
Chery, 36
Chestnut, 21
Chiat, 6
Childers, 19, 38-39
Childress, 13, 15, 26
Chisum, 4
Chitwood, 39-41, 60
Choat, 10
Chowning, 6
Christian, 73
Christopher, 31
Church, 22, 28
Cibb, 1
Cississm, 69
Clabber, 46-47
Clabeaugh, 46
Clackston, 73
Clanton, 36
Clariday, 67-68, 71
Clark, 3-4, 6, 9, 15-16, 20-21, 30, 35-36,
46-47, 49-51, 70, 74, 76, 79
Clarkston, 73
Claxton, 15
Clay, 13, 29, 32, 82
Clayton, 3, 20, 58
Cleabaugh, 48
Cleavbough, 45

Cleavland, 77, 83
Clemens, 15
Clements, 72
Clemmans, 72, 76
Clewer, 44
Clifford, 61
Clift, 56
Clifton, 53, 72
Climer, 77, 82
Clinard, 9, 11
Clonington, 52
Close, 73
Co_elm, 40
Cobb, 7, 9, 17, 48
Cochran, 9, 13
Cock, 35
Cocke, 18
Cockram, 72
Cockran, 26
Cocks, 72
Coe, 56
Coffee, 59, 72-73
Coffey, 18
Coggins, 73, 81
Cohea, 1
Coker, 77
Colby, 57
Coldwell, 51
Cole, 5, 22, 58, 62, 64
Coleman, 13, 31-32, 55, 58, 72, 75
Colewell, 29, 31
Colgin, 6
Collier, 29, 72
Collins, 27, 35
Colter, 35
Comer, 35-37
Compton, 46, 48, 61, 75
Conally, 27
Conatser, 44
Condett, 79-80
Condill, 79
Condor, 59
Cone, 6
Coner, 45
Conly, 8
Conn, 62
Connel, 8
Conwell, 80
Cook, 3-6, 23-24, 31, 40, 46, 51, 65, 70,
81-82
Cooksey, 68, 70
Coons, 52
Coonts, 21-22
Cooper, 35-37, 39, 79
Coopmoon, 63
Coopwood, 63

Cope, 47
Corbet, 55-56
Corbett, 62
Corble, 27
Corder, 31, 73
Corn, 15
Cornelius, 64
Cornig, 13
Cornwell, 79, 82
Coronahan, 14, 24
Corsey, 37
Cosby, 79
Costello, 81
Cothern, 5
Cotter, 35, 46
Cotton, 19, 21, 39
Cough, 56
Coul, 37
Course, 21
Coursey, 33
Courtney, 25
Cousins, 35
Couts, 6
Cove, 41
Covington, 5, 12, 24, 31-32, 36, 50
Cowan, 81
Cowder, 49, 51
Cowen, 28, 50, 52, 72
Cowgill, 57
Cowthern 25
Cox, 19, 25, 34, 62
Coybill, 64
Crabtree, 37, 39
Crafford, 10
Crafton, 37
Cragner, 21
Craig, 69
Craighead, 76, 79
Crance, 47
Crane, 55-56
Crap, 38-39
Crawford, 6, 18, 23, 33
Crayner, 21
Creekmore, 42
Crenshaw, 54-56, 58, 61
Creshaw, 56
Creswell, 50, 52
Crichlow, 13-14
Crick, 34, 36-37
Crigg, 34
Crocker, 22, 35-36
Crockett, 1, 9, 33-35
Croocke, 77
Crook, 75
Croslin, 24, 80-81
Cross, 24, 38-41

Crosthwait, 28
Crouch, 58
Crouse, 21-22
Crow, 49
Crowder, 17, 33
Crowly, 22
Crowson, 46
Crumpton, 20
Crunk, 1
Cruse, 13
Crutcher, 1, 9, 68
Crutchfield, 25, 29, 70
Culbertson, 9, 11
Culbreath, 77
Cullom, 79
Cumin, 14
Cummings, 4
Cunningham, 46, 50, 52, 69
Cunnings, 46
Curlee, 82
Curry, 31
Cusick, 51
Cuterell, 68
Dagly, 40
Dallis, 59
Dalton, 34
Dament, 82
Dandridge, 64
Danerson, 65
Daniel, 13, 22, 24, 28, 58
Darby, 64
Darden, 7-8
Darel, 17
Darrell, 37
Daughtery, 16, 69, 80
Dauherty, 42
Davel, 18
Davidson, 24
Davis, 1, 4, 13, 19, 21-22, 25, 28, 30-31, 33-34, 37, 49, 51, 56, 58, 61, 63-66, 72, 74, 76-79
Dawson, 71
Day, 68, 77
Deadrick, 64
Dean, 2-3, 33, 82
Deason, 31
Debdu_n, 73
Debow, 77-78, 83
DeChallenge, 56
Dedman, 73, 75
Dees, 62
Dejarnett, 20
DeLashenet, 53
Delaway, 5
Delbridge, 31
Delk, 41

Ellis, 7, 10, 12, 14, 32, 36, 49, 50, 52-53, 60, 62, 64
Ellison, 5, 17, 47, 49, 51
Elmore, 6
Elrod, 22-23
Eltel, 41
Embry, 41
Emert, 45-47
Empson, 5
England, 6
English, 15, 59
Enochs, 69, 76-77
Epperson, 54
Eppes, 31
Epps, 16, 64
Ernest, 48
Ervin, 83
Erwin, 16, 83
Eskew, 31, 72-73
Eskey, 76
Eskridge, 24
Eslinger, 45
Esprey, 29
Esslinger, 51
Est, 5
Estus, 76
Etheby, 68
Etherby, 56
Etheredge, 57
Etherton, 44
Eton, 47
Etter, 28
Eubank, 4-5
Evans, 17-18, 27, 45, 51, 78-79, 81
Everett, 69-70
Evett, 56
Evetts, 67, 82-83
Ewing, 68
Exum, 81
Ezell, 13
Fagala, 50
Fagan, 23, 74
Fagon, 76
Fan, 22
Fanner, 73
Fannin, 20
Fanning, 48
Farat, 72
Fardly, 13
Faringer, 15
Faris, 19
Farley, 60, 62, 71
Farlis, 14
Farm 30
Farmer, 1, 7, 9-10, 69, 72, 79
Farrar, 65

Farris, 26, 37
Fartherby, 20
Farthing, 1, 3-4, 7, 11
Fasacett, 29
Fatherby, 17
Faucett, 35, 62
Fauch, 73-74
Faulk, 54, 59
Fear, 22
Featherson, 64
Featherstern, 4
Featherston, 33, 35
Featherton, 13
Feazel, 47
Federick, 68, 70
Fellow, 64
Fellows, 12, 64
Felton, 48
Felts, 9-10, 65
Ferguson, 47, 49, 54, 60, 69, 79-80
Ferrell, 58, 62, 80
Field, 61
Fields, 14, 79
Filpipps, 36
Filpot, 29
Filston, 67
Finch, 29-30
Findley, 49
Finley, 81
Finney, 25
Fiser, 1, 7, 10
Fisher, 4, 67, 73-74
Fitzgerald, 56
Fitzpatrick, 79
Fiviash, 67
Flancers, 67
Flanikin, 59
Fleetwood, 60
Fleming, 13-14, 17, 20, 26, 32, 54, 59, 62
Flemings, 47
Flenar, 45
Fletcher, 12, 14-15, 24, 56, 61, 73
Flinn, 63
Flintoff, 8
Flippin, 68-69, 74
Floid, 23, 33
Flood, 1, 3
Floray, 58
Flowers, 26, 81
Floyd, 33-34, 48, 57, 74
Fly, 12
Foley, 76
Foot, 3
Forbs, 31
Ford, 21, 25, 48, 63, 68, 80
Forgis, 29

Fornin, 20
Fort, 8, 10, 21
Foster, 28, 30, 34
Fountain, 9
Fowler, 34, 47
Fox, 10, 17, 40, 44-45, 47-50
Francis, 44
Franklin, 45, 52, 79-80
Franshire, 46
Frazer, 33, 65
Frazier, 50
Freeling, 5
Freeman, 3, 13, 15, 25-26, 59
Freemont, 73
Frey, 1, 6-7, 9
Frie, 24
Fringer, 15
Frohawk, 68
Fry, 1, 43, 71, 76
Fulks, 15-16, 18, 24
Fulks, 71
Fuller, 20, 25, 30, 57, 75-77
Fulton, 3
Fuqua, 2, 9
Furgison, 37
Furguson, 25
Fyke, 1, 7
Gaddy, 68
Gainer, 29
Gaither, 54
Galaspie, 71
Gallagher, 65
Gallaher, 21-22
Gallet, 7
Gallick, 69
Galloway, 58, 62
Gally, 25
Galyean, 51
Gambell, 29
Gambill, 3
Gambrell, 29, 32
Gamman, 77-78
Gammon, 77
Gan, 69
Ganican, 17
Gann, 69, 74
Ganner, 44
Gant, 48, 62
Gantt, 47
Gardener, 19
Gardner, 6, 8
Gardon, 76
Garner, 15, 18, 29-30, 37, 51, 55, 81
Garratt, 36
Garret, 57-58, 80
Garrett, 1, 56, 61, 71, 77

Garrison, 74-75
Gartney, 76
Garver, 31
Garvin, 55
Gass, 79
Gate, 62
Gates, 32, 56
Gatlin, 52
Gavet, 25
Gee, 42
Geers, 55
Gent, 8
George, 5, 26
Gholston, 70
Gibbons, 64
Gibbs, 71, 81
Gibson, 17, 37, 39, 41
Gifford, 78
Gilbert, 5, 50, 65
Giles, 65
Gill, 8, 56, 68, 70-71, 75
Gillaspie, 36
Gilleland, 62
Gillespie, 60
Gillham, 54
Gilliam, 21, 24, 72
Gillshan, 79
Gilly, 18
Gilmore, 14, 62
Gipson, 46, 51
Gist, 53
Givinn, 53
Givins, 76
Gladden, 55
Glas, 70
Glasco, 14
Glenn, 32, 66
Glidewell, 5
Glimph, 32
Glipms, 32
Glissen, 7
Glisson, 54
Glover, 10, 80-81
Gobble, 48
Gober, 16
Goforth, 49
Gold, 72
Goldsby, 56
Gooch, 8, 15
Good, 12, 17-18, 39, 41, 79-80, 82
Goodall, 76
Goodlett, 15
Goodloe, 24, 60
Goodman, 8, 18, 25, 29, 55, 62
Goodrich, 63
Goodwin, 25, 55, 57

Harry, 17
Hart, 3, 26, 29, 58, 62, 77, 79
Harthen, 26
Harther, 51
Hartrell, 43
Hartwell, 20
Harvill, 75
Harwell, 59
Hasburg, 28
Hasking, 70
Hasten, 69
Hatcher, 46
Hatfield, 38-39
Hathaway, 57
Hatson, 36
Hauk, 68
Hause, 70-71
Haw, 19
Hawkins, 57, 67-68
Hawl, 74
Hawley, 56
Haye, 60
Haynes, 13, 29-34, 69, 81
Haynie, 78, 81, 83
Hays, 15, 22, 55, 60, 62, 69
Hayse, 30
Hazelwood, 16, 19, 28, 55, 65
Hazzard, 68
Head, 9-10
Hearn, 70
Hearry, 19
Heartley, 43
Heath, 31, 34
Hecklers, 61
Hedgpeth, 25
Hedrick, 46
Hefflin, 70, 72
Heflin, 8, 72, 74
Heilmanteler, 70
Helton, 24, 47
Henderson, 12-13, 29, 34, 46-49
Hendly, 46
Hendrick, 62
Hendrix, 36
Henley, 59
Henly, 3
Henry, 3, 6, 11, 34, 43, 49, 52-53, 58
Herald, 13, 16, 18, 24
Herendon, 20, 23
Herington, 52
Herndon, 30
Herod, 17
Herrald, 70
Herran, 64
Herring, 1, 55, 60, 80
Herrod, 83

Herron, 54, 56
Hester, 52
Heter, 28
Heutcheson, 70
Hewett, 37
Hewlet, 4
Hick, 12
Hickinlotte, 17
Hickman, 32, 36, 51-52, 68, 73
Hicks, 20, 27, 35, 50, 52, 67, 69, 74
Hide, 10
Hiett, 78
Higden, 24
High, 80
Highden, 23
Highsmith, 1
Hildebran, 64
Hill, 18-20, 22, 24, 29-30, 32, 40, 55, 58-59, 74
Hille, 48
Hills, 54
Hillsman, 13
Hilmantaler, 74
Hilmentaler, 72
Hilmintaler, 75
Hinds, 80
Hines, 60
Hinkle, 9
Hinton, 83
Hires, 69
Hix, 41
Hoard, 28
Hoberry, 24
Hocott, 57
Hodge, 27, 31
Hodges, 49-50, 53, 57, 64, 70-71
Hodgets, 49
Hodsden, 49-50
Hoe, 41
Hoffman, 1
Hogan, 37, 73
Hogg, 74, 82
Holden, 33, 35-36
Holder, 35
Holladay, 79-80
Holland, 1-3, 7, 78, 82
Hollaway, 7
Hollingsworth, 24
Hollis, 9-10
Holloway, 30
Holman, 1-3, 7, 64
Holmes, 9, 24, 58, 65
Holowell, 27
Holstead, 37
Holt, 54
Holton, 36

Honnycut, 40
Hoober, 47
Hood, 22, 79
Hooker, 15, 61
Hooks, 68
Hooper, 17, 56, 75
Hooston, 56
Hoover, 15-18, 24
Hope, 20
Hopkins, 36, 71, 80
Hoptson, 76
Horne, 60
Horsley, 78
Horthen, 26
Horton, 4, 13, 34-35
Houk, 44, 49-50
House, 3, 20, 29-30, 70
Householder, 49
Houser, 45
Housley, 52
Houston, 61
Howard, 3, 43-45, 49, 62, 64, 72
Howel, 59, 61
Howell, 30-31, 59
Howland, 15-16
Howman, 13
Howse, 30-31
Howze, 55
Hubbard, 34, 70-71, 80
Huchinson, 12, 20-22, 24
Huddleston, 1, 76, 78, 79, 81
Hudgens, 8-9
Hudson, 5, 53, 74
Huey, 3
Huff, 35, 48
Huffaker, 50, 52-53
Huffman, 4, 57
Hufft, 48
Huggins, 12-13
Hughes, 67, 69, 71, 75-76, 80
Hughett, 41
Hughs, 7-8, 13, 24
Hull, 35, 76
Hulsey, 10
Humphreys, 57
Hunnycutt, 40-41
Hunt, 9-10, 19, 21, 27-28, 66, 71, 74, 76
Hunter, 25, 28, 62, 80
Hurst, 43-44
Hurt, 19, 44
Husbands, 28
Huskey, 45-46
Husky, 8, 46, 61
Hutchens, 58
Hutcherdson, 27
Hutcheson, 1, 5, 37

Hutchins, 64
Hutson, 30, 32
Hutton, 35
Ight, 25
Imes, 65
Inge, 73
Innman, 47
Inscore, 1
Insel, 14
Ireland, 7, 17
Irwin, 66
Isler, 57
Isom, 59
Ivey, 24
Ivins, 24
Ivy, 2, 19, 21, 44
Jackson, 2, 8, 35-37, 56, 58, 63-64, 71, 73
Jacobs, 16-18, 35
James, 10, 23, 27-30, 46-49, 61, 71-72, 75-76
Jameson, 33
Jamison, 10, 15, 57, 80
Janaway, 34
Janican, 17
Jannaway, 12
January, 12, 14
Janway, 14
Jarman, 22, 44
Jarmon, 62
Jarnagan, 4-6
Jarnagin, 49
Jarner, 37
Jarrall, 28
Jarred, 81
Jarrett, 32-34
Jarrot, 20
Javansaw, 67
Jay, 63
Jeanes, 43-44
Jeanway, 52
Jeetter, 56
Jeffers, 37-39, 41
Jemison, 16, 20, 24
Jenkins, 28, 44, 49, 51, 56, 61, 70, 75-76, 82
Jennings, 22, 69
Jetton, 12-13, 18, 21
Jinkins, 46
Jobe, 31, 44
John, 31
Johns, 3-4, 19, 22, 27-28, 83
Johnson, 2-3, 5, 8-9, 13-16, 19-20, 24, 28, 30-31, 53-55, 65-66, 75-76, 78-79, 81-82
Joice, 64

Manor, 33
Mantlo, 1, 7
Manus, 57
Maple, 45
Maples, 43, 45, 47, 49
Marable, 29-30
Maran, 70, 75
Marchbanks, 17, 72
Marcum, 37-41, 55
Markins, 16
Marks, 61
Marlchain, 57
Marlin, 17
Marman, 79
Marrey, 77
Marris, 51, 67, 71
Marriss, 67
Marsh, 58
Marshal, 14, 22,
Marshall, 19, 78
Marter, 61
Martin, 10, 14, 16, 19, 22-23, 25, 28-29,
31, 33, 44, 61, 77, 79, 83
Mason, 2, 7, 25, 27, 29, 31, 33, 64, 66,
71, 79
Massengille, 39, 41
Massey, 56, 58-59, 63, 67, 79-80
Masthor, 33
Mather, 17
Mathers, 19, 21-22
Mathewes, 43, 57
Mathews, 7, 29, 33, 35, 43, 65-66, 78, 80
Matson, 63
Mattox, 46
Matz, 18
Maud, 59
Maxey, 8-9
Maxon, 2
Maxwell, 26, 28, 32-33, 36, 58
May, 33, 37
Mayfield, 14, 17
Mays, 7, 11, 29, 66, 81
McAden, 60
McAdire, 60
McAdoo, 19, 22
McAlister, 67
McBride, 56, 59, 73
McBridge, 75
Mcbrint, 46
McCabe, 35
McCall, 68
McCallie, 50
McCanless, 32
McCarley, 6
McCarmack, 74
McCarter, 45, 49

Mccarty, 64
McCathrine, 75
McCinsey, 46
Mcclaine, 72
McClam, 12
McClanahan, 77
McClannahan, 20, 29
McClary, 31, 52
Mcclay, 52
Mcclearry, 52
McClellan, 61, 71, 79, 81
McClennan, 75
McClinahan, 70
McClune, 36
McClung, 40
McCluran, 31
McClure, 36, 63
McColester, 27
McCollum, 57
Mccomes, 23
McCormick, 10, 82
McCowen, 50, 70
McCown, 49
McCrackin, 24
McCrag, 24
McCrary, 18-19
McCroskey, 49-51
McCrosky, 50
McCulloch, 13-14, 18, 21, 24, 26, 28
McCullough, 26, 34
McDanel, 19-20
McDaniel, 25, 27, 59
McDearmon, 25
McDermot, 12
McDonald, 3, 40-41, 62, 72-73
McDonold, 39
McDowel, 12
McDowell, 28, 61
McDuffy, 82
McEarvin, 22
McElhotten, 23
McElroy, 14, 17-18
McEwen, 22, 24
McFadden, 12, 28
McFadgen, 64
Mcfal, 46
McFalls, 46
McFarland, 18, 77
McGear, 36
McGee, 23, 42, 69, 72
McGhee, 58
McGill, 15, 46
McGinness, 81
McGinnis, 27, 73
Mcglaugher, 46
McGowen, 27, 33, 58

McGregor, 26
McGrue, 15
Mcguier, 4
McHenry, 7, 21
McHood, 79
McIntire, 26
McIntosh, 2
McIver, 63
McKee, 15, 17, 19, 23, 77
McKey, 35, 65
McKindley, 48
McKineon, 47
McKinness, 78
McKinney, 61, 71, 80
McKinneys, 78
McKinson, 79
McKinzy, 46
McKisic, 4
McKissick, 43
McKnight, 21, 23-24, 56, 58
Mclane, 73
McLean, 57
McLin, 12
McLuesovin, 29
Mcmahan, 43, 45, 47, 49
McMann, 4
McMenerway, 25
McMillan, 4
McMott, 49
McMunn, 4,
McMurry, 6, 15-16, 51, 77
McMurry, 83
McName, 65
McNeal, 25, 35
McNeely, 61
McNeill, 64
Mcnelly, 50
McNir, 59
McNoble, 16
Mcnutt, 49
McPeak, 26
Mcpherson, 51
McQuister, 23
McRae, 31
McSwain, 29
McSwine, 63
Meacham, 81
Meadows, 57, 79
Melton, 64
Mendenhall, 63
Menees, 7, 9
Mercer, 69, 70, 75
Meredith, 27-28
Merit, 19
Merrett, 33, 81
Merrit, 5

Merritt, 50, 52
Meson, 61
Michel, 44
Michelbery, 54
Midlens, 27
Midling, 22
Midloff, 20
Miggett, 75-76
Miles, 8-9, 17, 27, 30, 30, 52
Miller, 10, 12-16, 19, 22, 24, 26, 28, 35, 43, 45-46, 48, 50, 59, 63, 65
Milles, 52
Milliken, 59
Mills, 26, 53
Mims, 21
Mins, 21
Minter, 14
Minton, 69, 71
Mires, 21, 73
Mitchel, 20, 22, 24, 46-47, 49, 62
Mitchell, 7, 14, 27, 60, 63, 65-66, 79, 81
Modrall, 35
Monda, 51
Money, 13
Montgomery, 24, 62, 69, 75
Moon, 19, 20, 55-65
Mooneyham, 52
Mooningham, 67
Moore, 2, 6, 10, 18, 20, 23-24, 36, 52, 55, 57, 62-64, 68, 70, 74-76, 80
More, 50-51
Morefield, 69, 79
Morehead, 15, 56
Moreland, 63, 80
Morgan, 13, 16, 35, 64
Morris, 1, 7, 10-11, 25, 33-34, 56, 65, 71, 76
Morrison, 21, 26, 28, 65, 77
Morrow, 26
Mortain, 45
Morton, 14, 23, 25
Mosby, 12, 64
Moses, 40
Mosley, 31, 80
Moss, 5-6, 14, 22-23, 73, 76, 83
Motes, 69
Motley, 59
Mount, 52
Muckluoy, 68
Mullendore, 46, 49
Mullins, 19, 24-25, 28, 30-31, 58
Munglum, 61
Murfree, 12, 14
Murphey, 7, 10, 14
Murphy, 9, 32, 46, 50-51
Murray, 65

Parmley, 78
Parrish, 14
Parrot, 44
Parsley, 33
Parten, 72
Parton, 28, 45
Paschal, 70-72
Pat, 52
Pate, 45, 48, 82
Patera, 48
Patey, 76
Patman, 37
Patrick, 18, 23, 55, 61-62
Patten, 30, 49
Patterick, 26
Patterson, 4-5, 20, 22, 3-37, 41, 44, 47, 72, 74, 79, 83
Pattison, 59
Patton, 15
Patts, 29
Patty, 46, 52
Paty, 71-72, 76
Payne, 4-6, 30-31, 68, 70, 77-78, 80, 82-83
Peach, 31
Peacock, 33
Peak, 17, 23, 27-28
Pearce, 21, 27
Pearcy, 19-20
Pearson, 3, 14, 17
Peay, 24
Peebles, 31
Peel, 56
Pemberton, 41
Pendarvis, 80
Pendergrass, 80
Pendleton, 74
Penington, 33, 40
Penn, 67, 76
Pennington, 8, 10
Pennywell, 17
Pentecost, 9
Peoples, 21, 60, 66
Pepper, 1, 72-73
Perkins, 81
Perry, 1, 15, 25, 50, 52, 61, 80-81
Perryman, 14-15, 47
Person, 55, 63, 66
Persons, 66
Petteris, 72
Petters, 56
Petterson, 19
Petty, 14-15, 48, 53, 79, 81
Peyton, 26, 57
Pgher, 81
Phan, 57

Pharr, 57
Phelps, 23-24, 31
Phibbs, 71
Philips, 13, 20, 76, 78
Phillips, 37, 39-41, 49, 54, 57, 59, 63
Pickard, 81
Pickens, 49, 51
Picket, 20
Pierce, 51
Pierson, 65
Pigg, 53, 75
Pike, 1
Pilant, 9-10
Pilkington, 17
Pilson, 22
Pinkard, 15
Pinson, 5, 28
Piper, 78, 83
Pistole, 82
Pitt, 2, 6, 8, 10, 65
Pittman, 65, 74
Pitts, 2, 17, 20-21, 27,
Pitty, 13
Plummer, 56
Plunket, 73
Plunkett, 65
Poindexter, 15, 47
Polard, 52
Polk, 8, 32, 54, 58, 63
Pollard, 51-52
Ponder, 81
Ponds, 4-5
Pool, 59
Pope, 2-3, 7, 30, 37, 58, 69-70
Porter, 1, 6-7, 46-47, 49, 65, 76, 80, 82-83
Posey, 30-31
Posy, 24
Potter, 41
Potts, 57
Powel, 3, 16
Powell, 28, 35, 60-61, 79, 81
Prater, 15-18
Prawell, 76
Preeden, 59
Prentice, 73
Prescott, 56
Presley, 81
Preston, 69, 74
Prewett, 32
Price, 4, 20, 36, 68
Prichet, 14
Priddy, 61
Pride, 6
Primm, 36
Prince, 33

Prinom, 33
Prior, 57
Probles, 21
Proctor, 3, 76-77
Proffitt, 43
Pruett, 75
Pruit, 16
Pruitt, 16
Puckett, 30-31, 37
Pugh, 25
Puller, 73
Pulliam, 58
Pullun, 73
Pully, 18
Purnell, 68
Purser, 57
Pyher, 81
Pyrn, 61
Qualls, 20
Rackard, 50
Rafter, 62
Ragan, 45, 51, 65
Ragland, 65
Raglin, 72
Ragner, 22
Ragsdale, 19
Raines, 47
Ralls, 9
Ralston, 25, 28, 55
Ramack, 71
Rambo, 47, 50
Randler, 50
Randles, 49-50, 52
Randol, 61-62
Randolph, 3-4, 6, 26
Rankin, 13, 55
Ransom, 32-33
Ranson, 32, 34, 37
Rass_ann, 27
Rather, 12, 19, 27-28
Rauls, 68
Rauntree, 69
Rawland, 68
Rawlen, 74
Rawler, 74
Rawlings, 57
Rawllings, 50-51
Rawls, 9-10
Ray, 22, 31, 33, 37, 48
Rayner, 22, 58
Rayney, 21
Reach, 56
React, 58
Reactt, 56
Read, 9-10, 24, 67-68, 72
Reader, 9, 11

Readfeam, 4
Ready, 12
Reait, 58
Reasonauer, 75-76
Reasons, 8
Reaves, 55, 57, 68
Redd, 60
Reddin, 10
Redfeam, 4
Redman, 68
Redmond, 7
Reece, 77-79
Reed, 18, 27-30, 36-37, 39-40, 49, 51-52, 54, 68
Reede, 12
Reese, 25, 48, 52, 55
Reeves, 12, 21, 68-69, 76
Regan, 33, 37
Reid, 63-64
Rembert, 56
Renchar, 17
Reneau, 44, 47
Revees, 60
Revel, 62
Revil, 30
Rex, 24
Reynolds, 2, 16, 55
Rhodes, 62, 79
Riad, 7
Rice, 56, 61
Richards, 4, 29, 41, 48-49
Richardson, 20, 24, 28, 39, 47, 77, 79, 81
Richarson, 16
Riche, 41
Richerson, 16
Richeson, 46
Richmond, 3-4, 7
Rickets, 15
Ricks, 60
Riddle, 4
Rideout, 30
Ridings, 46
Ridley, 28-30
Right, 51-52
Rigsby, 69
Rigsby, 69
Riley, 61
Rimel, 46
Rinehart, 44
Rinkle, 51
Risen, 70, 76
Riser, 70
Roach, 58
Roark, 77
Robb, 25
Robberds, 31

Shahan, 48, 50-51
Shamlin, 50
Shanklande, 8
Shanklin, 12
Shannon, 5-6, 52
Sharber, 37
Shares, 73
Sharp, 20, 40, 45, 50
Shaw, 6, 10
Shelby, 55-56, 58
Shelly, 51
Shelton, 2, 17, 24-25, 32, 68
Shepherd, 70
Sheppard, 23
Sheron, 9
Sherrod, 8
Shields, 46, 48
Ships, 17
Shivers, 57-58
Shockley, 13-14
Shoemake, 80-81
Shoopman, 38-39
Shores, 73
Short, 27
Shother, 62
Shoulders, 55, 78
Shrader, 44
Shults, 45
Shutts, 45
Shy, 70
Sigler, 56-61
Sikes, 28, 58, 72, 76
Simmons, 3, 6, 9, 33, 36, 51, 80
Simms, 65
Simons, 80-81
Simpson, 16, 21, 58, 63, 73-74
Sims, 13, 26, 34, 74
Simson, 73-74
Sinclair, 25-26, 53
Sing, 51
Singleton, 29
Sink, 59
Skelton, 71
Slanton, 56
Slaren, 41
Slarun, 41
Slater, 59
Slaton, 21
Slaughter, 19, 70
Slo___, 13
Sloan, 55, 60
Sloane, 81, 83
Slough, 63
Small, 7, 63, 65
Smallen, 78
Smallwood, 43, 45

Smart, 25, 71, 77
Smelser, 2, 49
Smith, 2, 4, 11, 13-16, 19-22, 24-25,
27,38-44, 46-47, 50, 52-53, 55-57, 59, 61,
63, 65, 68-71, 75-79, 81-83
Smither, 38-40
Smithey, 31
Smithwick, 78, 83
Smoot, 18
Smotherman, 33, 36-37
Snapp, 47, 50
Snead, 54-55, 58, 80, 82
Sneed, 7, 23, 26, 29
Snell, 12-13, 32-33
Snider, 20
Snipes, 13
Snoddy, 50, 80
Soloman 76
Somers, 4
Sommerville, 4
Sorey, 7
Sott, 27
Soward, 61
Sowards, 60
Sowell, 34
Spain, 67
Spann, 25, 31-32
Sparkman, 58
Sparrow, 25
Spears, 61
Spence, 12, 33-35, 37
Spencer, 15, 63
Spickard, 25
Spring, 67
Springfield, 76
Sprouse, 6
Spurgen, 48
Squires, 70, 75
St. Clair, 25
Stack, 9-10
Stacy, 18
Stafford, 15, 17, 48, 77-78, 83
Stalcup, 83
Stallings, 70
Standback, 7
Stanford, 77
Stanley, 11, 40
Stanly, 41
Stanton, 56
Staples, 58
Starber, 37
Stark, 2-3, 61
Starkey, 46, 50
Starks, 54-55
Starnes, 73
Starr, 60

Steel, 3
Steele, 60
Stegall, 33
Stegar, 29
Stenett, 43-44
Stephens, 22, 32, 71
Stephenson, 17, 54, 63
Steprem, 33
Stevens, 40, 48
Stevins, 76
Steward, 60, 65, 69
Stewart, 5, 8-9, 19, 54-56, 65, 72, 79
Stockard, 27
Stoffle, 48-49
Stogner, 52
Stohl, 56
Stokes, 58, 73
Stoltz, 7
Stone, 3, 5, 72, 76, 78
Stott, 77
Stout, 64
Stovall, 4, 62
Stover, 48
Strain, 6
Strang, 76
Street, 9
Strickland, 5, 63
Stringer, 4
Strong, 56, 61
Strother, 80
Stroud, 8, 10
Strupe, 20
Strups, 20
Stubblefield, 78
Sturgis, 60
Stutman, 61
Sublet, 12, 14
Sublete, 19
Sublett, 15
Sudberry, 33
Suet, 67
Suge, 36
Sugg, 7
Suggs, 63
Sulivaan, 26
Sulivan, 23
Sullivan, 22, 62, 73
Summers, 16-17, 23
Sutton, 44, 78
Suy, 37
Swain, 19
Swan, 4-5, 13
Swancy, 15
Swane, 26
Swaney, 75
Swift, 6

Swink, 21-22
Tacket, 41
Talleforia, 15
Talley, 21, 61, 63
Talum, 31
Tanner, 65
Tarnel, 49
Tassey, 13, 22-23
Tate, 5, 61, 77
Taurinan, 60
Tawns, 25
Tayloe, 63
Taylor, 1-2, 12, 14, 16, 22, 24, 27, 30-33, 35-37, 40, 51, 55-57, 71, 80, 82-83
Teag, 52
Tedford, 53
Terry, 39, 41, 47, 76, 81
Thacker, 27
Thackston, 80
Thomas ,7, 12, 14, 21, 23, 33, 37, 39-40, 43, 45, 47-48, 50-52, 56-57, 60, 69, 71-73, 80-81
Thomason, 68, 74, 76
Thompson, 2, 10, 17, 20-21, 23-26, 28-29, 35, 38-41, 55, 57, 60, 62-63, 66, 69, 71, 75, 77
Thorn, 26
Thornton, 34
Thurman, 19, 29, 48
Thurmin, 60
Thweatt, 64
Timberlake, 79, 81
Timberlin, 2
Timmins, 54
Tinch, 24
Tipton, 51
Tison, 43
Tittis, 73
Titus, 64
Todd, 12, 16, 18, 24, 28-29, 35, 63-64
Tofly, 19-20
Tolbert, 52-53, 69
Toller, 78
Tombs, 32, 37
Tompkins, 27
Toomy, 49-50
Towns, 58, 77
Trail, 33, 37
Trammel, 40, 42
Trantham, 45
Traughber, 2
Travis, 12
Traylor, 25, 27-28, 31
Traywick, 79
Trezevant, 64
Trigg, 65

Wendel, 12
Wenders, 55
Wesson, 59
West, 3, 5, 33, 36, 40, 62, 79, 81-82
Westbrooks, 37, 58
Wetherford, 21, 24
Wetherly, 24
Whaley, 45
Whatley, 45, 52
Wheatley, 57, 66
Wheeler, 12, 27, 79
Wherry, 60
Whiless, 34
Whilly, 71
White, 4-6, 10, 15-16, 19, 22, 25, 29-30, 35-36, 46, 49-50, 54, 58, 65-66, 72, 74, 76
Whited, 8
Whitehead, 58
Whites, 10
Whitfield, 65
Whithead, 45, 55
Whitley, 60, 71-72, 74
Whitlock, 74
Whitmore, 25
Whitsett, 69
Whitson, 46
Whittle, 49-50
Whitworth, 14, 56-57
Whollaway, 41
Wickham, 57
Widner, 50
Wiett, 35-36
Wigs, 16
Wilbourn, 65, 77
Wilbourne, 78
Wilcox, 64
Wilcoxs, 51
Wiles, 61-62
Wilkerson, 70-71, 77
Wilkins, 4, 56
Wilkinson, 26, 82
Willerford, 57, 59
Willett, 58
William, 43
Williams, 2-5, 7-10, 14015, 17, 24-25, 31-32, 35-37, 43, 50, 56, 59-61, 63-66, 69, 72-74, 80-81
Williamson, 8, 28-30, 58
Williby, 71
Willie, 54, 57, 59-60
Williford, 18, 23, 74
Willis, 2-3, 37,56-57, 73-75, 77
Wills, 13-14, 20
Wilson, 4, 6, 10, 13, 15, 22, 24, 28, 33-36, 40-41, 43, 52, 55, 57, 62-65, 68-69

Wimberly, 8,
Wimberry, 56
Winchester, 57, 80-81
Windroud, 33
Windrow, 33
Winfield, 6
Winford, 62, 64
Winfree, 79
Winfrey, 72-74
Wink, 37
Winklee, 59
Winkler, 78-79
Winn, 6-7
Winset, 34, 36-37
Winston, 19, 35, 57
Wintel, 33
Winters, 10
Witherspoon, 21, 23
Witt, 79
Wo__rige, 65
Wolhup, 23
Woman, 12
Wommack, 56
Wood, 28, 30, 33, 35-36, 76, 78-79
Woodall, 4, 7, 26
Woodard, 1, 4, 6, 10
Woodcock, 79
Woodfin, 13
Woodle, 62
Woodliff, 37
Woodmore, 78
Woodruff, 10, 28
Woods, 12, 16, 20, 23, 47, 58, 67-69
Woodson, 10, 33, 60, 74
Woodworth, 62
Wooldrigee, 22
Woolsey, 59
Wooten, 34
Wooton, 68-69
Wootten, 15, 17
Wordfin, 23
Work, 14
Worthan, 60
Worthington, 59
Worthy, 68
Wraither, 27
Wrather, 27
Wray, 57
Wren, 65
Wright, 4-5, 7, 22-24, 28, 30, 37, 52, 63, 74-77
Write, 40
Wyatt, 81
Wyblood, 55
Wynne, 48, 55
Wysong, 51

Made in the USA
Coppell, TX
09 April 2022

76270988R00066